Gendering Elites

Economic and Political Leadership in 27 Industrialised Societies

Coordinated and edited by

Mino Vianello and Gwen Moore

Foreword by

Cynthia Fuchs Epstein

First published in Great Britain 2000 by

MACMILLAN PRESS LTD

Houndmills, Basingstoke, Hampshire RG21 6XS and London
Companies and representatives throughout the world

A catalogue record for this book is available from the British Library.

ISBN 0–333–77697–6 hardcover
ISBN 0–333–77698–4 paperback

First published in the United States of America 2000 by

ST. MARTIN'S PRESS, LLC,

Scholarly and Reference Division,
175 Fifth Avenue, New York, N.Y. 10010

ISBN 0–312–23213–6

Library of Congress Cataloging-in-Publication Data
Gendering elites : economic and political leadership in 27 industrialised societies /
edited by Mino Vianello and Gwen Moore ; foreword by Cynthia Fuchs Epstein.
    p.   cm. — (Advances in political science)
Includes bibliographical references and index.
ISBN 0–312–23213–6 (cloth)
   1. Leadership. 2. Elite (Social sciences) 3. Power (Social sciences) 4. Women
in public life. I. Vianello, Mino, 1922– II. Moore, Gwen, 1944– III. Advances
in political science (New York, N.Y.)

HM1261 .G45 2000
303.3'4—dc21

Selection, editorial matter and General Conclusions © Mino Vianello and Gwen Moore 2000
Introduction, part I © Gwen Moore, Mino Vianello, Eileen Drew and Renata Siemienska 2000
Introduction, part II © Gwen Moore, Silvia Sansonetti, Dawn Lyon, Jenny Neale and
Michael Palgi 2000
Chapter 10 © Gwen Moore and Deborah White 2000
Chapter 12 © Mino Vianello 2000
Other chapters © International Political Science Association 2000

This book is printed on paper suitable for recycling and made from fully managed and sustained
forest sources.

10   9   8   7   6   5   4   3   2   1
09 08 07 06 05 04 03 02 01 00

Printed and bound in Great Britain by Antony Rowe Ltd, Chippenham, Wiltshire

Gendering Elites

Advances in Political Science: An International Series

Members of the editorial board: **Asher Arian** (general editor), **Luigi Graziano, William Lafferty, Theodore Lowi** and **Carole Pateman**

As an expression of its commitment to global political science, the International Political Science Association initiated this series to promote the publication of rigorous scholarly research by its members and affiliated groups. Conceptual and theoretical developments in the discipline, and their explication in various settings, represent the special focus of the series.

Titles include:

Christa Altenstetter and James Warner Björkman (*editors*)
HEALTH POLICY REFORM, NATIONAL VARIATIONS AND GLOBALIZATION

Dirk Berg-Schlosser and Jeremy Mitchell (*editors*)
CONDITIONS OF DEMOCRACY IN EUROPE, 1919–39
Systematic Case-Studies

Klaus von Beyme
PARLIAMENTARY DEMOCRACY
TRANSITION TO DEMOCRACY IN EASTERN EUROPE

Ofer Feldman
THE JAPANESE POLITICAL PERSONALITY

Justin Greenwood and Henry Jacek (*editors*)
ORGANIZED BUSINESS AND THE NEW GLOBAL ORDER

Asha Gupta
BEYOND PRIVATIZATION

Mino Vianello and Gwen Moore (*editors*)
GENDERING ELITES
Economic and Political Leadership in 27 Industrialised Societies

Advances in Political Science
Series Standing Order ISBN 0–333–71458–X
(*outside North America only*)

You can receive future titles in this series as they are published by placing a standing order. Please contact your bookseller or, in case of difficulty, write to us at the address below with your name and address, the title of the series and the ISBN quoted above.

Customer Services Department, Macmillan Distribution Ltd, Houndmills, Basingstoke, Hampshire RG21 6XS, England

To all women who are fighting for a better world

Contents

List of Figures and Tables

Figures

Tables

Foreword

Cynthia Fuchs Epstein

The barriers against women attaining high political positions were so strong in past decades that most scholars attributed their relative absence from political élites to what were thought to be immutable differences between the sexes. Conventional perspectives of the time held that women were unsuited to decision-making roles. Some believed this was women's nature – that is, they were assumed to possess emotional and cognitive attributes different from those of men; others believed that they were socialised to assume subordinate roles in society. Few predicted there would be a time when women would be leading players on the political stages of modern societies. Many scholars in such fields as psychoanalysis and psychology, anthropology and sociobiology suggested that it was the nature of women and not societies' political and organisational structures that limited female participation in the top jobs of the political and business arenas.

Indeed, the few scholars who analysed women in management or in the political process turned their attention mainly to their activities as voters and as supporters of political parties. For example, political scientists such as Fred Greenstein in the United States and Harriet Holter in Norway compared how women and men voted across the political spectrum and found that women were more conservative in their choice of parties and in their voting behaviour. This empirical finding was interpreted by many as indicative of women's nature. Today, quite the reverse seems true and we find women to be more liberal than men in certain societies. In Iran, for example, President Khatami, the more liberal candidate, reportedly was elected because of the margin provided by women's votes; and in the United States, President Bill Clinton was voted into office for a second term in 1996 partly because a significantly larger percentage of women voted for him than for the Republican candidate, Bob Dole. In North America the phenomenon has been referred to as the 'gender gap', and indeed, it seems to reinforce the notion of women's basic difference from men. Holter was one of the first social scientists to point to the phenomenon of different voting patterns of women and men as lodged in their different positions in the social structure and in the degree to which they are expected to play different roles. There were also marked differences in behaviour between groups of women stemming from their different positions in society. Indeed, in her study Holter (1970) deconstructed the categories studied at the time in Norway to show that single women accounted for the gender gap she found – they voted more conservatively than men – and although it is true that today married women and single women tend to vary in their voting behaviours, married women tend to be more liberal than those who are not married – at least for the moment.

In my own early work (Epstein, 1970), I inquired why political sociologists sought only to explain women's voting behaviour and not their systematic exclusion from the routes to decision-making positions in society – the routes to power (Epstein, 1974). Noting that their outlooks and behaviour were variable and that many women had attempted to achieve power, it seemed important to me to search for the patterns of exclusion of women from decision-making spheres of society.

As part of this inquiry, Rose Laub Coser and I convened a conference on women and élites at Cambridge University in 1977 bringing together social scientists of political and organisational behaviour from eight countries in Western and Eastern Europe, Britain and the United States, to explore the issue of women's under-representation in élites. The meeting resulted in the volume *Access to Power: Cross-National Studies of Women and Élites* (Epstein and Coser, 1981), which I believe was the first attempt to understand through comparative analysis the structural and cultural factors that facilitate or undermine women's access to power.

Scholars of the sociology of knowledge should be curious about the absence of comparative study of women's place during the 20 years in which they have made such enormous strides – although most would agree that they have far to go to reach true equality – in a number of countries. Scholars have turned their attention to women's continued exclusion in various countries, but efforts to compare systematically their situation have not engaged many researchers. The book *Gender Inequality* by Mino Vianello and Renata Siemienska (1990) published a decade ago is a notable exception.

Thus we welcome this book co-ordinated by Mino Vianello and Gwen Moore, bringing together data on women's participation in élites from no fewer than 27 countries – in fact, the 27 major industrial countries of the world.

Many of the findings reported in this book challenge often widely held assumptions. For example, it was found that bias and structural barriers impede women's attainment of decision-making roles in politics and business, not their personal qualities or attitudes. Perhaps the most important finding is the overarching one that culture has more influence in determining political and business leadership attributes than does gender. Furthermore, the studies reported in this volume show that across countries and cultures, women exercise and regard power with the same range of styles that men do. They show that women and men holding high positions in leadership hierarchies tend to hold similar views and demonstrate similar leadership styles. Other researchers, such as Collinson and Hearn (1994) in their path-breaking work on managers, have also found this to be true. As Vianello points out, for example, women and men have similar perceptions about power, and they exhibit similar styles of leadership.

These findings do not mean that women and men follow the same paths to leadership. Stereotyping as well as structural impediments make women's route to the top more problematic. I found in my own studies of women lawyers (1970; 1981) that women who 'make it' in a prestigious occupation tend to come from more privileged backgrounds than do men in similar positions. They tend also to have more cultural capital in the form of education, and more social capital as well. Data from the 27-country study reported in this volume show this to be the case. Furthermore, the studies of these countries show it is more important for women to have mentors clearing the path on which they embark.

Of enormous interest is the issue of childcare. Although a smaller proportion of women than men in leadership roles are married and have children, most women leaders are mothers. Many observers marvel at the high proportion of women serving in the governments of the Scandinavian countries. But weaving in information about the social context in which women make decisions to immerse themselves in politics sheds new light on this phenomenon. In the Nordic countries we find that 50–80 per cent of children aged 3–6 years are in day care. This not only means that women can begin their careers knowing their children are well cared for, but that Nordic societies accept the norm of surrogate care for small children and do not impose guilt on parents who use it.

Time is another issue treated in this book. Although many observers recognise that men and women are directed and persuaded to use time differently, the 'politics' of time allocation is rarely studied. For example, it is considered normal for more women than men to work part-time (Epstein, et al., 1999) and for women to work fewer hours than men in paid employment. Yet the studies in this book show that the pressures on women to curtail paid labour because of the work they are expected to do in the home is often arbitrary. When opportunities are open to both sexes in political and business life, we find women's and men's schedules follow different timetables. Surprisingly, women political leaders work as hard or harder than their male counterparts. Indeed, in the category of those working more than 90 hours a week we find more women than men. This may be a consequence of another finding – that women feel they have to achieve more than men to attain equal recognition. Women business leaders do not put in more hours of work per week than men do, but we find across the board that women put in more hours of work in their households than do men. Of course, most women leaders use paid household help, a category not often explored in surveys of housework but the usual solution for couples who hold high-power positions.

The cultural capital women rely on can also be found in the support given by husbands. It has always been my view that the focus on division of house-hold labour between husband and wife in professional families neglects the factors most important to understanding the dynamics of the family. In families where both spouses work at high-level jobs there is usually sufficient money to purchase services, and the support of husbands ought not to be measured in terms of the percentages of time each partner spends in house work or even in childcare. Like the élite women I studied, this volume's com-prehensive overview shows that women in positions of power find invalu-able support from husbands who also hold élite positions (fully 73 per cent of the partners of female leaders occupy these positions). In these families, husbands may provide not only emotional support, but also valuable infor-mation about career tracking and access to networks of political knowledge and connections. Husbands, and in some cases fathers, may be the role models for women.

Then there is the question of whether women's leadership is compa-rable to that of men. Although several women have become presidents and prime ministers of their countries, women's acquisition of key leadership roles does not match that of men. Women tend to be clustered in political roles linked to the 'soft', people-related support services. Yet, as the writers of this volume point out, people-related services in social policy areas like social welfare and education administer the largest budgets in most countries.

The investigators of this study have a number of observations to make with regard to moving women towards equality. They suggest that the most important factor in furthering women's equal access to leadership roles is for a society to have a deeply rooted culture of equality. Referring to Pierre Bourdieu's work (1984: 292), they suggest that as a 'battlefield for the maintenance and change of dominant categories to perceive the world . . . the political arena is probably one of the most important providers of cultural change toward the equality of the sexes'. They also state that it is imperative that organisations and leaders actively integrate women and support them – as they start the movement toward normative change. This comparative study shows that differences exist in perceptions of inequality in various societies and how value systems affect perceptions of gender inequalities. Economic development and the existence of a democratic system also aid in providing women with access to leadership positions.

The essays in this volume lend support to the idea that gender is a dynamic phenomenon. As Renata Siemienska writes, it is created and reproduced in interactive processes, affected by both cultural and social factors. It is part of the symbolic order of a culture and it is always related to power relations. What this book shows, through its careful and sys-tematic analysis, is that women as well as men can move to leadership positions and perform them well, providing they receive the same or comparable supports that men do. It also shows that many women have moved to the top in spite of many obstacles and have forged the way for others to follow.

History of the Research and Acknowledgements

The history of this study dates back to 1973, when Mino Vianello was able to organise a one-week meeting to explore the feasibility of a comparative research on women's participation in decision-making in the upper echelons of public life. Colleagues from 12 countries took part in that meeting, but it soon became clear that, at that time, the overwhelming majority of them were interested in studying gender issues from other points of view, such as the labour market, the family and civil rights. So, three years later a much reduced group met again for five days in Assisi to begin the lengthy work of organising the above research. The following year, at a three-day meeting in Ariccia (near Rome), the group was able to finalise the research design and to decide on the appropriate tools for the collection of the data. The results of this study were published in 1990 by Sage under the title of *Gender Inequality.*

But by then the issue of women's exclusion from public life had become an integral part of mainstream sociology. So, in 1990, Mino Vianello's proposal – backed by the moral sponsorship of the International Political Science Association, the International Sociological Association, the United Nations Centre for the Advancement of Women – for another study, which became the present one, drew the eager attention of colleagues in as many as 27 countries (including Italy) – in fact, the 27 most industrialised nations of the world.

Since then, for nearly a decade – through seven research group meetings and innumerable communications – the collaborators in this project worked towards the common goal of a comparative study of gender and power in industrialised nations. Even with agreement on the overall goal, such a lengthy and complex collaboration among a large group of scholars from various disciplines is never simple. Yet, believing that a deeper understanding of women's access to elite positions is critical for both scholars and the international community, group members persevered.

In November 1990, thanks to the support of the local administration, it was possible to organise a three-day meeting in Bevagna (Central Italy), which was attended by 15 colleagues from as many countries.

Basic principles for the research were agreed upon. First, each participant could study her/his specific area of interest on gender and power by including items in a common questionnaire. Second, there would be a co-ordinator to facilitate the collaboration. Mino Vianello offered to co-ordinate the project. Third, the project would focus on elites in politics and business. If we had included non-elites, we would have had the added dimension of being able to study the mobility of non-élites into élites (as had been done in the previous study mentioned above). But, by excluding the former, we increased our ability to examine gender differences and similarities within elites, as was the original topic of the research. Finally, all agreed to use a common questionnaire and the same sampling method. Participants were responsible for obtaining funding for and carrying out the study in their own countries. In return, all participants were guaranteed the right to contribute a chapter on a topic of their choice to this volume and to have free use of the data set for all countries once the project's volume is published.

The adoption of the first principle reflected the criteria, on one side, of giving equal standing to each participant, but also, on the other, of avoiding the impervious difficulties of trying to develop a common set of hypotheses. Yet, to a certain extent, common hypotheses and measures for specific topics such as social origins, power exercise, and values, were developed by thematic sub-groups. In general, however, participants started from different theories, and obviously the choice of variables was not uniform. In accordance with this principle, each participant eventually wrote a chapter on a topic of her/his choice. The price paid for this autonomy is that the book is somewhat discontinuous. Yet, we believe that its fragmentary, and for the hurried reader confusing, character also has some advantages. Different patterns of analysis, different comparisons based on the same items, different groupings of variables allow – given the richness of the material collected – the exploration from different perspectives of the issue of the gender gap in elites, illuminating aspects that a more centralised treatment would have neglected.

In 1991, after testing a preliminary questionnaire, some members of the group (along with a new one) met again in Bevagna for three days. At this meeting, Vianello proposed that Gwen Moore should also assist in the co-ordination of the project. From then onwards, all decisions concerning the study were taken Jointly by the two co-ordinators. The research design as well as the questionnaire, both described in the methodological chapter, were elaborated in the course of that work-shop.

A subsequent meeting was held the next year in Rome.

At this point, data collection was supposed to begin. Fortunately, it started only in Israel, because the Norwegian colleague, Kari Skrede, who had not attended the last workshop, subsequently insisted that her set of questions be included in the already finalised questionnaire, and this was done. A grant from the Italian National Research Council helped our Israeli colleague to rerun part of the data collection already completed in that country.

Data collection took place in all countries between 1993 and 1995. It was financed by local sources as it is specified below; the European Union countries also obtained a grant of ECUs 200,000 in the framework of the Human Capital and Mobility Programme (HC&MP) of the European Commission.

In July 1994 a large group of participants met in Bielefeld for half a day to monitor the progress of the research and deal with some collateral problems (such as the unexpected withdrawal of the Norwegian colleague).

At the end of 1996 another two-day meeting was held in Rome. The purpose of this meeting was to resolve some problems concerning coding and data analysis.

The full data set from all 27 countries was sent to all team members in 1997 so that they could write a chapter based on it for this volume. Draft chapters were then circulated to all collaborators and underwent a multistage process of critique and revision.

In April 1998, during a ten-day meeting in Bevagna, the first drafts of the chapters were discussed in detail and changes proposed. The meeting was attended by 16 participants.

Following further revisions by the authors, a few months later, in Montreal, J. Esseveld, G. Moore, M. Palgi, R. Siemienska, L. Nicolau-Smokoviti, M. Vianello and A.E. Woodward re-examined the manuscript, which in the following months was reviewed again by Vianello and still later again by Moore. They had to face the delicate task of eliminating overlappings and establishing links between the various chapters written autonomously by their respective authors. The ensuing draft was then edited by Sara Griffith, Lecturer in English at the Faculty of Statistics of the University of Rome La Sapienza.

Needless to say, each chapter's hypotheses, analysis and interpretation are the exclusive responsibility of its author. Indeed, peer reviewers of some chapters recommended changes that authors declined to make. As equal collaborators, authors were the final arbiters of the content of their chapters.

We said that this study has a long history. In fact, it is not over. For many of the contributors to this book, the results presented here have become the premise for another research on gender and power, this time of a qualitative nature and based on depth interviews.

*   *   *

Unfortunately, some participants, who collected the data in their countries, were unable to contribute a chapter to this book. We want to thank them for their invaluable assistance. They are: Lois Bryson in Australia, Maria Cermakova in the Czech Republic, Julia O'Connor in Canada, François de Singly in France, Yoko Hosoi in Japan, Katalin Koncz in Hungary, Valentina Konstantinova in Russia, Ilona Ostner in Germany. Bjørg Aase Sørensen unfortunately collected only a few questionnaires in Norway.

*   *   *

The obligations incurred in carrying out this research are many and varied. We are indebted above all to the many scholars, mostly women, who have long been working on gender issues. This book has also benefited decisively from the stimulating criticisms that came from many sides: we cannot name all the colleagues who generously contributed helpful critical comments on the whole or parts of the manuscript.

With regard to funding, before listing the national contributions, we want to thank the International Political Science Association, the International Sociological Association and the United Nations Centre for the Advancement of Women for their moral support; the University of Rome 'La Sapienza', the Faculty of Statistics, and in particular the Department of National Accountancy and Analysis of Social Processes, of the same University, for making available to us its facilities and supporting our applications for funding; the Italian Consiglio Nazionale delle Ricerche; the municipality of the city of Bevagna; and at the individual level Sylvia Sansonetti for her help in the international co-ordination of the research and Maria Luisa Rocco for the hundreds of often lengthy documents and letters she promptly wrote and mailed over all these years.

Individual participants special thanks are listed below:

Jeannette Bakker, the Faculty of Social and Behavioural Sciences, Dpt. of Education, University of Amsterdam; J. Dronkers; *Maria Carrilho*, the Instituto Superior de Ciencias do Trabalho e da Empresa and H. Carreiras; *Gertraud Diem-Wille*, the Ministry of Science, Communication and Art and the Fund for the Advancement of Scientific Research; R. Fischer; *Eileen Drew*, R. Johnson, E. Michelsen, K. König, E. Mullins; *Johanna Esseveld*, the Research Council for the Humanities and Social Sciences; *María Antonia García de León*, the Universidad Complutense de Madrid, M. Romero Torres, A. Pascual, A. Zappone; *Lis Højgaard*, the Danish Social Science Research Council; *Bogdan Kavčič,* the Slovenian Ministry of Science and Technology; *Jaana Kuusipalo*, the Dpt. of Political Science and International Relations of Tampere University, the Finnish Institute of Occupational Health; the Academy of Finland; T. Huuhtanen, P. Järvinen, A. Peltomaa; *Joanna Liddle*, the Nuffield Foundation and the University of Warwick; *Brigitte Liebig*, the Swiss National Science Foundation; Prof. Thanh-Huyen Ballmer-Cao; *Gwen Moore*, the Research Foundation of State University of New York; the Dpt. of Sociology, College of Arts and Sciences, and the College of Social and Behavioural Sciences at the University at Albany; D. White, C. Fuchs Epstein, E. Pellegrino, D. Beaulieu, C. Meeks, H. Pearce, Y. Shen, S. Sobieraj; *Jenny Neale*, the Victoria University Internal Grants Committee; E. McLeay, J. Craven, D. Peterson; *Litsa Nicolaou-Smokoviti*, the University of Piraeus Research Center; V. Kavvada, S. Paroutis, D. Halamandaris; D. Smokoviti, G. Tzourvakas; *Michal Palgi,* the Institute for Research of the Kibbutz and the Cooperative Idea in the University of Haifa, the Emek Yezreel College, the Italian

National Research Council; E. Orchan and V. Mayn; *Renata Siemienska*, the Friedrich Ebert Stiftung; the UNESCO Interdisciplinary Research Section on Gender; *Mino Vianello*, the Italian National Research Council, the University of Rome 'La Sapienza', C. Fuchs Epstein, N. Glazer, J. Mossuz-Lavau, C. Pateman, S. Verba; *Alison Evelyne Woodward*, the Belgian National Science Fund; E. Michielsens.

*   *   *

Gwen Moore would like to acknowledge her appreciation of Mino Vianello's vision and commitment in not only imagining such an ambitious project, but also in co-ordinating the research even when its ultimate success sometimes seemed unlikely.

Mino Vianello would like to thank Cynthia Fuchs Epstein who introduced him to Gwen Moore, with whom 'a marriage of true minds' came into existence, without which this work would have been much more difficult to accomplish.

*   *   *

The royalties of this book will be given to the United Nations agency for the reconstruction of the Women's Hospital in Kosovo.

List of Contributors

María José Alonso Sánchez, Fellow, Centre of Sociological Research, Madrid, Spain.

Gunnar Andersson, Assistant Professor, Department of Sociology, University of Lund, Sweden.

Jeannette Bakker, graduate student, Faculty of Social and Behavioural Sciences, Department of Education, University of Amsterdam, The Netherlands.

Burt Baldwin, Professor, Department of Sociology, Central Connecticut State University, USA.

Maria Carrilho, Professor, Higher Institute of Business and Labour, Portugal.

Gertraud Diem-Wille, Professor, Interuniversitäres Institut für Interdisziplinäres Forschung und Fortbildung, Abteilung Schule und Gesellschaftliches Lernen, Vienna, Austria.

Eileen Drew, Senior Lecturer, Department of Statistics, Centre for Women's Studies, Trinity College, University of Dublin, Ireland.

Johanna Esseveld, Professor, Department of Sociology, University of Lund, Sweden.

María Antonia García de León, Professor, Department of Sociology, Faculty of Education, Complutense University of Madrid, Spain.

Lis Højgaard, Associate Professor, Institute of Political Science, University of Copenhagen, Denmark.

Kaisa Kauppinen, Senior Researcher, Department of Psychology, Finnish Institute of Occupational Health, Finland.

Bogdan Kavčič, Professor, Faculty of Economics, University of Lubljana, Slovenia.

Jaana Kuusipalo, Senior Researcher, Department of Political Science and International Relations, University of Tampere, Finland.

Joanna Liddle, Lecturer, Centre for the Study of Women and Gender, University of Warwick, UK.

Brigitte Liebig, Fellow Lecturer Institute of Psychology, Social Research Department, University of Zurich, Switzerland.

Dawn Lyon, Researcher, European University Institute, Italy.

Marjana Merkač, Professor, GEA College of Entrepreneurship, Portoroz, Slovenia.

Elisabeth Michielsens, Fellow, Westminster Business School, University of Westminster, UK.

Gwen Moore, Associate Professor, Department of Sociology, State University of New York at Albany, USA.

Jenny Neale, Associate Dean (Research), Faculty of Humanities and Social Sciences, Victoria University of Wellington, New Zealand.

Litsa Nicolaou-Smokoviti, Department of Business Administration, University of Piraeus, Greece.

Iira Nuutinen, student, Department of Psychology, Finnish Institute of Occupational Health, Finland.

Michal Palgi, Senior Lecturer and Chair of Women and Gender Studies, Yemek Iezreel College; Senior Researcher, The Institute for Research of the Kibbutz and the Cooperative Idea, University of Haifa, Israel.

Helena Rodriguez Navarro, Fellow of the Department of Sociology, Faculty of Education, Complutense University of Madrid, Spain.

Silvia Sansonetti, student, Faculty of Statistics, University of Rome La Sapienza.

Renata Siemienska, Head of the Department of Sociology of Schooling and Education, Institute of Sociology, University of Warsaw, Poland.

Mino Vianello, Professor, Faculty of Statistics, University of Rome 'La Sapienza', Italy.

Deborah White, Graduate Student, Department of Sociology, State University of New York at Albany, USA.

Alison Woodward, Professor, Vesalius College, Free University, Belgium.

Judith Ziegler, Researcher, Interuniversitäres Institut für Interdisziplinäres Forschung und Fortbildung, Abteilung Schule und Gesellschaftliches Lernen, Vienna, Austria.

If non-violence is the law of our being,
the future belongs to women.

Gandhi, *Young India*, 10 April 1930

INTRODUCTION

1
A Theoretical Framework

Eileen Drew, Gwen Moore, Renata Siemienska and Mino Vianello

The persistent concentration of economic, social and political power in a relatively small group has been a traditional subject of investigation by social scientists, but the fact that women are hardly ever among these power-holders in the public sphere, even in advanced democracies, has been generally ignored in mainstream social and political science. With the important, but relatively recent, exception of feminist scholarship, most analyses of élites and of leadership ignore the gender aspect of power and decision-making. Changes in gender relations in the family, labour market, education, sexual behaviour and political participation have attracted considerable academic interest in recent decades (e.g., Epstein, 1988; Walby, 1990). Yet the relative absence of women among power élites seems to be a more central issue to journalists than to non-feminist political and social theorists.

Since World War II, women's participation in higher education and the labour markets of industrialised countries has burgeoned, but their growing participation in paid employment has not been matched by an equivalent presence in decision-making positions in economic and political life. In 1998 fewer than 13 per cent of the world's parliamentarians were women and virtually no top economic organisations were headed by women (United Nations, 1995; Siemienska, 1996; Inter-Parliamentary Union, 1998). In spite of this male dominance of élite positions, women's presence in such posts has increased in recent decades (Epstein and Coser R.L., 1981; Randall, 1987; United Nations, 1995).

In this book we focus on the small number of women who have achieved top business and political posts in industrialised societies as well as on similarly situated men. Recognising that public power is concentrated in male élites and that advantaged groups seek to maintain their dominance, we seek to understand the backgrounds, actions and attitudes of the few women in decision-making positions in comparison to their far more numerous male counterparts.

The import of women's equal participation in decision-making and power is stressed in the *Beijing Declaration and Platform for Action* of the Fourth World Conference on Women in 1995. The Declaration states: 'We are convinced that: women's empowerment and their full participation on the basis of equality in all spheres of society, including participation in the decision-making process and access to power, are fundamental for the achievement of equality, development and peace.' We believe that careful study of women (and comparable men) in decision-making positions will contribute to the understanding of how gender equality can be achieved.

The mechanisms that produce and maintain men's advantage are both structural and cultural (e.g., Connell, 1987; Randall, 1987; Walby, 1990; Acker, 1991; *Beijing Declaration*, 1995). Unequal opportunities based on race, class, gender and other factors are part of organisations and societies. Our research is a contribution to both élite theories, which refer to global societies, and leadership theories, which refer to organisations. The study of women and men in key business and political positions offers a unique opportunity to gain insights into the experiences, achievements and social conditions which facilitate or hinder advancement in organisations and societies.

The terms 'élite' and 'power' have been given varying definitions by scholars. We define élites as people occupying senior decision-making positions in powerful national institutions and organisations (Dogan and Higley, 1998). We use a positional definition of élites, identifying such people by the formal positions they occupy at the top of powerful organisations. We define power as the ability to make binding decisions with wide-ranging consequences for society. In this study we focus on two powerful institutions in industrialised democratic societies: politics and big business.

Élite theories

The study of élite composition has a long tradition. In all its varieties it is concerned with the issue of inequality (Bottomore, 1993; Etzioni-Halevy, 1997). Since the inception of philosophy in Greece 2,500 years ago, numerous theories have been developed to explain the causes of social and political power. After Machiavelli founded the discipline of political science, the concept of 'élite' slowly moved to the centre of attention. Weber spoke of the 'Vorteil der kleinen Zahl', and the Italian school – from Mosca to Sartori – can be considered an outgrowth of Machiavelli's treatment of the phenomenon of power.

For the purposes of this study, it is necessary to distinguish only two strands of élite theory. The sociological strand, represented especially by Pareto, studies élites chiefly in the context of the analysis of social stratification and conceives of élites as grounded in the process of natural selection and individual abilities, a perspective that led in the late 1930s and 1940s to the structural-functional perspective. The political science strand of élite theory deals with the phenomenon of the unequal distribution of power, especially as discussed in Mosca's influential treatise (1896). Our study belongs to the latter perspective. In it, the goal of élite studies is not the correlation between resources and position in the social hierarchy, but an emphasis on the small number of people who hold economic, political and cultural sway. Hence the focus is not on the opposition between élite and class (Bottomore, 1993), but between rulers and ruled – a distinction that led Mosca to reject Pareto's equivalence of aristocracy and élite in favour of the concept of 'political class'.

A critique of liberalism, democracy and socialism, based on the concept of oligarchy, which quickly moved to the centre of this approach, is beyond the scope of this introductory chapter. We note, though, that in both the Marxist (e.g., Gramsci) and in the pluralist (e.g., Bentley) approaches there is no reference to women's exclusion from power in the public sphere. This lack of interest characterised the works of the founders of élite theory as well. For Mosca, Pareto and Michels the factors that bring about the formation and renewal of élites are military might, wealth, technological training, political acumen, and wisdom. They never considered whether women had these attributes, or, if they possessed them, why women remained excluded from power positions.

Later important developments of élite theory (Lasswell, 1936; Burzio, 1945; Lasswell and Kaplan, 1950; Schumpeter 1941; Dorso, 1955; Mills, 1956; Djilas, 1957; Burton and Higley, 1987) also ignore the issue of the relationship between élite and gender. This way of thinking has survived also in authors investigating political transformations in contemporary societies (e.g., O'Donnell, Dahl, Offe). This state of knowledge is symptomatic of male ideological domination. Yet, this omission of gender is even more surprising, given the tendency of political theorists, from Lasswell to Schumpeter, Dahl, Bachrach and Sartori, to consider democracy as essentially preserved by pluralism, which depends to a crucial extent on the permeability and enlargement of élites. This omission is perhaps the most marked contradiction in analyses of the democratisation process in contemporary societies (Walby, 1997).

In the past, in both the realms of political and economic life, élites in most societies were recruited from a group of families or, to a lesser extent, certain professions or institutions. Élites were often tied by bonds of kinship or friendship and were frequently graduates of the same schools, which prepared them for their roles in adult life (Mills, 1956; Miliband, 1969; Domhoff, 1998). The supposition was that members of the élite were characterised by the ability to rule effectively, knew how to gain access to necessary resources and could correctly calculate avenues to success (Baltzell, 1958). These qualities were believed to result from the experiences accumulated by generations and passed on by the family, the school and certain professions.

Such traditional recruitment of élites no longer dominates in the societies that grew in an era of rapid industrialisation. Mass migrations to cities, a rise in educational levels, growing affluence benefiting a majority of people, ideas of democracy, citizens' participation in the process of major decision-making, all caused radical changes which provided opportunities for members of previously excluded groups to gain access to power. The remnants of the traditional élites came to play only a marginal role in European and other industrialised countries. In order to consider broadly similar societies, we restrict this study to modern, industrial or post-industrial societies in which élite positions are not limited to traditionally powerful groups.

Élite positions in modern industrial nations are no longer hereditary. Nevertheless, studies of élite recruitment in advanced capitalist democracies concur in finding that economic and, to a lesser extent, political élites are drawn primarily from men with privileged social origins and higher education (e.g., Putnam, 1976; Dogan, 1989; Norris and Lovenduski, 1995). Putnam (1976: 32) concludes that women are statistically the most under-represented group in political élites world-wide; he also contends that the advantage of highly educated, high-status males grows as the level of authority of positions increases (Putnam, 1976: 33; also see Epstein and Coser R.L., 1981). Thus, individuals of both sexes who hold top decision-making posts may be even more likely than lower-level élites to enjoy cultural and social capital from their family of origin (Bourdieu, 1977). By contrast, some scholars have found that women élites have often offset the 'handicap' of gender by social origins even more privileged than those of their male counterparts (e.g., Moore, 1988).

Leadership theories

Leadership theories have sought to discover how certain people succeed in mobilising human and material resources to promote the efficiency and motivations that are the basic conditions of organisational efficacy. Leadership theories have developed mainly, though not exclusively, in the study of organisational management and can be considered part of élite theory. We define a leader as a person who has the ability to induce others to follow her/him, and in doing so acts in a way that is beyond ordinary, daily, routine behaviour, especially when a crisis erupts. We concentrate on leadership positions in governments and firms.

Historically, women have rarely been leaders. Traditionally, with some notable exceptions, leadership has been synonymous with masculinity. One explanation offered is that women lack the personal and experiential qualities of leaders; for instance, they may be seen as having difficulties making and implementing choices (see Walby, 1997, on women's apparent 'choices'). Others point to women's situational and structural disadvantages – including networks, job segregation and limited career ladders – in work organisations (e.g., Hennig and Jardim, 1976; Kanter, 1977; Epstein, 1988).

In addition, involvement in family and community life impinges in quite different ways on the aspirations and achievements of men and women.

Leadership theories have dealt mainly with the characteristics of leaders, both in management and politics (where attention to charismatic leadership has been central), and more recently with the interactions between leaders and others in their own organisation and outside of it. A central concern has been the selection of leaders and the mechanisms influencing such selection (co-option, nomination, ability to adjust, elections and inheritance). The earliest leadership theories sought to identify the common traits held by leaders in different kinds of organisations. Compiling a large range of personal attributes did little to explain the advancement of some people within organisational structures. The focus then shifted towards an examination of leadership styles, stressing the importance of adopting measures inspired by the concept of human relations, but still reflecting a traditional, prescriptive orientation along the classical line founded by Weber, that centred on the concept of formal organisation (on one side, Urwick, Fayol and Mooney, and, on the other, Taylor). These developments paved the way for a more motivational emphasis in management, shifting from autocratic to more democratic leadership forms. When tested empirically, the limitations of this doctrine (autocratic or democratic), too, emerged.

This led to an extension of the behaviourist approach that focuses on the concrete group situation, in contrast to explanations based on the personality traits and style of the leader. Fiedler's contingency theory (1967; also see Heller, 1992) seeks to include the context of the decision-making process such as the nature of the task, authority relationships and group dynamics. Hersey and Blanchard (1977) further developed these ideas in 'situational leadership'. More recently, concern has shifted from sole emphasis on productivity to the importance of quality and excellence in products and service. A Total Quality Management (TQM) approach emphasises people management skills and leaders with vision to embark upon transforming organisational cultures (Atkinson, 1997).

Kanter's path-breaking work (1977) on gender and organisations emphasised the effects of organisational structures and cultures on women (and men) in managerial and other positions. She introduced gender – a previously ignored factor – into leadership studies and demonstrated the importance of structural factors – such as sex ratios, mobility opportunities and 'homosocial' reproduction of managers – in shaping ambition, opportunities and power for women in work organisations. (See Rosener, 1990; and Vianello, 1996, for related work.) As far as selection to the top is concerned, the mediating role of informal networks is of paramount importance and we devote much attention to this. Since the time of Bryce and Michels little has been added to what was already known in general, and only in recent decades have women been studied in this perspective.

Our study aims to explore gender differences and similarities in the process of formation and selection of leaders and to highlight how – or whether – gender correlates with leaders' positions, informal access, preferences, approaches and behaviour (Epstein and Coser R.L., 1981). It considers the phenomenon from a behaviourist point of view, concentrating on circumscribed realities like governments, legislative committees and firms. For further insights into gender inequality in élites and leadership in business and political decision-making, we now examine the contributions of feminist and gender theories.

Feminist and gender theories

Writing on élites and leadership has much company in its inattention to gender. Women were largely absent from scholarly analyses in the social sciences, except those addressing the family, until the early 1970s or later. Gender was generally ignored in social science scholarship, while the generic 'worker' or 'politician' (but not 'parent') was implicitly defined as male (Acker, 1991). As feminist movements and women's studies have developed in the past several decades, feminist scholars have drawn attention to the bias of much social science theory and research.

Feminist scholarship is diverse in subjects, theories and methods (Evans, 1994; Brooks, 1997). Varying feminist explanations of the origins and maintenance of gender inequality have been proposed, including class divisions and the family structure of the capitalist system and the sexist domination of women in organised patriarchy. While feminist scholars hold diverse views, they are generally united in seeing social institutions and cultural values as structuring gender roles and relations.

The feminist challenge to social science has directed attention to gender inequality in access to resources, including public power, and to male control of dominant social institutions. To many feminist scholars, gender is a central aspect of all institutions and organisations (Chafetz, 1988). Feminist and gender analyses have sought to redress the imbalance within male-dominated disciplines and to offer alternative perspectives on topics of major societal interest such as domestic work, labour market segregation, sexuality, access to public power (e.g., Connell, 1987; Epstein, 1988; Walby, 1990; Acker, 1991), and reproduction (even today, in fact, the most virulent controversies in the political arena about women concern sexuality and rights concerning their own bodies).

While traditional social and political analyses generally leave implicit women's rare presence in formal positions of power, feminist scholars typically recognise the near-absence of women from powerful public positions (e.g., Epstein and Coser R.L., 1981). Some authors write of 'gender regimes' and the 'institutionalisation of gender' throughout social structures (Connell, 1987; Walby, 1997). Connell (1987: 99) sees the division of labour, the structure of power and the structure of sexuality as major elements in all gender regimes, which he defines as historically constructed patterns of power relations between the sexes as well as definitions of masculine and feminine. The institutionalisation of gender in the economy, politics and the family makes routine and maintains women's subordination. Such male advantage is not readily ceded. Epstein, too, argues that social structures and cultural patterns both create and maintain gender distinctions (1988: 5). She affirms that the social arrangements of women and men shape the structures and ideology of work, family and politics, maintaining male advantage in these major social institutions. Both formal structures and informal relations in organisations work to the advantage of men (Epstein, 1988; see also Kanter, 1977).

All gender theories acknowledge that gender disparity exists in access to decision-making in public life. The overarching theory of 'patriarchy' (social systems of male domination over women) identifies the various arenas in which women are subordinated (e.g., Walby, 1997). Walby distinguishes public patriarchy – based in employment and the state – from private patriarchy sited in household production (1990: 24). She sees the gender imbalance in power as lying within systems of patriarchal household work, paid employment, male violence, sexuality, culture and the state. These private and public patriarchal structures are neither immutable nor inevitable, and they interact in different ways to exclude, segregate or integrate women and men, thus affecting gender relations throughout society. Walby (1997) discerns a recent shift in Britain and other industrialised societies toward public patriarchy, where women are not excluded from public life, but are segregated and subordinated within the public sphere (while still remaining largely subordinate in household production).

Since gender inequality is seen by feminist scholars as socially structured, it is subject to change. Many feminist writers go beyond scholarly analyses to position women in a proactive role: 'women need to change management, to change structures, relationships, values and ways of working' (Coyle, 1989). Cockburn (1991: 7) reminds us that 'just as capitalism is only one of successive modes of production, so patriarchy is only one of other possible sex/gender systems'.

Conclusion

In this book, we seek to employ elements of élite, leadership and gender theories in our analyses of economic and political élites in industrial societies. We recognise the centrality of gender in such analyses, and ask to what extent the women and men in key decision-making positions are not only different from but also similar to one another (Epstein, 1988).

Our research focuses on economic and political élites, measuring the impact of gender, not only in achieving such positions, but also in the exercise of power in these posts across 27 industrial nations. Focusing solely on those who have 'made it', we study pathways to power and the consequences of holding a powerful position in public life. In this book we examine the family and social backgrounds of leaders, seeing the family as a primary agent of socialisation and of reproduction of élites. We ask if privileged social and cultural origins (including education) typically characterise not only male élites, but also their female counterparts. In addition, we examine the interplay of current public positions of power and leaders' private lives outside the workplace.

As discussed above, deeply embedded cultural patterns and gendered social structures also advantage men in the attainment of, and performance in, leadership positions. The upper echelons in public life are not only numerically male-dominated, but they also have male-defined informal cultures (Kanter, 1977; Morrison et al., 1992). Women tend to be marginal to male-centred informal networks of the powerful and are often in 'gender-appropriate' formal positions as well (Randall, 1987; Norris and Lovenduski, 1995). As a result, women may less often enjoy sponsorship to advance in their careers or access to informal information or advice. If the small numbers of women political and economic élites in each country are relatively isolated from their overwhelmingly men counterparts, they are hindered in further upward mobility and in exerting power.

Cultural images (such as stereotypes) shape conceptions of women's and men's roles and gender relations at all societal levels, from families to the highest levels of public power. Women are caught in the patriarchal ideology that underpins these images even when such ideology appears to work against their interests. We also investigate cultural dimensions of gender inequality, including élites' views of, and explanations for, women's under-representation in positions of power and whether these views differ across sectors and nations.

Much recent writing focuses exclusively on differences between women and men. Yet, Epstein reminds us that an exclusive focus on gender distinctions 'obscures the overwhelming similarities between men and women' (1988: 240). In this volume, we seek to discover both the similarities and the differences between important economic and political decision-makers of both sexes in modern industrial and post-industrial countries, taking into consideration their differing histories, cultures and socio-economic conditions.

In her book *Gender Equity* (1988), Chafetz identifies male control of élite positions as crucial in maintaining gender inequality. Thus, she argues that 'equal representation for women among a society's élites constitutes the single most important change required to produce a system of gender equality' (1988: 220). With this investigation, we aim to advance the long-term goal of gender equality in key decision-making posts throughout the world.

2
Methodology

*Silvia Sansonetti, Dawn Lyon, Gwen Moore, Jenny Neale
and Michal Palgi*

A running methodological debate divides cross-national and comparative social researchers into two camps (Goldthorpe, 1997: 1). One group favours quantitative, variable-oriented methods with the goal of uncovering similarities and general patterns across nations (Przeworski and Teune, 1971; Teune, 1990), while the other advocates qualitative case-studies, with detailed attention to historical and cultural variations across nations (Dogan and Pelassy, 1984; Ragin, 1987; Rueschemeyer, Stephens H. Stephens J.D., 1992; and Goldthorpe, 1997). In this research we use a variable-oriented survey method and statistical analyses to uncover similarities and differences across a set of industrial and post-industrial nations. This method is well suited to our goal of uncovering general patterns of gender (in)equality in élites in a comparative, cross-national context, though we recognise that this method minimises the opportunity to consider in detail specific social and historical contexts in these nations.[1]

The sample

The 27 countries[2] covered by this study were chosen from among the most advanced countries in the world. Although we regret not having been able to include other countries, there are good reasons for it. The first is that it seems reasonable to assume that women's generalised access to the top of public life is more probable in societies characterised by high educational standards and a democratic system. The second is a methodological reason. Even if we had succeeded in collecting the data in other countries, we doubt that we could interpret findings coming from societies so widely different in terms of culture, family customs and laws, political organisation, economic development, educational level, demographic structure, etc. The third reason is that extending the study to other countries implied costs that we would not been able to cover. The unique feature of this study is that women in élite positions are the point of departure in the sample construction. Since élites are overwhelmingly male, random surveys of this group cannot explore in depth issues of gender similarities and differences; thus we chose a purposive sample. This permits comparisons between male and female leaders, and thereby an analysis of the role of gender amongst those in positions of power. After identifying important economic and political organisations, we then selected individual élites within these organisations in each national study, in accordance with the following strategy.

We defined various levels for both political and business sectors and we selected the sample starting from the top level moving down to the next only when it was not possible to find women at the highest level. We identified all women in the highest positions in the selected organisations in business and politics and then selected men from the same or similar organisations at the same level. We sought to include at least the top 15 women in politics and the highest ranking 15 in business from each country and an equivalent size-matched male sample. Strictly speaking, we do not have a sample of top women in each country, but rather the universe of élite women excluding only those who refused to participate in the survey.

For political leaders we defined four levels of political positions. The most powerful (level 1) are members of the government, presidents of national assemblies and those in executive decision-making posts in the main parties in power. The second level includes governors/presidents of regional/provincial bodies, individuals in executive posts of the main opposition parties, presidents of parliamentary commissions/select committees, and mayors of major cities. The third level consists of elected representatives of the upper or lower parliamentary assemblies. The fourth and last level includes representatives in local bodies of major cities. In the political sector, the majority of women respondents are at level 3 (see Table 2.1), most often members of national parliaments. While we aimed for top-level women and began

Table 2.1   Level of Respondents by Gender and Sector[a]

Career Level	Political Leaders			Business Leaders			Total		
	Women	Men	Total	Women	Men	Total	Women	Men	Total
Level 1	20.4	18.8	19.6	22.5	26.9	24.6	21.5	23.0	22.2
Level 2	15.4	16.0	15.7	33.0	31.7	32.4	24.7	24.1	24.4
Level 3	59.4	62.9	61.1	36.5	33.4	35.0	47.3	47.7	47.5
Level 4	4.8	2.3	3.6	8.0	8.0	8.0	6.5	5.2	5.9
Total	100.0	100.0	100.0	100.0	100.0	100.0	100.0	100.0	100.0
	(397)	(388)	(785)	(449)	(413)	(862)	(846)	(801)	(1647)

[a]There are 39 missing cases belonging to the category 'Political Leaders' since the 33 cases in Poland (14 women and 19 men), 2 in Spain (women), 2 in the Nederlands (1 woman and 1 man) and 1 woman in Greece were coded separately as bureaucrats; moreover one woman in the Norwegian sample was incorrectly coded.

with all those at level 1, in some nations there were few or none at this level. In addition, overall completion rates (measured as the number of women participating as a proportion of all women in eligible positions) varied across the 27 national studies, with most from 65 per cent to 95 per cent, but a few under 50 per cent (France, Greece, Japan, US).

For business leaders, we identified the 250 most important enterprises in terms of turnover and the top ten banks and insurance companies ranked by premiums and deposits. Women were selected from these businesses according to the following classification. The first level includes managing directors and chief executive officers; level 2 members of the central boards of the enterprise who are in managerial or financial functions; level 3 other senior managers; and level 4 department or branch managers. Once again, women were scarce at level 1 in the business sector, requiring selection of at least some respondents from level 2 or below in all national samples. Table 2.1 shows that the majority of women in the business sample held level 2 or level 3 positions. The female completion rate in the business sector was generally a little higher than that for politics, with four countries reporting rates below 50 per cent (Australia, France, Ireland, Japan).[3]

A matched sample of men was constructed. For each woman, a man was selected at the same level from the same or similar organisation (in a few cases, more than one man was included as a match for a particular woman). Where possible, men were of the same age (±5 years).

Included are a substantial proportion of the total population of women in élite positions, while the male respondents do not constitute a population or a representative sample of male leaders. This sampling strategy does not, strictly speaking, permit the use of inferential statistics. Many of the chapters do use inferential statistics as aids in evaluating the findings, but not as the basis for generalising beyond the group studied.

Questionnaire

The questionnaire focuses broadly on gender and power. Its more than 100 (mostly closed-ended) questions measure access to and exercise of power, and related activities and attitudes. Also included are measures of education, family, career, current professional and domestic situations, as well as attitudes about gender and policy measures.

The first section measures the current position of the respondent, details of her/his position in organisational hierarchies and the scope of her/his current responsibilities.

The second measures participation in networks and access to informal channels of communication/information within or outside one's sector of activity.

Third is a set of questions about the respondents' occupational history, including the position, organisation, years of employment, level of responsibility and the main factors in obtaining and leaving the post, as well as mentoring activities. Respondents' aspirations for the future and their perception of factors that have helped and hindered their careers are also addressed. Another series of questions measures organisational memberships, media visibility and service on corporate and non-profit boards.

Next is a section on family background and present domestic situation. This includes information about their family of origin such as the size of the family, the education level, occupations and levels of responsibilities of their parents, and the relative wealth of their family when they were 14 and now. In this section are also questions on marital status, partner's/spouse's education and occupation, number and ages of children and children's perceived impact on their careers.

Finally, a series of attitude questions about the gendered distribution of power in society and a set of standard demographic questions are asked. We also collected systematic data about the organisation (business or party) the respondent belongs to, as well as about the national context s/he comes from.[4]

To avoid distorting question meanings in translation, the questionnaire was translated from the original English into the respective languages of the participant countries, and then each was retranslated into English by another scholar to locate any discrepancies in wording. A final questionnaire in the national language was then constructed.

Methods of delivery

In most countries data were collected by mailed self-administered questionnaires, with extensive follow-up mailings and telephone calls to increase response rates. In some cases researchers determined that only personal contact would succeed in gaining élites' participation in the research, so personal interviews were conducted. In a few cases, a combination method of data-gathering used personal interviews for some respondents and mail questionnaires for others.

Analyses

Contributors were free to select theories, topics and analytic methods for their individual chapters. However, throughout the chapters, the analysis is conducted using the variables of gender, leadership sector (political or business) and – in most chapters – country grouping. The latter clusters countries on theoretical grounds to see if results differ across these clusters. Countries are grouped in different ways depending on the hypothesis tested, but many chapters employ the following grouping scheme to increase comparability of results:

Less developed market economies and recent democracies (Czech Republic, Hungary, Poland, Russia, Slovenia, Greece, Portugal).

Market economies and stable democracies (Australia, Austria, Belgium, Canada, France, Germany, Ireland, Israel, Italy, Japan, New Zealand, Spain, Switzerland, United Kingdom and USA).

Social democratic market economies (Denmark, Finland, Norway, Sweden, and the Netherlands).

The first two categories correspond to the World Bank classification (1995). The third is derived from Inglehart's (1997) cross-national study of modernisation and postmodernisation.

The data were weighted because of differing numbers of respondents in some countries. Most national studies collected 60 questionnaires, but four gathered fewer (Hungary, Israel, Norway, Russia), while France and Poland had much larger samples. Chapter authors weighted cases in the analyses so that each national sample contributes equally to the results.

Notes

1. We find strengths in both approaches, with quantitative research excelling at identifying general patterns and similarities across nations, and case-oriented approaches more suited to emphasis of the unique historical and cultural contexts of different nations. A second phase of our research, now underway, is based on the case-oriented approach.
2. All Western European countries, except Iceland, the five major Eastern European countries (Russia, Poland, Czech Republic, Slovenia, Hungary), North America, Japan, New Zealand and Australia, and Israel.
3. Unfortunately, we do not have data for completion rates from all national studies. The discussion here is based on 18 nations reporting.
4. The questionnaires are available from the volume editors.

SUBSTANTIVE CHAPTERS

Part I
Pathways to Power

Introduction

The aim of Part I is to explore why and how women and men are included in positions of power, focusing on the kinds of backgrounds from which female and male top leaders come, and the other factors which help them to reach those positions.

It is natural to speculate on whether women followed the same pathways as men or attained power by different routes and alternative strategies; whether they drew on the same resources men did; whether they needed more extensive resources than men to reach the same levels of power.

We have centred this part on the concept of 'pathways to power', because it combines elements of both structure and agency: various different pathways exist, but people take decisions about which routes to walk.

We shall also examine whether there are differences between the business and the political sectors, and between various country groupings, and will attempt to explain these differences.

The chapters in Part I look at four main categories to understand gendered pathways to power: family cultures, class background, education and career routes.

Some well-known women who have reached the highest positions of power have argued that they attained them entirely through their individual efforts. This part, however, shows that there are important structural and cultural features in their backgrounds, which help to account for how and why they attained those positions.

Chapter 3, on gender, capital and public power, investigates whether women and men in top positions come from different class backgrounds.

Chapter 4, on cultural capital, looks at whether women require a greater degree of cultural capital than men to succeed in the fields of business and politics, and asks how significant was the influence of different levels of education and fields of knowledge in men's and women's routes to power.

Chapter 5, on gender and career, examines how far women's career paths differed from men's and whether or not men and women employed different strategies in the progression of their careers.

Chapter 6, on political leaders, explores whether gender makes a difference in political careers and offices.

3
Gender, Class and Public Power
Joanna Liddle and Elisabeth Michielsens

Introduction

The question we are asking in this chapter is: does class background differentiate men and women in positions of public power, and if so how? Our hypothesis is that women leaders come from higher class backgrounds than male leaders, and the evidence suggests that, in most of the dimensions of class examined, there is a significant relationship between gender and class in the direction proposed.

In most industrialised countries it is no longer the case that women are confined to the domestic sphere and excluded from public life. Despite radical changes in gender relations over the last 50 years, however, women's participation in institutions of public policy- and decision-making, such as business and politics, has had limited effects in changing the gender balance of public power (see Appendix). Where women are participating in public life, it is not where it matters; and in many countries they are largely excluded from positions of power, so that their interests cannot be effectively represented.

Research questions and conceptual approach

Several explanations have been put forward to understand women's segregation into low-value, powerless positions in public life (see Collinson D.L., Knights and Collinson M., 1990: chapters 1 and 2 for a review). The most influential explanations have attempted to understand women's exclusion or marginalisation from power within the context of the intersection of important structural divisions in society such as class, gender and race (for example, Walby, 1990, on the labour market; Norris and Lovenduski, 1995, on political recruitment). Two major conceptual approaches, which emerged from particular theoretical perspectives and were developed in the 1980s and early 1990s, are Marxist feminism (for example, Barrett, 1980; Beechey and Perkins, 1987) and the 'dual systems' thesis (for example, Cockburn,

1985; Walby, 1990). Each of these perspectives has been extensively criticised (Collinson D.L., Knights and Collinson M., 1990; Pollert, 1996) for leading to 'an impasse, regarding the relative significance of class and gender. Where reductionism or dualism threaten' (Coole, 1996: 24). Marxist feminism has tended to reduce the operation of gendered power to the class structure, whilst the dual systems thesis treats gender relations as if the systems of race, class and gender were separate and additive, suggesting that a particular woman or man could be gendered alone, without this gendering itself being constituted by, and constitutive of, the dimensions of class and race (Spelman, 1988: 115).

Into the gap created by this impasse in materialist theorising has stepped postmodernist feminism with its focus on discourses of difference and debates about diversity. Yet, as Diana Coole points out, amid all the discussions of difference amongst women, differences of class are rarely 'even mentioned in the capacious lists of significant differences' (1996: 17). The decline of class politics in its traditional forms in many established capitalist countries in the context of global economic restructuring, and the breakdown of the communist system in Eastern Europe, have both led to an erosion of the resonance, if not of the significance, of the concept of class, and this political eclipse of class has contributed to the analytical disappearance of the concept within feminism. Yet, its importance to questions concerning gender and power still makes itself felt in women's everyday lives.

In the last decade women have made significant encroachments into areas of public influence, in which even 20 years ago women were considered exceptional, if not abnormal (Adler, 1996: 135–8). It is, therefore, appropriate at this stage to ask: why and how is a minority of women able to achieve representation in influential positions in the managerial and political hierarchies, given the gendered nature of the power relations operating to exclude women from public decision-making in many parts of the world? Are women in powerful positions simply to be regarded as exceptions, or can their participation be understood with reference to the same structural features which figure in the theories of women's exclusion or marginalisation from public power? Do women who have reached positions of power present a challenge to or a confirmation of such explanations? The specific research questions we will address in this chapter, then, are:

1. How far is class background associated with women's entry into positions of public power compared with men?
2. What different dimensions of class, if any, are associated with women's achievement of positions of public leadership in comparison with men?
3. How are gender and class related, if at all; that is, what is the direction of any relationship?
4. Which dimensions of class, if any, show the strongest relationship with gender?

5. How far are any significant relationships maintained when the business and political sectors, and various country groupings, are examined separately?

Our hypotheses in relation to these questions are as follows: first, that class background will be associated with women's entry into positions of public power, and will significantly differentiate female from similarly placed male leaders; second, that all the dimensions of class under examination will be associated with women's achievement of leadership positions, in comparison with men; third, that the direction of the relationships will show that women leaders' class background will be higher on all dimensions than that of male leaders. The fourth above-mentioned question will be addressed after it becomes clear from the analysis which dimensions, if any, are statistically significant. Fifth, that the business and political sectors will be equally affected by any significant relationships, whilst the countries classified as 'full capitalist' will be more affected by any class–gender associations than countries categorised as 'post-communist' or 'social democrat'.[1]

What we are examining, therefore, is the socio-economic and class origins of the men and women in our sample, to assess how far women in positions of public power come from more privileged backgrounds than their male counterparts. We intend to use several different indices of class, drawing on a range of approaches to the concept. Broadly, we will use class as a descriptive concept to refer to a number of aspects of social life, which differentiate hierarchically ordered groups in society materially and culturally.

First, we will use class as a description of social status or prestige, a concept that has emerged from Weber's idea of status groups (Crompton, 1993: 10, 13). As Crompton points out, occupational prestige scales measure the relative distribution of rewards, reflecting the outcome of class processes, rather than explaining the structure of class relations which brought those outcomes about (1993: 57). She further suggests that employment-based measures of class, whilst not comprehensive, are both effective and essential for a class analysis of structured social inequality (1993: 118–19). We will operationalise our use of class as social status by using two occupational class indices based on the employment of the respondents' parents. One of these is a measure of the occupational prestige of the mother (where relevant) and father when the respondent was 14, assessed by Treiman (1974). The second index is a simple measure of whether or not the job of the respondent's mother (where relevant) and father included supervisory and managerial responsibilities. We will refer to these measures as occupational class.

Second, following both Coole (1996: 17) and Crompton (1993: 119), we will use class as a description of structured social inequality, where material differences are stable over time and reproduced within a group. We will operationalise this use of the term by having recourse to Erik Olin Wright's 'class map', which aims to measure class differences in terms of the social relations of production, rather than in terms of a scale of occupational positionings. Ideas of exploitation and control within production relations as a way of understanding the outcomes of class relations are central to Wright's models, as opposed to Weberian models based on exchange relations in the market (Crompton, 1993: 57, 70–1). Wright's second class map produced 12 categories based on the ownership or control of labour, capital, organisations and skills or credentials (Wright, 1985; see Crompton, 1993: 69–75 for an outline and review, and Marshall et al., 1988 for a British study). We will use this map to assess the social class of the mothers and fathers when the respondents were 14. We will refer to this measure as social class.

Third, in the absence of reliable objective data on family income and assets when the respondents were 14, we will use a subjective measure of economic capital based on a five-point scale which asked them to assess the economic position of their family at that age. We will refer to this measure as subjective economic capital.

Fourth, we will use two indices based on Bourdieu's concept of cultural capital, as indicators of cultural and educational knowledge (Bourdieu 1984). Although educational and cultural capital are not synonymous, Bourdieu regards them as sufficiently close to allow educational credentials to serve as an index of cultural capital: '[educational qualification] ... guarantee cultural capital more or less completely and so it is an unequally adequate indicator of this capital' (Bourdieu, 1984: 13). The indices we will use consist of the highest level of educational qualification attained by the respondents' mothers and fathers. We will refer to this as cultural capital.

Fifth, we will use several indices of social capital, based on Bourdieu's and Passeron's idea of social networks (1979) and Ishida's broader concept of the social circumstances surrounding childhood development (1993: 53, 80). This will comprise family size and birth order, the engagement of the respondents' natal families in political and professional associations and networks, and the availability of mentors in the respondents' progression into public life. We will refer to this as social capital.

Clearly none of these measures is a perfect or objective index of class, and each has specific problems associated with it. For this reason we do not regard any one of the measures as adequate on its own. However, examining a range of indices representing several different dimensions of class will enable us to have greater confidence in the results.

Methods of data analysis

This chapter looks at the combined international data as a whole, then at the business and political sectors separately, and at three country groupings.

It does not examine the different processes by which these positions of power are obtained by men and women, for which qualitative studies are needed.

The following five sections discuss the results of the statistical tests on the international sample, assessing the significance of gender differences in the five aspects of social stratification identified above, that is: occupational class, social class, subjective economic capital, cultural capital and social capital. After this, we look at how far these patterns are maintained by sector and country grouping. Tables are presented only when the data show statistically significant patterns.[2]

Occupational class

The first set of measures consists of the occupational prestige index of the respondents' mothers and fathers when they were 14. A large proportion of the respondents' mothers (55 per cent) did not engage in paid work at that time, and these mothers are excluded from the analysis. Tables 3.1 and 3.2 show the occupational prestige index grouped into eight categories.

The associations in the two tables are significant for both mothers and fathers in the sense that the occupational prestige of the female respondents' parents is significantly greater than the occupational prestige of the male respondents' parents.

The second set of measures of occupational prestige consists of mothers' and fathers' supervisory functions (if they were in paid work) when the respondent was 14. These categories look at whether or not the parents' jobs involved a supervisory role.

Table 3.1   Mothers' Occupational Prestige

Mothers' Prestige Index	Sex of Respondents %	
	Male	**Female**
0 to 30	35.1	27.0
31 to 40	12.6	13.6
41 to 50	16.9	19.9
51 to 60	25.0	24.8
61 to 70	7.9	9.4
71 to 80	2.5	5.2
81 to 90	0	0
91 to 100	0	0
TOTAL	100.0	100.0
(N)	(357)	(405)

Kendall's tau-b: 0.022.

Table 3.2   Fathers' Occupational Prestige

Fathers' Prestige Index	Sex of Respondents %	
	Male	**Female**
0 to 30	7.9	4.7
31 to 40	16.2	13.2
41 to 50	19.1	18.3
51 to 60	26.8	26.2
61 to 70	18.8	20.6
71 to 80	10.1	16.7
81 to 90	1.0	0.3
91 to 100	0	0
TOTAL	100.0	100.0
(N)	(611)	(647)

Pearson chi-square asymp. sig. (2-sided): 0.003.

Table 3.3   Mothers' Job Supervisory Functions

Supervisory Functions	Sex of Respondents %	
	Male	**Female**
Yes	28.3	38.4
No	71.7	61.6
TOTAL	100.0	100.0
(N)	(305)	(354)

Pearson chi-square asymp. sig. (2-sided): 0.006.

Table 3.4   Fathers' Job Supervisory Functions

Supervisory Functions	Sex of Respondents %	
	Male	**Female**
Yes	67.8	75.4
No	32.2	24.6
TOTAL	100.0	100.0
(N)	(612)	(642)

Pearson chi-Square asymp. sig. (2-sided): 0.003.

Table 3.5 Fathers' Class (Wright 2)

Wright 2 Index	Sex of Respondents %	
	Male	**Female**
Bourgeoisie	7.0	11.8
Small employer	5.6	5.3
Petty bourgeoisie	19.7	18.4
Expert manager	24.5	29.1
Expert supervisor	1.5	2.5
Expert non-manager	7.5	5.7
Semi-credentialled manager	8.0	7.4
Semi-credentialled supervisor	3.6	3.3
Semi-credentialled worker	9.0	6.4
Uncredentialled manager	1.3	0.5
Uncredentialled supervisor	1.3	0.9
Proletariat	6.0	4.4
Outside Wright 2 Index *(unemployed or unpaid work at home)*	5.0	4.2
TOTAL	100.0	100.0
(N)	(602)	(635)

Pearson chi-Square asymp. sig. (2-sided): 0.049.

These associations are highly significant, showing that a higher percentage of the parents of women leaders had jobs involving supervisory responsibilities than the parents of male leaders.

The statistics in this section indicate that the women come from a significantly higher occupational class background than the men in the sample.

Social class

The social class measure is based on Wright's second class map, comprising 12 categories.

The statistic for the social class of the mothers is not significant and is not shown. However, the statistic for the social class of respondents' fathers shows that women leaders come from a significantly higher social class backgrounds than do male leaders, based on Wright's measure of their father's class position.

Subjective economic capital

This consists of a subjective measure of the family's economic position when the respondent was 14. The question asked was: 'Where on the following scale would you place your family's economic position when you were 14?' to be answered on a five-point scale from 'very comfortable' to 'not very comfortable'.

This measure too is significant, and suggests that, according to the self-perceptions of the respondents, the families of the women leaders were economically better off than the families of male leaders.

Cultural capital

The possession of cultural capital is assessed by the educational level of the respondents' mothers and fathers.

Table 3.6   Subjective Economic Capital

Family's Economic Position when 14 years old	Sex of Respondents %	
	Male	**Female**
Very comfortable	4.8	8.6
Comfortable	18.2	20.1
Average	42.9	42.9
Less comfortable	22.7	18.6
Not very comfortable	11.5	9.8
TOTAL	100.0	100.0
(N)	(692)	(726)

Pearson chi-Square asymp. sig. (2-sided): 0.016.

Table 3.7   Mothers' Education

Mothers' Education	Sex of Respondents %	
	Male	**Female**
Elementary not completed	2.0	1.6
Elementary school	22.8	15.8
Junior secondary	23.7	21.0
Senior secondary	22.5	23.4
Vocational training	11.0	16.1
Bachelor degree/College	11.6	14.7
Master	5.2	6.1
Doctorate	1.2	1.3
TOTAL	100.0	100.0
(N)	(653)	(685)

Pearson chi-Square asymp. sig. (2-sided): 0.007.

These two indices are both highly significant, indicating that the educational level of women leaders' parents is significantly higher than that of male leaders' parents, and suggesting that women in positions of power possess significantly greater amounts of cultural capital than comparable men.

Social capital

Social capital comprises measures of family size and birth order, the natal family's political and professional activism, and mentoring. Ishida (1993: 53) defines it as the social circumstances surrounding childhood development, including number of siblings and, we would argue, birth order. He argues that parents of large families will have less time and money to invest in each child, and therefore smaller families result in greater social capital for the child (Ishida, 1993: 54). We would suggest further that being a first child produces family circumstances in which he/she is often constructed as a leader in the family, providing both a learning experience and a sense of identity which may facilitate the achievement of leadership positions in later life.

Bourdieu's concept of social capital concerns social networks, which we have measured in terms of the respondents' access to mentors in their political or professional lives.

We have also used the respondents' subjective view of the political and professional activism of their natal family as a measure indicative of both social networks and the circumstances of childhood development.

The results show that neither family size and birth order, nor natal family's activism in political and professional associations are statistically significant

Table 3.8 Fathers' Education

Fathers' Education	**Sex of Respondents %**	
	Male	**Female**
Elementary not completed	2.3	0.7
Elementary school	15.8	9.1
Junior secondary	19.1	14.4
Senior secondary	16.4	15.6
Vocational training	12.3	16.9
Bachelor degree/College	16.7	20.9
Master	13.1	16.0
Doctorate	4.4	6.4
TOTAL	100.0	100.0
(N)	(667)	(699)

Pearson chi-Square asymp. sig. (2-sided): 0.000.

in differentiating between male and female leaders in positions of public power. However, the availability of certain kinds of mentors is reported in significantly different numbers by men and women. We do not show detailed tables for the mentor measures, because this question is covered in more detail in chapter 7 below, but report significance levels in summary form.

The only male mentors who significantly differentiated women from men leaders were family members. This index of social capital was highly significant, showing that women in positions of power were much more likely than men to have had male family members who acted in a mentoring capacity. The other mentors important in differentiating between male and female leaders were all women: colleagues and supervisors at work, friends or colleagues in other organisations, and political acquaintances. The results in this section do not necessarily mean that men failed to act as mentors to women other than within the family, but that, except in the family, male mentors were equally active or inactive in a mentoring role for both male and female leaders.

In terms of social capital, then, Ishida's concept of the social circumstances surrounding childhood development is not important in distinguishing men's and women's access to positions of public power, whereas Bourdieu's more limited idea of social networks, as operationalised in mentoring activity, is of value in understanding gendered access to public power. This form of social capital is itself gendered, since mentors from the public arena who facilitate women's access to power (as opposed to those from the private sphere of the family) are exclusively female. These results reveal the importance of female networking in terms of the mentoring role for the achievement of positions of public power by women.

Sector and country differences

Finally, we examine how far the significant gender differences in the various dimensions of class demonstrated so far on the whole international sample are maintained when the sample is divided first by political or business

Table 3.9 Type of Mentor Significantly Differentiating Male and Female Leaders

Type of Mentor	Significance Level
Male relatives	0.000
Female work colleagues	0.001
Female supervisors	0.000
Female friends/colleagues in other organisations	0.000
Female political acquaintances	0.015

sector, and second by particular country groupings. In this section we look at all the indices except mentors, since this is examined in chapter 7. Table 3.10 reports the significance levels of the gender–class associations by sector for each class measure.

Five of the eight measures continue to show significant differences when the business sector is examined alone, namely mother's and father's education, mother's and father's job supervisory function, and subjective economic position, but only three of the eight remain significant when the political sector is examined alone, all of them concerned with the position of the respondents' fathers: that is, father's education, father's job supervisory function and father's job prestige. Only two of the measures remain significant for both sectors: these are father's education and father's job supervisory function. The results suggest that the association of gender and class is stronger for women's entry into top positions in the business world than the political world. This difference may be associated with the argument that a democratic institution which excludes important sections of the population is hardly democratic at all, and so perhaps the requirements for women gaining access to political power are less class-bound than in the business world. For those measures that remain significant in the political milieu, it does seem that it is the position of the father rather than of both parents that is particularly important, and this may relate to sectoral differences in the extent to which the mothers of male and female respondents undertake paid work. In terms of the two class measures which remain significant in both sectors, it seems that father's education and father's job supervisory function are of particular importance in differentiating women and men leaders, and therefore we can reject the assumption that gender operates independently of the cultural capital and occupational position of the father in the two sectors.

Table 3.10 Significance Levels for Gender–Class Relationship by Sector

Class Measure	Significance Level	
	Politics	**Business**
Mother's job prestige	0.438	0.126
Father's job prestige	0.024	0.155
Mother's job supervisory	0.254	0.004
Father's job supervisory	0.041	0.034
Father's Wright class (2)	0.164	0.094
Subjective economic position	0.464	0.037
Mother's education	0.780	0.032
Father's education	0.003	0.010

Table 3.11　Significance Levels for Gender–Class Relationship by Country Grouping

Class Measure	Significance Level		
	Post-communist	**Full capitalist**	**Social democratic**
Mother's job prestige	0.768	0.144	0.130
Father's job prestige	0.300	0.001	0.527
Mother's job supervisory	0.654	0.003	0.586
Father's job supervisory	0.867	0.002	0.200
Father's Wright class (2)	0.996	0.016	0.282
Subjective economic position	0.374	0.022	0.492
Mother's education	0.515	0.016	0.006
Father's education	0.288	0.000	0.069

Table 3.11 reports the significance levels by country groupings of the gender–class associations for all the class measures except mentors. We have modified the World Bank country groupings slightly for reasons of theoretical consistency. We will use three categories: post-communist, full capitalist and social democratic. World Bank groupings are based on economic ratings of development, placing Greece and Portugal with the less economically developed countries in the 'post-communist' group. For this study, however, it is vital to group together countries with a similar political-economic structure, rather than rely on purely economic ratings, since the history of class politics is likely to affect how class divisions interact with gender. We have therefore moved Greece and Portugal to the 'full capitalist' grouping, whilst Norway, Sweden, Finland, Denmark and the Netherlands, with long histories of welfare capitalism, are grouped in the 'social democratic' category.

What this analysis shows is that class effects on gender are highly significant in the full capitalist countries, whereas in the post-communist and social democratic countries, where conscious attempts have been made at the level of state policy to break down the class structure or to mitigate its impact, the effects of class on gender are much reduced. In other words, when all the countries in the sample are looked at together, we can reject the idea that gender operates independently of class on the variables tested, but when we look at the different country groupings separately we can see that in the full capitalist countries the class impact on gender is strongly maintained.

Gender, class and power

The statistical evidence suggests that there is a significant relationship between gender and class. The remarkable feature of the statistical analysis is that, for all the dimensions of class and for almost all the specific measures, a strongly significant association is found across the entire international sample of nearly 1,500 men and women belonging to the élite of public power. The fact that these relationships are revealed consistently across the various dimensions and definitions of class, often at very high levels of significance, suggests that what is being identified here is an important structural relationship rather than a statistical artefact or accident. It also suggests that the various measures used to operationalise the different concepts of class may be valid assessments of structural divisions occurring in society at a global level.

The direction of the associations follows that predicted by the hypotheses, demonstrating that women in powerful positions show consistently higher or more privileged class backgrounds than comparable men. The occupations of women's parents are more prestigious, their fathers come from a higher social class, their families are seen as possessing more economic capital, their parents possess more cultural capital in the form of education, and the women have greater access to social capital compared with their male counterparts.

The measures showing the strongest relationship with gender are father's occupational prestige, mother's and father's job supervisory function, mother's and father's education and four of the five mentor measures. Finally, the class–gender correlations are maintained more strongly in the business than in the political sector, which may be connected to the greater legitimacy of ideas of democratic representation in the political than in the business arena. The significant association between class and gender is much more strongly maintained in the full capitalist countries than in the post-communist and social democratic countries, suggesting that attempts to break down class disadvantage do erode class-related effects on women's access to power compared with men. This finding gives some support to the validity of the measures of class used in this study, since the theoretical basis on which they are constructed would predict that class impact effects on gender would be greater in full capitalist than in post-communist or social democratic countries.

It is clear, therefore, that the hypotheses are supported – except for mothers' social class, the broader definition of social capital, and the sectoral imbalance in the gender–class relationship. The evidence from the international sample demonstrates that structural, status, subjective, cultural and social dimensions of class are significant in the gendered production of public power and leadership, and that these relationships are maintained more in the full capitalist countries and in the business sector.

How to explain these class differences between male and female leaders is the next task and cannot be determined from a quantitative analysis alone. What we can say, however, is that it is a mistake to see women in leadership positions as merely exceptional. On the contrary, there are very clear class patterns in the production of gendered power; and it is likely that the inclusion and participation of women in public power may be understood with reference to the same conceptual frameworks which help to explain their exclusion or marginalisation from economic and political leadership. Class, in whatever way we wish to define it, is central to women's challenge to men's monopoly on public power at a global level.

Notes

1. We departed, as later explained, from the tripartition presented in the methodological chapter.
2. Whenever possible we have used Pearson's chi-square to test statistical significance. Where this is not possible, because more than 20 per cent of the cells have expected counts of less than five, we have used Kendall's tau-b.

4
The Élites' Cultural Capital[1]

María Antonia García de León, María José Alonso Sánchez and Helena Rodriguez Navarro[2]

Introduction

An élite can be shaped by different factors and can also be studied from different angles. Frequently, the élites are analysed from an economic perspective, and it is also customary to study them by determining class origin.

In order to expound succinctly the above (solely for introductory purposes), we could say that there is an 'external' approach to the study of the élites that is mostly based on political science and revolves around the problem of power. From another angle, there is a mainstream of theoretical debate that focuses on analytically confronting two concepts: élite and social class (Scott, 1990). A third study approach focuses on investigating 'internally' the configuration of élites. In this method, the processes of acquisition and reproduction by the élites of different kinds of capital (economic, social, cultural, symbolic) are the primary target of analysis. The main source of inspiration for authors working along these lines is Bourdian sociology (Bourdieu, 1985; Bourdieu and Passeron, 1970).

This chapter is based on the third approach, but focuses the analysis exclusively on the study of the élites' cultural capital as viewed specifically from the educational perspective.

The term 'education' is a very broad concept. It is an enormous frame of reference in comparison to the concrete realities and situations that are normally linked to it. In this respect, this chapter will use one of the aspects encompassed by the term education and which the sociology of education basically deals with: the school system. Specifically, the objective is to assess the weight of education in obtaining positions of power. To do so, the evaluation will be based on the credentialist criterion, according to which social positions would be determined by the investment in education, whereby the higher the individual's educational credentials, the more possibilities that individual will have to achieve high social positions. In this respect, Bell (1970) would say that education-based specialisation is the basis of power and social position in post-industrial society.

In the purest style of human capital theory, it is believed that certain individuals gain advantages and maintain them through education. It is an investment in a life insurance policy that yields long-term benefits, as these individuals achieve a recognised social status. However, this does not mean that education is only of interest to the more socially well-positioned classes to maintain their status. Meritocratic society has set up the school as the primary dispenser of privilege, and therefore all social groups are obliged to use it as a reference for their expectations of mobility.

On the basis of the above, which is a perspective widely shared by many authors, we will test the following hypotheses:

1. There is a positive relationship between the educational level of the parents of the political and business élites and the educational level attained by these élites.
2. Education plays a relevant role in the configuration of both the political and business élites.
3. Women in positions of power have required more educational capital than men in the same positions. The aim is to confirm if there is a 'super-meritocratisation' of the female élites.

With the first two hypotheses (the ones described in terms of social reproduction), the aim is to confirm the role of cultural inheritance, i.e., the weight of the educational levels of the élite's family of origin on the educational horizons of these élites. We consider that the higher the educational level of the parents, the greater will the educational demands imposed on the children be. If the results confirm this 'reproductive hypothesis', what we would undoubtedly be witnessing is an educational accomplishment that is achieved in advance, or at least determined to a great extent in advance, which would lead us to speak quite correctly of 'selection of the select' (Bourdieu and Passeron, 1970).

The third hypothesis is developed on the plane of individual choices. Society views school in terms of social mobility, or more accurately as a space open to individual choices that can be translated into upward social mobility. Thus, women find in the educational system their particular panacea. In this sense, it is observed that schools promote gender equality more than any other social institution. Although it is a formal egalitarianism, in that the school offers a mostly androcentric vision of the world, the school is the social space that most encourages democratic gender relations.

At the same time as this phenomenon of 'scholastic democracy', an important social change is occurring, i.e., the access of women to positions of power or to 'essentially' masculine professional positions. This is based on certain super-pluses: on family input (high socio-economic origins) and greater professional demands and personal costs than is the case for their male colleagues. Therefore, in the case of these women, a 'social over-selection' occurs. The need to acquire and accumulate these biographical super-pluses thus becomes *per se* a discriminatory factor for élite women, turning them into 'discriminated élites' (García de León, 1994).

This third hypothesis will be used to study one of the aspects of this social over-selection: whether or not educational over-selection exists. More precisely, we want to verify whether a super-meritocratisation of the female élites is occurring in the context of a school that promotes gender equality, at least in formal terms.

The concept of cultural capital

The theoretical reference for this chapter is defined by the concept of cultural capital outlined by Bourdieu and Passeron. In general, it can be affirmed that cultural capital involves many of the factors that help to achieve scholastic success, such as motivations and abilities, mastery of the 'linguistic code' on which the school places a premium, the type of family socialisation dispensed, etc. All these, at the same time, are encompassed in the scholastic notion of 'habitus'. More specifically, Bourdieu breaks down the concept of cultural capital into three dimensions:

1. Cultural capital can exist in an incorporated state, i.e., in the form of long-lasting natural aptitudes of the individual, such as introduction of one's self, manners, language and relationship with the school and with culture. In other words, the habitus as set forth above.
2. Cultural capital can exist in an objectified state, i.e., in the form of cultural goods such as paintings, books, dictionaries, instruments, etc. It should be noted that it does not suffice to transmit these goods: the way to use these goods must also be transmitted.
3. Cultural capital has an institutionalised form: i.e., guaranteed by the school institution by way of a diploma. The form cultural capital assumes is directly convertible into economic capital via the labour market. But, even in this case, having a scholastic degree does not guarantee access to a specific position, since one must know how to make good use of it. The school explosion and unemployment have heightened competition between holders of academic degrees, and thus it is necessary to resort to other forms of cultural (and also social and economic) capital to devise a strategy to make use of a diploma. In this respect, social inequalities in careers or scholastic success would be the result of prior social inequalities in the distribution of cultural capital. To these inequalities, we must add the socially determined individual aptitudes/choices: the habitus. According to Bourdieu, the habitus is a principle that shapes the representations and conducts of social agents.

It is the incorporated form of the social class (or fraction of class) to which one belongs.

On the cultural inheritance of the political and business élites

Cultural capital has basically been approached from two perspectives. Each of these, in turn, involves two diverging directions in the under-standing of social structure and social mobility. The former focuses on cultural practices, preferences and educational options of the students them-selves which lead them to a certain social status (Duncan, 1967). It is a per-spective that focuses on the subject proper and avoids any reference to structural determination. The second perspective examines the effect of the parents' socio-economic resources and cultural habits on the possibilities of their children's scholastic success, in which social structure is conceived as a structure of classes.

The data presented in this section refer to the second perspective. It is considered that a high investment in education or a high educational level of the parents influences the educational level attained by the children. A high educational level of the parents is often converted into a favourable disposition towards schooling which the children will absorb.

This effect of the studies of the élites' parents must be taken in a relative sense. The educational capital[3] of the family of origin is only part of a more extensive variable that involves other forms of capital (social, economic, etc.), which have a significant influence on attaining an educational level. In addition, from the perspective of class, the weight of each kind of capital varies in terms of the different social groups (a further major element to be considered, although we will not discuss that here).

Educational portrait of the élites' parents

The paternal educational model

We will begin with the educational level obtained by the fathers of political and business leaders. It is observed that for both élites the fathers' educational background is high: around 35 per cent in the category of university studies, although the percentage for the category of interme-diate studies is similar. Both data are highly significant, if we consider the historical period during which these fathers studied, when the ceiling of educational prestige was located at the intermediate or secondary level of the school system.

If we distinguish the data by gender, we discover major differences. In both the political and economic élites, the fathers of women in positions of power are notably more educated than the fathers of men in the same posi-tions. The fathers of the female élites are always found in higher propor-tions at all university levels (bachelor's, master's and doctoral) than fathers of the male élites: 45.5 per cent for fathers of the female business élite as opposed to 26.0 per cent of fathers of the men in this élite; and 49.4 per cent for fathers of the female political élite as opposed to 31.1% of fathers of the men[4] in this élite. The clear university orientation of the fathers of political women is especially noteworthy.

These results also reveal that the fathers of the political élites in general are only slightly more educated than the fathers of the business élites. This underlines the fact that the gender variable has a greater explanatory power than type of élite in determining the paternal educational differences.

To describe the reproductive process from parents to children in matters of education, the father's education and child's education variables for each of the élites under consideration have been cross-tabulated (see Tables 4.1 and 4.2). Each cell indicates the percentage resulting from crossing the

Table 4.1   Educational Reproduction: Business Leaders

Child's Education (%)	Father's Education (%)					
	Junsec.	**Sensec.**	**Voc.**	**Coll.**	**Master**	**Doctoral**
Junsec.	4.8	1.7	1.6	0.7	0.7	
Sensec.	11.2	8.3	8.1	2.1	5.8	1.9
Voc.	7.2	3.3	9.7	4.9	1.4	1.9
Coll.	39.2	36.4	30.6	**42.3**	12.3	13.2
Master	29.6	41.3	33.1	33.1	**64.5**	**45.3**
Doctorate	8.0	9.1	16.9	16.9	14.5	37.7
Total	15.5	15.0	15.3	17.6	17.1	6.6

Pearson chi-square sig.: 0.000.

Table 4.2   Educational Reproduction: Political Leaders

Child's Education (%)	Father's Education (%)					
	Junsec.	**Sensec.**	**Voc.**	**Coll.**	**Master**	**Doctoral**
Junsec.	1.5		3.1			2.7
Sensec.	10.8	6.4	5.2	2.3	7.2	2.7
Voc.	10.8	3.6	9.3	3.1	2.4	
Coll.	33.1	45.5	39.2	**56.6**	12.0	24.3
Master	26.9	28.2	29.9	14.7	**60.2**	24.3
Doctorate	16.9	16.4	13.4	23.3	18.1	**45.9**
Total	18.6	15.7	13.9	18.5	11.9	5.3

Pearson chi-square sig.: 0.000.

different educational levels of the father (independent variable) with the same values for the children (dependent variable). This is intended to demonstrate only approximately what is called 'educational reproduction', i.e., the influence of the education of the élites' fathers on the education of these élites.

The data show a clear tendency towards 'educational reproduction' between the élites' fathers and the élites, especially at university level. The most outstanding percentages result from the coincidence between fathers' and children's undergraduate studies (42.2 per cent for the business élite, 56.6 per cent for the political élite), and between master's studies (64.5 per cent for the business élite and 60 per cent for political élite); finally, high percentages are also observed where fathers' and children's doctoral studies are crossed (38 per cent for the business élite and 46 per cent for the political élite). It is thus concluded that the higher the educational level of the father, the more likely it is that the children (in this case, the élites) will reach at least this educational level.

The maternal educational model

The data regarding education of the élites' mothers reinforce the thesis of the strong educational background of the families of origin of the leaders.

In general, a high educational level of the mothers of the political and economic élites is observed. These women are concentrated in the intermediate level and at a relevant rate in the university levels of the educational system. In the case of male political leaders, the percentage of mothers with secondary studies is 44 per cent and for the mothers of female political leaders the percentage is 45.5 per cent in this category. For the business élite, the mothers of the men have intermediate studies in 46 per cent of the cases and the mothers of the women in 42.3 per cent. As regards university level, the percentage of mothers with university studies is 17.5 per cent and 26.1 per cent for the male and female business élites, respectively, and 17.1 per cent for mothers of both male and female political élites.[5]

These data show the higher educational level of mothers of women in positions of economic power as opposed to mothers of political women, whose results more closely resemble those of male political leaders. In addition, the mothers of female business leaders have a higher rate of university education than the mothers of the male business leaders. Gender again becomes the fundamental explanatory variable.

Therefore, the studies of mothers of the economic élites strongly influence their daughters' studies.[6] This is a key finding, if we take into account that these same mothers also perform managerial tasks in more than 40 per cent of cases (as opposed to 23.6 per cent of the mothers of male business leaders), and especially if we review the social and educational history of women in the Western world. It is a well-known fact that the phenomenon of women being involved in professional activities and attending universities in large numbers is a fairly recent occurrence. We are, thus, speaking of enterprising women who were unique for their time and could very well serve as models for their daughters in an historical context in which the generalised status of mothers was to be in non-salaried work. Therefore, the female business leaders probably acquired an early professional socialisation in their families of origin, in this case influenced also by the maternal model.

In the case of mothers of the male business élite, a lower level of university education (17.5 per cent) is noted than is the case of mothers of female business leaders, and also of mothers in managerial positions (23.6 per cent). In this respect, it can be argued that the families of male business leaders followed a traditional family pattern, in which the gender division of work linked women to the private sphere and men to the public sphere. Therefore, the marked labour and educational differences between mothers of the male and female business élites would lead us to conclude that the family types for men and women in this élite are different.

What do we observe as regards the education of the mothers of the political élite? As we indicated above, the mothers of the male and female political élites have obtained an university education at the same rate (17.1 per cent). This is a homogeneous trend which repeats itself in the percentage of these mothers who have occupied positions of responsibility in their jobs (32.5 per cent for mothers of male political leaders and 35.9 per cent for mothers of female political leaders – just slightly higher than the former figure). If these data are compared to the data regarding the mothers of the business élite, we see that the differences between the mothers of both male and female political and business leaders are primarily educational. The mothers of the female business élites are more university-oriented, but only slightly more professionally-oriented, than the mothers of women in positions of political power. This may be due to the fact that the social capital in families of the female political élites has a higher weight as compared to a greater degree of objective factors, such as educational credentials, in the business families.

A correlation between the mothers' education and the children's education shows that, in general, the same level of educational reproduction as observed in the case of the fathers does not exist. In other words, there is less of a coincidence between the studies of mothers and fathers of the élites. This is obvious, as the mothers have a lower educational level than the fathers of the élites[7] and for each examined category the children have a higher educational level than their mothers.

Using the business élite as an example, we can see that their mothers are concentrated in intermediate studies. The highest percentages appear at the crossover between the secondary educational categories of the mothers and the bachelor's and master's categories of the children (élites). In other words, when the mothers' level is junior secondary school, the higher percentage for the children is found at the bachelor's level (36.7 per cent) and at the master's level (33.3 per cent). When the mother has a senior secondary school level, the highest percentages appear at the crossover of this stratum with the bachelor's level (33.5 per cent) and master's level (41.0 per cent) of the children. Therefore, it is concluded that, in general, the élites have reached an educational rung in the school system one step higher than their mothers.

Educational background of the spouse/partner

The husband's or wife's educational background is provided as a complementary variable to the family of origin's education. This will help to reinforce the idea of reproduction of social and educational situations, completing the realm of the different manifestations of this reproduction.

For both political and business leaders as a whole, it is observed that their partners have a high educational level. Most of them are concentrated at the same university level of the educational cycle as the élites themselves. This strong homogeneity is not surprising, as we are dealing with people in positions of political and economic power who seek partners who are very much like themselves socially and educationally.

Some significant differences do appear when we control the partner's level of studies variable by the gender variable of the élite. This shows that, while 80 per cent of the partners of the female political and economic élites are in the university categories, only 63 per cent of the partners of their male counterparts are in the same categories. In addition, the partners of male leaders are also represented in the 'lower', or intermediate level, educational categories. In the case of male political leaders, the percentage of wives with senior secondary school studies is 61.5 per cent as opposed to 38.5 per cent of the partners of female political élites. The same pattern is observed in the case of business leaders: 77.2 per cent of the partners of the male business élites are concentrated in the senior secondary school category, which contrasts starkly with the 22.8 per cent of the partners of the female economic leaders.

All this indicates that, unlike men, women in positions of power find invaluable support in highly qualified husbands who also hold élite positions in many cases (73 per cent of the partners of female leaders occupy these positions as opposed to 46.5 per cent of the partners of male leaders). It could be said that, with regard to the female élites, these partners act as a dynamic element for these women either as a second role model to be emulated (together with the father) or else as mentors for these women in the professional world.

Finally, there are no statistically significant educational differences between the two types of élites in terms of educational credentials obtained by the husbands/wives. As we have seen, in general they have university studies, although the political élite shows a greater tendency towards obtaining a doctorate and the business élite a master's degree.

Cultural capital of the political and business élites

Level of studies of the élites

This section focuses on educational levels in terms of the type of formal education attained by the élites. In this sense, cultural capital is defined by a series of academic credentials acquired in the official educational systems.

The first fact that should be noted is the high percentage of members of the élites who have attained higher education. Of the élites under study, 86.6 per cent have a bachelor's degree and either a master's degree or doctorate. If we distinguish between the political and the business élites, this percentage ranges from 85.5 per cent for the former to 84.5 per cent for the latter. Obviously, this difference is not significant enough to affirm that education has a greater weight in the political élite. However, the educational differences between the two are determined by the type of higher studies that they choose. The political élite is more inclined to choose doctoral studies (more academic), whereas the business élite mostly prefers the master's degree. According to the business logic, the rule of 'effectiveness of the investment' translates, in the educational arena, into the selection of more specialised studies with which to obtain a greater market advantage.

The question now is: are there significant differences between the political and business élites depending on their gender? *Grosso modo*, there are some enlightening patterns. If we look at the percentage of élites that do *not* attain higher studies, the figures are similar for the male and female élites (15.5 per cent of the men in positions of power do not have university degrees as compared to 14.3 per cent of the women for the élites in general). In both cases, they belong to the older élites: i.e., the ones born approximately between 1925 and 1950. In these cases, it is assumed that membership in the élites results from factors others than education, such as family origin or a career of professional promotions. However, in this latter case (professional promotions) and for the age group in question, it would be easier to find male examples. This is because the working life of men has been and continues to be more stable and continuous than for women.

If we look at the élites that have obtained a higher education (84.6 per cent of the male élites and 85.7 per cent of the female élites, for the élites in general), we observe major differences depending on the age variable. We can see that, in spite of the similarity of the percentages between genders, there is a predominance of the older males of the élites in higher studies (born between 1910 and 1946), whereas there is a higher percentage of women in the younger age groups (born between 1947 and 1970) in these university studies. This is because élite women have begun to have access to the higher education resource more recently.

Table 4.3   Educational Levels by Age and Sex: Men (%)

(*)	(1)	(2)	(3)	(4)	(5)	(6)
Coll	9.1	38.3	33.3	27.1	26.6	47.6
Master	9.1	28.9	28.3	39.6	35.4	38.1
Doct	45.5	18.0	23.9	18.8	16.5	4.8
Total	1.4	16.5	38.3	30.9	10.2	2.7

Pearson chi-square sig.: 0.000.

Table 4.4   Educational Levels by Age and Sex: Women (%)

(*)	(1)	(2)	(3)	(4)	(5)	(6)
Coll	20.0	37.5	37.9	33.4	33.6	33.3
Master	20.0	26.9	32.4	42.5	43.7	43.3
Doct		10.6	12.9	14.0	11.8	16.7
Total	0.6	12.7	31.1	37.5	14.8	3.6

Pearson chi-square sig.: 0.009.
(*) (1) 1910–25 (2) 1926–37 (3) 1938–46 (4) 1947–54 (5) 1955–62 (6) 1963–70.

As we can see, age significantly marks a difference between élite men and women in relation to higher educational levels. A clear dividing line can be established in the year 1947. Up to that date, men predominated over women in terms of the levels of higher education attained. The differences between men and women were not very significant at the bachelor's level, but they shot up at the master's and doctoral levels. After 1947, age has a positive effect on equality at the higher educational levels. For men, it means a higher rate of representation in doctoral studies, while for women it means a predominance at the bachelor's and master's levels. In the last age group (women who today are between 28 and 36 years of age), the percentage of élite women at the doctoral level greatly exceeds the number of men, although this is not the general rule.

If we distinguish between the political and business élites, we find that the differences in the former are not as appreciable as in the latter. In the political élite there are almost no age or gender differences in the percentage of this élite in university studies (49.6 per cent of the male political leaders fall into the university categories as compared to 50.4 per cent of female political leaders). The most outstanding fact that can be deduced from these data is that here also there is a slight predominance of female political leaders at the bachelor's and master's levels. This trend changes direction in the case of doctoral studies, where a higher number of men are found.

In the case of the business élite, there is a higher percentage of women in higher studies than men (53.1 per cent of women in the university education categories as compared to 46.9 per cent of men). In the younger age groups (under 51 years of age), the differences between men and women in the business élite are considerable at the bachelor's level (28 per cent of the men are included at this level as compared to 32 per cent of the women). There are also outstanding differences at the master's level: 35.4 per cent of the men from the business élite are in this category as compared to 43.2 per cent of the women.

Two conclusions can be drawn from these data:

• Education has more weight in the business than in the political élite.
• Women need educational 'pluses' to counteract the inequalities that occur in the job market in favour of men.

At the same time, it is in the business élite where most of the young female leaders are numerically concentrated. This confirms the market logic: an environment of free competition and, therefore, of free access, but also of free demands. Therefore, as indicated above, it is the market where educational credentials have a stronger power of differentiation. Here, education has become a commodity with a usage and an exchange value.

Years of training

Years of training are directly related to the level of studies achieved. Since a majority of both élites have higher education, a high percentage of them (76.1 per cent), stay in the educational system from 15 to 20 years of age. However, the educational character of each élite can be better defined by observing the training pluses in years that are produced, once university studies have been completed.

It is observed that there is a higher percentage of individuals from the business élite (77.2 per cent), whose stay in the educational system corresponds to the bachelor's level and beyond, as compared to the political élite (73.3 per cent). This reconfirms the fact that there is a greater instrumentality in the use of education by the business élite. For this élite, once the university credentials required by the market are obtained, the educational career comes to an end. The logic followed by the political élite is different. Although the bulk of this élite is also found in the interval of 15 to 20 years, it is observed that this élite is more inclined than the business élite to pursue doctoral studies.

As regards gender, women at the bachelor's level are comparable in both élites. There are no significant differences between genders in years of formal education attained. However, the most noteworthy fact is that the female élites are mostly concentrated at the bachelor's level and very few women continue to postgraduate studies. In accordance with the more academic character of the political élite, the number of political women with more years of education is higher than in the business élite, although lower than in the case of the male political élites (6.7 per cent of political women have obtained more than 21 years of education as opposed to 8.7 per cent of political men). In the case of the business élite, these percentages are lower for both genders, although in this élite it is also observed that women have fewer years of education (3.6 per cent of women in the business élite receive more than 21 years of training as opposed to 5.2 per cent of male business leaders).

Selected courses of study

Many of the differences that can be sociologically categorised as social dichotomies are reproduced through the selected course of study. In this chapter, the division between the sciences and the arts would be the most obvious dichotomy, although to this we will add other social dualities of a binomial structure such as: masculine/feminine, theory/practice, politics/economics, etc.

By framing both élites in terms of these dualities of social structure, we see that the selection of a course of study is also based on the same co-ordinates. The courses of study chosen by the political élite include law (20.9 per cent), social sciences (13.2 per cent), economics (10.8 per cent) and the humanities (9 per cent). The business élite, on the other hand, opts for economics (15.3 per cent), business studies (15.3 per cent), law (10 per cent) and natural sciences (7.8 per cent). We see that the academic profile changes from one élite to the other, although there are courses shared by both élites. Law (for the political élite) and economics (for the business élite) are specific fields of job application in each of the élites, but both subjects provide essential knowledge for the professional work of the élites in general (both courses appear with a high percentage in the educational preferences of both élites). It could said that the élites in question specialise in certain careers that mostly fall into the sphere of the social sciences.

It should be noted that in the careers that rank highest among each élite (law and social sciences for the political élite, and economics and business studies for the business élite) there are no significant differences by gender of the élite. However, it should always be remembered that we are speaking of a particular stratum of the population. The fact that, in this case, women share the same careers as men does not mean that there are no gender differences in choice of career in the general population: here we are speaking of élites, and of very specific élites linked to certain studies, which explains why career choice is so similar between men and women. This fact is verified when we approach the careers least related to the professional profile of the élites. In this case, it is observed that the gender, although we are speaking of élites, become increasingly similar to the bipolarities found in society regarding study choices.

Table 4.5   Selection of Course of Studies: Political Élite

	Men (%)	Women (%)	Total (%)
Law	51.1	48.9	20.9
Social science	47.2	52.8	13.2
Economics	72.6	27.4	10.8
Humanities	27.9	72.1	9.0
Engineering	84.6	15.4	1.9
Medicine	34.4	65.6	4.7

Pearson chi-square sig.: 0.000.

Table 4.6   Selection of Course of Studies: Business Élite

	Men (%)	Women (%)	Total (%)
Economics	50.0	50.0	15.3
Business	47.3	52.7	15.3
Law	35.6	64.4	10.0
Natural science	64.9	35.1	7.8
Engineering	77.6	22.4	6.7
Medicine	16.7	83.3	0.8

Pearson chi-square sig.: 0.000.

For example, the differences can be appreciated in the political élite when we move away from the two most frequently chosen careers. In economics and the humanities, we can see a gender difference in choice. The former is chosen mostly by men, whereas the latter is chosen mostly by women. This fact is reinforced if we look at other studies such as engineering, medicine, etc. The same is true of the business élite. The similarity of career selection between men and women in this élite occurs in economics and business studies. The selection begins to differ by gender in law (chosen more by female business leaders) and natural science (chosen more by men). Course of study choice in the business élite also begins to differ in the careers least related to their professional profile. This is demonstrated in Table 4.5.

Conclusion

Based on the most relevant data regarding the cultural capital of the political and business élites and taking into the account the basic hypotheses, the following conclusions can be drawn:

1. As regards the cultural inheritance of the élites, it emerges that the educational levels of the family of origin heavily influence the qualifications

attained by the élites themselves. In this respect, determining high paternal educational levels is more relevant that determining the influence of maternal studies. In the case of fathers, this pattern of educational reproduction occurs not only in relation to study levels, but also in the type of postgraduate work preferred by each type of élite. For example, in the case of the political élite, there is an obvious preference for doctoral studies, which is the same preference observed for the fathers. On the contrary, the business élite tends to choose master's studies, just like their fathers.

On the other hand, it is seen that the fathers of both the female political and business élites have a higher educational level. The fathers of the male élites would thus be men with a high educational level, but their proportion in the category of university studies would be considerably lower than that of the fathers of the female élites. This demonstrates the tremendous influence that the fathers of the female élites can have on these women. In this respect, the gender variable has a greater explicative power than type of élite.

As for the mothers, a high educational level is observed in general, although it is significantly lower than the fathers'. In this case, the influence of maternal education is understood to be key only in the case of the female business élites, whose mothers are more educated and professional than the mothers of the men and political élites. Perhaps the real influence of the mother could be better analysed by using techniques of in-depth interviews rather than on the basis of objective survey data. In view of the fact that women have traditionally lagged behind in their access to social spaces (such as the school), future research should consider the possibility that the maternal influence has developed on a more intimate, subjective plane.

2. As regards the cultural capital of the élites, there is an obvious disposition towards the university. The difference between the political and business élites lies in the type of postgraduate studies chosen by each one. For example, the former seem to prefer doctoral studies, perhaps because of the academic nature of the university careers that they follow (e.g., law). The latter, on the other hand, mostly opt for master's studies, which is related to the practical nature that characterises the bachelor's studies they have obtained (economics, business studies).

The educational differences between men and women are related to age. There is a greater proportion of older male élites at the university levels, where younger women predominate. The latter is especially significant in the case of female business leaders, as they are the ones who accumulate more educational credentials and where younger women are found at university levels. This points to how important university degrees are for these women in their professional strategies. It is in this case that we can speak quite rightfully of 'super-meritocratisation' of the female élites.

Although there are no notable gender differences in choosing the type of university studies in the most preferred careers, differences do appear when we address other courses of studies that are not as critical to the professional profile of the élites. These differences manifest themselves on a normal topical or social basis (for example, economics, natural sciences and engineering for men, as opposed to humanities, medicine and law for women).

3. The most marked differences between men and women of the élites in question occur above all in the educational credentials of the family of origin. The fact that these élites have been investigated when they have already attained a certain position of power perhaps obscures the obstacles that women have had to overcome to arrive at these positions. Further research is required to explore this process: i.e., the channels of access to prestigious professional worlds monopolised by men, and in this way confirm that this similarity in the professional profiles of the élites is only an effect of the position itself.

Notes

1. This section reproduces Oeuvrard's explanation of cultural capital. F. Oeuvrard, 'Tendencias actuales de la Sociología de la Educación en Francia', in García de León et al. (1993).
2. Marcial Romero and Alicia Pascual have collaborated in obtaining the data for this survey.
3. We have begun to speak in terms of educational capital because there is no direct measurement of the source family's cultural capital. Thus, the mother's and father's educational capital is methodologically considered as a *proxy* of cultural resources. Therefore, both terms can be viewed in this restricted sense as interchangeable. For more information, see Aschaffenburg and Maas (1997) and Blossfeld and Shavit (1993).
4. Using a chi-squared test, the difference between the results for male and female leaders is statistically significant. In the case of political leaders (men/women), the Pearson chi-square significance (p value) was 0.002. For business élites (men/women), the p value was 0.021.
5. The p values were statistically significant: 0.085 in the case of male/female political élites, and 0.031 in the case of male/female business élites.
6. At first we thought that this influence was a result of the age of the élite in question. It was thought that the younger female business élites would reflect this influence more. As they are younger, their mothers would also be younger and therefore would have had more opportunities to continue their schooling. To check this, we crossed the élite's age with the educational levels of their mothers. No statistically significant results were obtained that would have validated this hypothesis.
7. We can see this clearly if we examine the distribution of the fathers' and mothers' secondary studies, where the mothers are more predominant than the fathers. For example, in the case of political leaders, the figure of the mothers at that educational level is 45 per cent, while for the fathers it is 34 per cent.

5
Career Trajectories:
Convergence or Divergence?

Eileen Drew

Introduction

Women's access to, and advancement within, formal labour markets in the industrialised nations has been well documented (OECD, 1985; Norris, 1987; Jenson, Hagen and Reddy, 1988; Kicková and Forkasová, 1993; Drew and Emerek, 1998). However, the process of feminisation has occurred at an uneven pace and does not generally mirror the patterns of men's labour market activity in Western industrialised countries (a notable exception is the position of Finnish women). This pattern has relegated them to what Jane Lewis (1993: 21) has termed 'women's unequal position in the work-force'. Though women now spend more of their life-cycle than previous generations in paid employment and less time on unpaid domestic and caring work, there has been little alteration between the genders in the division of labour within the home. Moreover, it is women's labour that has traditionally provided labour market flexibility, mainly through part-time employment, within most OECD countries. Part-time employment emerged during and after the Second World War in response to labour shortages. It gained the support of governments and trade unions in enabling married women with domestic responsibilities to combine paid employment with domestic commitments (Charles, 1993). No similar policy or action was adopted to encourage men to adapt to the demands of childcare.

The disadvantages attached to part-time working have been much debated, particularly within the EU, in terms of the lower pay and status attached, and terms and conditions of employment (Drew, 1990). Many of these disadvantages are not due to the hours worked, but to the nature of the part-time jobs (e.g., cleaning and personal service) and/or the insecure nature of the employment contract (e.g., part-time, hence temporary teachers). Research shows that even professional and skilled women who return to the labour market following child-rearing, do so to 'jobs which are lower in pay and status than those held prior to the birth of their first child' (Charles, 1993: 60). In post-communist states where full-time employment had been the norm for all workers it is women (though not men) who are seeking not to leave the labour force completely, 'but to work part-time when they have children under three years' (Funk and Mueller, 1993: 326).

The 'choice' to exit from the labour market and/or work part-time must be seen in the context of 'familial ideology', reflecting what 'ought to happen' (Charles, 1993: 68) in families. This influences decisions concerning women's and men's labour market participation and the domestic division of labour. Duane-Richard (1988: 266) asserts that the social construction of a trajectory for women and of their workplace identities can only be understood 'via an appreciation of women's double lives – both at work and at home'. These must also be viewed against the mechanisms of domination, which characterise formal institutions and public life. Cockburn reiterates the assignation of women's disadvantage in work and public life to 'their disproportionate responsibility for domestic work, including care of the young, old and ill' (1991: 12). She shows that this disadvantage is exploited by employers through the adverse consequences for women, though not men, seeking to combine paid and unpaid work: 'The absence of any serious policy to extend such 'privileges' to men, and men's unwillingness to make use of them when they exist, are identified as a significant form of resistance by men to women's progress in organisations' (Cockburn, 1991: 12).

The asymmetrical arrangement of working life in which women work fewer paid hours, while men work more, is accompanied by the uneven division of labour within the home so that men earn more, work fewer total (paid and unpaid) hours and hence have more leisure time. Their permanent attachment to the labour force facilitates their advancement, allowing them to attain higher status 'partly because their hands are not tied by domesticity, partly because they have the power to keep women down' (Cockburn, 1991: 18).

The resulting imbalance in the allocation of work within and outside the household has been the subject of considerable debate. Becker (1985), arguing from a position of rational economic choice, would claim that women and men choose to allocate their time between paid work, housework and leisure, in proportions which reflect the earning power of respective partners. Partners (usually male) with greater earnings would remain in continuous employment, while the other (female) partner, possessing lower human capital, would be more likely to opt for greater involvement in housework and childcare. This supply-driven approach has been heavily criticised for ignoring the structural and institutional constraints which operate selectively to exclude, segregate and discourage women's advancement in business and political life.

Walby addresses Becker's economic rationality in stating that women 'make choices, but not under conditions of their own making. Women choose the best option that they can see, rationally, though usually with imperfect knowledge, but only within the range of options open to them' (1987: 25).

The consequences of exercising these 'choices' can be observed in the life/career patterns of women workers (for example, Elias and Main, 1982; Martin and Roberts, 1984). Compared with men's continuous full-time careers, women's are more often characterised by discontinuity, a mix of part-time and full-time work and time spent out of the labour force. In labour markets which tend to equate 'numerical flexibility' with marginality, it is women who have provided cheaper, sex-segregated and highly flexible workers.

Even for women with equivalent or higher levels of social capital, relative to men, 'the structure of a management career, based on men's experiences, needs and life-cycle patterns, assumes a history of continuous full-time employment' (Wajcman, 1996: 262). Wajcman's study of five multinational companies underlined her claim that managerial 'work itself is conceptualised as involving constant action. . . . Thus, the social construction of management is one in which managerial competencies are intrinsically linked to qualities attaching to men' (Wajcman, 1996: 262).

An appraisal of women's public and political identity cannot be viewed in isolation from their involvement in the labour market. Neither can it be assumed that political participation occurs in tandem with economic involvement. Women's reproductive role pre-dates the industrialisation process, through subsistence and outworking, while female emancipation was not achieved widely until the twentieth century. While feminisation is recognisably occurring in many industrialised labour markets, women have not been as readily accepted into the political arena. As Chapman (1993: xi) notes: 'with a very few and arguable exceptions among the industrialised nations, women remain outside the centres of decision-making throughout the world and the forms of status, influence and power which are available to men continue to elude them.'

Mechanisms, similar to those used historically (see Walby, 1986) within the production process, have been employed to control women's access to public power: exclusion, segregation and (partial) integration. Chapman (1993: 13) refers to the 'exclusion of out groups per se, or discrimination as it is nowadays perceived. . . . Discrimination may be open, or, in the case of élites under severe pressure, disguised by a semblance of equal opportunity; it may be conscious or take the unwitting form of prejudice.'

A further inhibitor for women in political life, as distinct from the labour market constraints already referred to, is the nature of the recruitment process in politics and the unique nature of political appointments in parliamentary systems from the pool of elected representatives, by a single leader or small group of, usually male, leaders.

Norris (1987: 117) concurs with this observation that there 'have been few women in cabinet office in any of the countries under comparison, although again there is a consistent pattern since the countries with the most women in their elected assemblies also have the most women in government'. Gelb (1986: 111) notes that 'in the main, the more significant a policy-making body is, the fewer women it has on it'. Norris (1987: 122) states that one of the primary functions of political parties is to 'nominate and support suitable candidates for office'. Randall (1987) acknowledges that the 'exclusiveness' which pervades political institutions constitutes a barrier to women, as Rogers (1988) has shown in her investigation of other men's organisations. Randall (1987: 143) refers to women's exclusion from the most powerful informal US House caucuses and the pigeonholing of women into 'traditional "feminine" fields as far as government appointments go and in committee assignments in Congress'. She notes that in general, and even in Scandinavia, women are absent from finance committees and over-represented in family and cultural committees.

By the 1980s, women could no longer be actively excluded from business and public office, yet as Haavio-Mannila et al. (1985: 165) show, 'a vertical and a horizontal division of labour between genders are to be found in political life'.

The remainder of this chapter concentrates on the survey data to confirm or contradict the conclusions drawn from the review of international literature. It examines the career advancement of female and male leaders by testing key hypotheses relating to gendered career paths. As the literature reviewed has shown, men's careers are typified by their continuity in full-time, continuous employment, following a clear trajectory of advancement. Women's careers have not always followed this pattern (though the closest matches were found in former Eastern bloc countries), as is illustrated by the divergent employment of leaders' mothers and fathers.

The chapter explores whether, even among successful women leaders of this generation, their pattern and history of employment diverges from the male 'norm' of 40 hours a week, throughout the year and over 40 years of a life span (Drew, 1987). Hence, it examines the number of full-time jobs held, the policy and functional areas in which leaders are appointed/employed. It analyses the work histories of male and female leaders to ascertain whether significant differences exist in their previous careers in terms of occupational prestige/class.

Given the overwhelming dominance by men in the area of political appointments, to cabinet, ministerial office and committees, this chapter analyses where political women/men are positioned relative to their desired committee involvement. Finally the chapter looks at the degree to which women and men in leadership positions have experienced conflicts between home/family and work, and whether these have been resolved, according to gender lines, by recourse to 'atypical' working patterns in the form of career breaks and part-time working.

Career histories

Male and female leaders differ significantly in terms of the number of full-time jobs they have held – this variable is used as a proxy for 'career ambition', based on the assumption that men are more likely to change (full-time) jobs to secure advancement and promotion (Elias and Main, 1982). Women will be less likely to have achieved upward mobility, due to their more frequent adherence to the logic that 'I'll stay on and do my job better' (Davidson and Cooper, 1992; Flanders, 1994) and, if they make career shifts, these are less likely to be exclusively in full-time jobs.

The results using all the (unweighted) data show that male leaders held more full-time jobs than female leaders – 62 per cent of men and 69 per cent of women in the sample had four jobs or less. Using a statistical test,[1] the difference between male/female results was statistically significant (p = 0.004). Using weighting to control for uneven numbers of male/female leaders across country samples, on average men held 3.8 full-time jobs and women 3.6. The weighted mean was higher for men in socio-democratic countries (4.6) and less economically developed countries (4.2), compared with 3.5 in full market economies. There was less variation among female leaders, though the pattern was consistent with that of men's in relation to country groupings. Male business leaders had, on average (weighted) 4.2 full-time jobs, compared with 3.8 for their female counterparts. The average level of full-time jobs was lowest among female political leaders (3.3), compared with 3.6 for their counterparts.

These findings show a consistently higher level of full-time jobs by male leaders, which holds for sector (business/political) and across country groupings. The statistically significant gender difference supports the hypothesis that male leaders will have gained more experience and enhanced their career prospects through working in a greater number of full-time jobs than female leaders.

Occupational prestige

The hypothesis tested is that male political and business leaders are more likely than female leaders to have achieved higher levels of occupational prestige in their first, last but one and previous posts. The data were coded according to the Treiman index (1974). Since the responses ranged in occupational prestige score from 0 to 92 they were recoded for analysis into ten prestige categories (0–10, 11–20, 21–30, etc.) and the results for each of the three jobs held can be seen in Tables 5.1, 5.2 and 5.3.

The mean prestige level (weighted) of the first positions held by business and political leaders was 56.4 for men and 56.0 for women, suggesting a marginal difference. In the position before last the mean prestige score was 61.4 for men and 60.4 for women, suggesting a minor, but increasing, gap.

However, in the last position held the means were closer: 64.6 for men and 64.0 for women.

Whilst the analysis using the mean prestige score suggested that men ranked higher, the scores need to be examined against the results in each occupational prestige category. It is clear that in each position, from first to most recent, female leaders dominate in the very high prestige levels, reflecting a score in excess of 80. Male leaders are more prominent in the 70–80 score category and, with the exception of first position, in the 60–70 score category. The complex pattern is best examined in Tables 5.1–5.3.

Class

Although the number of class categories was small – (1) owner with more than nine employees, (2) owner with 0–9 employees, (3) manager, (4) no supervisory function – the results of the analysis show a significant difference between male and female leaders in relation to first job ($p < 0.0001$), in last but one job ($p = 0.001$) and at a 5 per cent level for previous position ($p = 0.015$), suggesting that the gender gap in relation to class was reduced between leaders' first and most recent jobs.

The male/female differences emerge in relation to the higher proportion of female leaders who did not hold supervisory positions (see below) and the lower proportion of them in management positions. Even in previous positions, owners of a business employing staff represented less than 10 per cent of all leaders in the sample.

Supervisory role

The hypothesis tested is that male political and business leaders are more likely than female leaders to have held a supervisory role in their first, last but one and last posts. These questions relating to respondents' job history showed that there were statistically significant differences in the (non-)supervisory nature in each of the previous jobs held.

In first jobs, 66 per cent of female and 53 per cent of male leaders held no supervisory position. Among the latter 38 per cent held a lower/middle or top management position compared with 25 per cent of female leaders. The differences were statistically significant ($p < 0.000$). Moving to the position before last there was no supervisory function in the jobs held by 27 per cent of women and 20 per cent of men leaders. For the latter, 43 per cent had achieved a top management position in their previous post, compared with only 26 per cent of women. The difference between male/female leaders was again statistically significant ($p < 0.000$). Finally, examining the last posts held by male and female leaders, 18 per cent of women still held no supervisory function, compared with 11 per cent of men. A total of 59 per cent of men had achieved positions as senior managers compared with 44 per cent of women. The male/female difference was statistically significant ($p < 0.000$).

Table 5.1   Main Policy Areas in which Political Respondents were Involved in Last Year (based on multiple responses of 793 respondents)

Policy Area	No. Female Respondents Involved	No. Male Respondents Involved	% Female	% Male
Male (10)				
Premier	5	5	50	50
Internal Affairs	62	104	37	63
Economic Affairs	82	146	36	64
Fiscal Policy	35	70	33	67
Public Works	6	17	26	74
Defence	21	42	33	67
International Affairs	84	81	49	51
Constitutional Affairs	28	55	34	66
Industrial Policy	13	23	36	64
Agriculture	19	27	41	59
TOTAL	*355*	*570*	*38*	*62*
Female (10)				
Labour	56	43	57	43
Health	81	45	64	36
Education	86	63	58	42
Justice	56	44	44	56
Welfare	72	45	62	38
Family Affairs	53	11	83	17
Gender Equality	127	6	95	5
Migrants	32	21	60	40
Assistance to Elderly	15	9	63	37
Human	39	20	66	34
TOTAL	*617*	*307*	*67*	*33*
Neutral (11)				
Environment Affairs	48	56	46	54
Disarmament	10	7	59	41
Transportation	11	23	32	68
Energy	10	13	43	57
Traffic Problems	8	11	42	58
Monuments	9	4	69	31
State Property	5	14	26	74
Cultural Affairs	23	14	62	38
Mail	1	5	17	83
Misc. specified	23	31	43	57
Other	30	61	33	67
TOTAL	*178*	*239*	*43*	*57*

Table 5.2 Political Issues Handled by Committees of which Respondents were Members (based on multiple responses of 467 respondents)

Policy Area	No. Female Respondents Involved	No. Male Respondents Involved	% Female	% Male
Male (12)				
Premier	31	28	53	47
Internal Affairs	33	51	39	61
Economic Affairs	42	91	32	68
Fiscal Policy	20	58	26	74
Public works	7	23	23	77
Defence	28	43	39	61
International Affairs	43	61	41	59
Constitutional Affairs	29	45	39	61
Industrial Policy	12	18	40	60
Agriculture	11	14	44	56
TOTAL	*256*	*432*	*37*	*63*
Female (12)				
Labour	38	25	60	40
Health	52	26	67	33
Education	55	32	63	37
Justice	45	38	54	46
Welfare	61	27	69	31
Family Affairs	48	9	84	16
Gender Equality	65	8	89	11
Migrants	19	20	49	51
Assistance to Elderly	30	19	61	39
Human	28	21	57	43
TOTAL	*441*	*225*	*66*	*34*
Neutral (12)				
Environment Affairs	27	34	44	56
Disarmament	15	11	58	42
Transportation	6	20	23	77
Energy	11	17	39	61
Traffic Problems	6	9	40	60
Pres. Monuments	11	6	65	35
State Property	6	10	38	62
Cultural Affairs	18	15	55	45
Mail	2	1	67	33
Misc. specified	15	29	34	66
Other	29	64	31	69
TOTAL	*146*	*216*	*40*	*60*

Table 5.3 Summary of the Five Most Important Areas for the Political Profile of Leaders' Parties (based on multiple responses of 455 respondents)

Policy Area	No. of Male Responses	No. of Female Responses	Total Responses
Economic Affairs	153	136	289
Education	105	88	193
Welfare	94	83	177
Labour	90	83	173
Health	77	71	148
Fiscal Policy	86	57	143
International Affairs	75	59	134
Internal Affairs	68	46	114
Justice	44	51	95
Women	20	51	71
Family Affairs	29	33	62

Current positions

Ranking of current position

Respondents were asked to rate their satisfaction with their career progress. The hypothesis tested here is that male leaders would express a significantly higher ranking of their present position than their female counterparts. In fact, no significant difference emerged. In all, two-thirds of men ranked their present position in terms of being highly satisfied, compared with 63 per cent of the female respondents.

Satisfaction with career progress

Business and political leaders were asked the same question in rating their satisfaction with their career progress in civilian/political life. I hypothesised that male leaders would express higher levels of satisfaction with their political or business careers to date than female leaders. On the contrary, there were no statistically significant differences in the levels of satisfaction among male/female business and political leaders.

Involvement in main policy areas – political leaders

The next hypothesis was that male and female political leaders work in significantly different policy areas and hence are occupied with different policy issues. The questionnaire allowed respondents to identify up to three main policy areas in which they were involved in the last year. These were not ranked in any order of preference or importance. The results showed statistically significant differences in the policy areas identified by men and women ($p < 0.0001$ for each of the three areas).

While interesting, this finding does not in itself imply any important imbalance in the policy allocation. Therefore, to draw further conclusions about the implications of the gendered involvement in policy areas, the responses to the three areas were merged, to obtain an overview of all the responses to a question. The hypotheses tested here was that:

- men would be more involved in the 'hard' economic areas: fiscal and economic policy, international affairs;
- women would be more often involved in 'soft' policy areas: social welfare, health, family, education, women's affairs;
- men and women would be more evenly represented in 'neutral' areas such as: infrastructure, environment.

This required an allocation of the 31 policy areas into 'male', 'female' and 'neutral' to produce Table 5.1. Table 5.1 illustrates that, with the exception of 'premier' and the policy areas of international affairs and to a lesser extent agriculture, women are under-represented in the 'male' policy areas. Male leaders are even less likely to be involved in the 'female' policy areas. While not equally represented, the 'neutral' policy areas do show a better balance among male and female leaders, (though mail, state property and transportation tend to be male-dominated areas).

When the 31 policy areas were allocated to three categories 'male', 'female' and 'neutral', the responses to main policy area involvement indicate statistically significant gender differences ($p < 0.000$ for each round of three responses).

These results will be further compared with responses to committee involvement of politicians and the importance assigned by leaders to the same policy areas.

Functional section of employment – business leaders

The equivalent approximation to policy involvement among business leaders was in relation to their functional division or area in their company. The hypothesis tested here was that male and female business leaders are employed in significantly different functional areas:

- male leaders in strategic, financial, production and raw materials;
- female leaders in administration, human resources/personnel, and marketing.

Analysis of the ten main functional areas showed that female business leaders were under-represented at the top strategic apex, and were over-represented in organisational development, personnel, management information and finance. Male business leaders were over-represented in marketing, production and top management. Similar proportions of male and female business leaders were found in Accounting, and Research and

Development. However, the differences were not statistically significant at a 5 per cent level (p = 0.080).

Directorships of major corporations – business and political leaders

All leaders were asked if they had ever held directorships of corporations. The responses of male and female leaders differed significantly (p < 0.000). Among women, 75 per cent had never held such positions, whereas this applied to only 65 per cent of men.

The (weighted) average number of directorships (including those who held none) for men was 0.7 and for female leaders 0.5. These differences were reflected in the results for leaders according to sector. Male business leaders held an average of 1.0 directorship, compared with 0.7 for female business leaders. The level was lower for political leaders: 0.5 for male and 0.3 for female political leaders.

When asked about the number of current directorships held, the level was somewhat lower. For men the (weighted) average was 0.6 and for women 0.4. The level of holdings was considerably higher for business leaders than political leaders, suggesting that political leaders give up, or are forced to give up, previously held directorships on entering politics. For male business leaders the current average was 1.0 and for female 0.7, in contrast to male and political leaders with an average of 0.2 and 0.1 respectively. The gender difference for currently holding directorships showed borderline significance at a 5 per cent level (p = 0.046).

Committee involvement – political leaders

Respondents were asked to identify up to five political issues handled by the parliamentary/senate committees of which they were members. The SPSS multiple response function was used to compile a composite table incorporating the range of responses from political leaders. The results are shown in Table 5.2.

The hypothesis tested in this section is that male and female political leaders are appointed to committees reflecting significantly different policy areas:

- men in the 'hard' economic areas: fiscal and economic policy;
- women in 'soft' policy areas: social welfare, health, family, education, women's affairs.

The analysis of these issues showed that there were statistically significant differences between male and female leaders when each of the five, or fewer, areas were compared (p = 0.000, 0.000, 0.000, 0.013, 0.011 respectively).

When the responses were assigned to 'male', 'female' and 'neutral' categories the results were statistically significant for each of the five committee-related issues (p = 0.000, 0.000, 0.000, 0.003, 0.001 respectively). These results provide further evidence of the gender segmentation of political involvement through committees membership by leaders. These will be examined against the first and second preferences of political leaders and the five policy areas which political respondents considered most important.

Preferred committee involvement – political leaders

Political leaders were asked to state what their first and second choice of parliamentary/senate committee would be. Given the gendered nature of the membership of committees, it is natural to ask whether these committees reflect the different wishes of the male and female leader or, alternatively, whether men and women are assigned to committees, not on the basis of their personal preference, but of gender stereotyping. The hypothesis tested is that male political leaders are significantly more likely than women leaders to be serving on committees which match their stated choices.

The analysis of male and female first preferences showed that there was no statistically significant difference between those of men and women (p = 0.061). The top three preferred committees were the same for men and women: international affairs, economic affairs and fiscal policy. Some policy areas, most notably education, constitutional affairs, justice, defence, environmental affairs and public works, attracted similar levels of first preferences from male and female leaders. In others there was some divergence in relation to health and labour, where more women expressed a first preference, while male leaders were twice as likely to seek internal affairs and marginally more likely to be involved in welfare.

Analysis of second preference membership of committees revealed a more complex picture in which the differences were statistically significant between men and women (p = 0.001). The largest number of responses was for international affairs, by both men and women, fiscal policy sought mainly by men, followed by education and economic affairs preferred mainly by female leaders. More women expressed an interest in welfare, while defence and justice emerged as the next more preferred areas among men.

Most important areas for their parties' political profile – political leaders

Respondents were asked to list the five areas which they considered most important for the political profile of their party. The hypothesis tested is that men and women hold similar views on what are the important issues in political life and that these coincide with the areas in which men are most heavily represented. The first part of this proposition is borne out by the results comparing men's and women's views on what are the important issues. For each of the five listed areas, there were no statistically significant differences between the male and female political leaders. Using the SPSS multiple response function to synthesise the views of political leaders, Table 5.3 shows the ten most important areas according to gender.

The results show that men and women do not differ significantly in assigning the most important policy areas and that these span the 'hard' economic and policy areas traditionally dominated by male politicians as well as the 'soft', people-related service support areas.

The analyses of policy involvement, committee representation, preferences and assignation of importance attached to policy areas support the views of Haavio-Mannila. Women are more involved in 'promoting issues relating to the situation of women, children, the sick and other underprivileged groups' (1985: 165). The authors state that it is tempting, but oversimplistic, to conclude that 'where women are, power is not, and where power is, women are not', since it is the 'social' policy areas like social welfare and education that administer the largest budgets in most countries. What is clear from Haavio-Mannila's study of the Nordic countries and from this survey is that, while women and men share similar views on the importance of both 'hard' and soft' policy areas, women are not appointed to the planning, productive and financial functions and committees to the same degree as men.

Reconciliation of career/family/other life

Career disruptions

Due to family/work conflicts, it is hypothesised that women leaders are more likely to have experienced disruptions in their career advancement than male leaders, with the exception of disruption due to military service. Respondents indicated the extent of career disruption from several family and other responsibilities (1 = 'not at all' to 5 = 'very much'). Taking each potential reason for career disruption, we tested for statistical significance. In relation to military service there is a statistically significant gender difference, in which only 13 women compared with 160 men had been affected (p < 0.000). The impact of spouse's career emerged as a statistically significant difference among male and female leaders (p < 0.000). To some degree (excluding 'not at all' responses) spouses' careers affected 32 per cent of female leaders, while the equivalent among men was 20 per cent.

Respondents were asked if their spouse's attitude to their work had interfered with their career. There were no significant differences between men and women. Care of children/relatives was posed as another potential career disruption. While 59 per cent at men had been totally unaffected by this, only 41 per cent of women stated to have been *totally* unaffected. The gender differences were significant (p < 0.000). In fact, 14 per cent of female leaders noted that childcare or care of a relative had interfered much/very much with their careers, compared with 5 per cent of men.

A major and significant gender divergence emerged in relation to the experience of career interruptions due to housework obligations (p < 0.000). While 70 per cent of male respondents cited that housework had not in any way interfered with their career, this applied to only 47 per cent of female respondents. In fact, 11 per cent of the women stated that housework had interfered much/very much with their careers, compared with 3 per cent of men.

Family commitments also differentiated the men from the women in the sample, with statistically significant differences (p < 0.000). In fact, 61 per cent of the men stated that family commitments had not interfered with their career, compared with 49 per cent of the women. Almost 9 per cent of female leaders stated that family commitments had interfered much or very much, compared with less than 4 per cent of men.

Conflict between dual demands of work and life outside work

Due to the gendered division of labour within households, it is hypothesised that female leaders are more likely to have experienced conflict between the demands of their work and the demands of life outside work than male leaders. A question asked how often (1 = 'very often' to 5 = 'never') the respondent experiences a conflict between the demands of the position held and the demands of life outside work, the differences between men's and women's experience of conflict in reconciling their dual roles were statistically significant (p = 0.008). The same percentage of men and women stated 'never' (5 per cent), while 15 per cent of women and 12 per cent of men responded 'very often'.

Reasons for and duration of part-time working

As the literature review has shown, societal expectations are placed on women in relation to their primary responsibility for rearing children, caring for relatives and housework. It is hypothesised that women are more likely than men to have worked part-time as a strategy to resolve the conflicting demands on their time.

Respondents indicated whether and for how long they had worked part-time for a variety of specified reasons.

Almost 99 per cent of the male leaders had *never* worked part-time to care for a child or relative; this was the case for 83 per cent of the female leaders (p < 0.000). In fact, 5 per cent of women leaders had worked part-time for eight years or more. This applied to none of the male leaders.

There was no statistically significant difference in the number of years worked part-time by men and women in order to further their education – an option for 3 per cent of male leaders and almost 5 per cent of female leaders – or for political or trade union activity.

Gender differences, significant at the 1 per cent level (p = 0.001), were observable for years worked part-time through change of residence due to a partner. However, the cells were very small and those who worked part-time for this reason accounted for less than 3 per cent of female leaders.

There was no statistically significant difference between men and women at a 5 per cent level between the years worked part-time for political or trade union activity. In fact, 3 per cent of male leaders and almost 4 per cent of female leaders had worked part-time for this reason, most commonly for one year.

Recourse to part-time working by women, mainly to cope with childcare or care of relatives, may help to explain the less gender-differentiated response to conflicting demands covered above, since it is among the female rather than male leaders that part-time working was used as a reconciliation strategy.

Career disruptions

It is hypothesised that women leaders' careers are significantly more likely to have been subject to disruptions of more than six months than men's and that these disruptions are more likely to have been for childcare/family reasons. When male leaders have experienced disruptions, it is significantly more likely that these will have been for military/education reasons. Hence, men's disruptions will enhance their career prospects, while women's disruptions will hinder their career advancement, under prevailing personnel practices.

There were statistically significant differences in the male/female pattern of career disruption for military service (p < 0.000). As anticipated, this disproportionately affected 11 per cent of male leaders, but only three women in the sample. Most of the men who had taken a break for military service had experienced only one disruption.

There were no significant differences between men and women in leadership positions experiencing disruptions due to illness; to start a new business, although twice as many women (24) had done so compared with men; to further education; for political or trade union activity; unemployment or other reasons.

The statistically significant difference between men's and women's career disruptions arise in relation to time out for childrearing or care of relatives (p < 0.000). Less than 1 per cent of the male leaders had interrupted their careers for these reasons, compared with 17 per cent of the women leaders. Most had taken one (5 per cent), two (3 per cent) or three (1 per cent) breaks in their careers for caring responsibilities.

Significantly more female leaders had experienced a disruption due to having to move with their partner. This affected more than 3 per cent of the women, but only one man. The significant level is high (p < 0.000), but only very small numbers were affected.

Conclusion

This chapter provides evidence of gendered career paths even among top-level leaders. Male leaders were significantly more likely to have built up their previous job histories and to have remained in full-time employment, without interruption, throughout their working lives. Female leaders were significantly more likely to have had fewer full-time positions. On average, the women held fewer managerial and supervisory positions than men, and attained a marginally lower occupational class in their previous careers than their male counterparts.

Among political leaders, men were significantly more likely to be involved in policy areas, most notably via committees, which matched their 'hard issue' policy preferences. This was not true of female political leaders, who were clustered in the 'softer' social policy areas, although this did not necessarily reflect their preferences. It was mainly women political and business leaders who had disrupted their careers and/or worked part-time to care for children or other family members.

It is clear from this study that men's and women's career trajectories were dissimilar, since it was female leaders who more frequently experienced conflicts between home/family and work and who were more likely to resort to 'atypical' working patterns to resolve these conflicts.

Note

1. All of the statistical tests referred to in this chapter are based on Pearson's chi-squared test.

6
Men and Women in Political Leadership

Maria Carrilho

The explanations and justifications for women's marginalisation from public life run from those rooted in certain ideological-religious beliefs to philosophic theories on 'natural' (recently, biological) differences and roles. But in the end they can be narrowed down to deep-rooted ideas, namely that women have their own sphere of influence, which is the 'private', while men have to master the 'public' (Pateman, 1989).

On the other hand, we find the idea (expressed by a long strain of thinking within the feminist movement) that men and women have different capacities and values and bring different behaviour to politics and to the organisation and exercise of power. This assumes that women are more humanistic-oriented and should thus bring a higher moral standard to politics.

It is probably no exaggeration to say that a rather 'Leviathanesque' understanding of the state and of politics is implicit in all these views.

The least we can say is that there is no evidence for any of the above-mentioned ideas. However, the attempt to shed some light on such questions is generally present in the mind of the researcher on gender and politics.

If we search for support in the literature, we find much important work has been done in the social sciences explaining the origins and continuity of gender inequality in political participation. However, the same does not apply to the study of differences/similarities in style and ways of acting in the political field. Democratic theories seem to assume that norms and desirable practices in democracies are clearly defined and societies only have to go further in the right direction. The lack of substantial findings on gender and power may in part be explained by the small number of women in world politics until recently, but may be influenced by some stereotyped ideas as well. While some feminists hold that democracy today does not exist, since it is not egalitarian, others believe that women would bring nothing new to it from a qualitative point of view.

This chapter will not discuss theoretical aspects of the main issue of democracy, gender and power. However, some authors are central to our research, among them Almond and Verba (1963), Verba, Nie and Kim (1978), Lijphart (1977; 1984), Dahl (1989) and Pateman (1989).

Since democracies – and all the countries in our sample are democracies – have been and still are structured mainly by parties expressing different and even opposite tendencies, we can consider, at least for the time being, political parties to be the axis of political life. To go deeper into the study of gender and politics a better understanding of whether and how the internal characteristics of political parties influence political behaviour is required. Indeed, they were created by men, shaped by men's traditional lifestyles, and their history developed in a context of male dominance of the family as well as of the economy and politics.

This chapter cannot go deeper into this issue, but will try to provide answers to some of the main questions. The first section examines the adjustment of the main collective actors and instruments of democracy (parties) to the democratic principle of equal opportunities. The second identifies gender differences/similarities in political attitudes and judgements that can, or cannot, support the idea of a different gender management of power.

Statistical analysis involved not only the main variable (gender), but tested several country associations as well, and found no major differences as far as our main topics are concerned, although some asymmetries regarding a few aspects emerged in Europe when we compared Northern and Southern countries, and in post-communist states as well. Since our focus is on gender, we include in this chapter only tables pertinent to this variable, and those we found to be most significant.

Gender and political parties: a problematic relationship

Political parties have had greater appeal to men than to women, since affiliation constitutes a main asset for beginning and developing a political career. But in a democracy it is to be expected that on joining a party women should have the same opportunities as men. However, as a classic study demonstrates (Verba, Nie and Kim, 1978), when women are members of a party, 'such affiliation has less pay-off in terms of increased political activity'.

Our data do not focus on the relationship between political engagement and the conquest of power positions. However, by means of data on men and women and political leadership we can analyse some characteristics of their political background and understand better their relationship with parties.

A main topic is to understand whether parties are 'neutral' towards men and women and whether the two genders share the same attitudes towards them. One way to elucidate this issue is through data on specific questions such as: Have political leaders, men and women, spent the same number of years in general political activities and, specifically, in party activities? Do they follow the same path, from local to national positions? Do parties offer the same support to men and women in electoral campaigns? What is the influence of women in party decisions?

We begin by referring to data on political involvement in general, and specifically on party activities (Table 6.1).

Lengthy political and party engagement is a characteristic of political leaders (both elected and appointed). The average time spent in politics ranges from 15.3 years (women, party activity) to 18.3 years (men, political activity). Men have spent more time than women in both general political activities and party activities, but a statistically significant difference is found only for years in politics.

As we would expect, the number of years spent by women and men in political and party activity is somewhat lower in more recent democracies (Portugal, Spain, Greece and post-communist states) than in long-established democratic states (the most notable difference is in the United States and the Nordic countries).

Party activity at the local, regional and national level is common in political careers (data not shown). In the overwhelming majority of cases the same people have held office at both the local and national levels at different periods of time. Nevertheless, there is a gender difference: women have generally held more positions at the regional level, namely, in regional assemblies ($p < 0.03$) and fewer positions at the national level than men (among those who did not, 44.6 per cent were men and 55.4 per cent women).

Involvement in 'civil society' activities is also common among political leaders, especially in top positions in non-profit organisations. This is true for all groups of countries considered, and there are no significant gender differences.

What support do men and women find within the party for inclusion on an electoral list and a successful election? It is well known that formal

Table 6.1   Party Membership and Political Involvement

	N		Mean		P
	M	**F**	**M**	**F**	
Number of years of party membership	401	400	16.8	15.3	0.07
Number of years active in politics	418	432	18.3	16.4	0.02*

*Significant for $\alpha = 0.05$.

and informal support can both be important. However, formal financial support is fundamental in electoral campaigns. Table 6.2 shows financial resources and media coverage on a scale from 1 (+) to 3 (–). Respondents compared their finances and coverage relative to other candidates in their own party.

The data reveal a problematic situation, since women perceive that they are not treated in the same way as men (2.2 versus 2.0). We find that of the 22.9 per cent men and women who said they had had less support than others in their party, 56 per cent were women.

With regard to media access, more dependable on personal resources than party resources, women perceive fewer difficulties, and there are no statistically significant differences between men and women.

It is worth mentioning that analysis by countries shows a significant difference between Northern and Southern Europe, as the access of politicians to the media is easier in the North (Northern Europe 1.6, Southern Europe 2.1), but no noticeable difference is found when we consider the gender variable.

Although all these differences are narrowing as new generations enter politics (Verba, Nie and Kim, 1978: 267), they have made the situation of women in the power structure of political parties less comfortable than that of men. This is reflected in the women's department of the party, which both men and women tend to consider has little influence: 36.3 per cent of respondents say that its influence is slight or very slight, and only 27.9 per cent consider its influence noticeable or very noticeable. Even when women take part (sometimes via quotas or affirmative action) in party decision-making structures – such as nominating committees, for example, for lists of candidates to elections or to party leadership – data reveal that men and women take part in these structures in similar percentages. We can conclude that women involved in such positions tend to promote women's participation, since activism in women's associations is quite a common finding in the biographies of women who are members of parliament or govern-

Table 6.2 Support for Election

	N		Mean		S. D.		P
	M	F	M	F	M	F	
Access to financial resources during the campaign	278	258	2.0	2.2	0.6	0.6	0.02*
Access to the media during the campaign	279	273	2.0	2.0	0.8	0.7	0.34

*Significant for $\alpha = 0.05$.

ment (62.3 per cent of women in our sample have been active members of women's organisations).

In conclusion, the above results suggest that some features remain that make the parties not fully egalitarian or 'neutral' democratic instruments for men and women, at least as perceived by women leaders.[1]

Gender and management of power

Political power means more than occupying a position in parliament or government: it has to do with the distribution of responsibilities through the main areas of government.

A significant aspect in the allocation of power has to do with the areas of political activities prevailing for men and women. Just what issues are chosen to deal with?

As we saw in the preceding chapter, regarding the distribution of power there are clear differences.

It could be said that women occupy precisely the areas they are more interested in. However, the data do not confirm this common-sense idea, since when we asked in what field those interviewed would like to work, a large number chose economic affairs, which are preferred almost equally by men and women.

Although this situation may in part be determined by the most common areas of specialisation among women, namely due to their educational background (see chapter 4), it probably has to do with women's smaller influence within their own parties. This situation is evidenced either by their small numbers within the party's governing bodies and/or by the degree of influence of the women's department in party decision-making.

This brings us back to the question of the degree of representation necessary in an organisation or social group for the various sectors represented to exert a real influence. The case of the Scandinavian countries is demonstrative of this direction: only when women reach a substantial proportion (Kanter, 1977), can they reproduce or even increase that presence, and eventually their influence.

One of the most common questions in the discussion on gender and political leadership is whether women can bring to politics anything different and more beneficial to societies and individuals (Giddens, 1991: 228–31). Yet this is a misleading point, which has nothing to do with the discussion of democracy in its present state. The basic question is about representation in democracy, with balanced distribution of the various social groups throughout the various bodies that formulate and make political decisions. But if the representativeness of a group is based on the supposition that the individuals in it have inherently different intellectual and emotional capacities, according to their sex or colour, this supports a rationale for discrimination and a contingency principle in democratic theory.[2] Keeping in mind the democratic theory framework, the principle to take into account is that of individuals in their condition (which includes gender, colour, etc.) and their right to be represented and to take part in the decisions that can affect their lives. This is the case even if this does not bring 'salvation' with it, or is unable to do 'better' than the others, but does simply the same thing.

That said, we can redraft our original question. Instead of guessing what human society might be in a situation where men and women globally divide the responsibilities of political management, we shall for the present limit our questioning to aspects that we can clearly point out: Are there any indications that women who currently hold positions of power have styles of wielding that power that are different from men in the same situations? Do women view their own power in a different way?

We will focus on some aspects central to the definition of the styles of power-wielding: instrumental values in career strategies; personal contacts with people representing the various socio-political sectors; formal/informal connections; evaluation of and relationship with the group; distribution of time in political activities in parliament.

Assets in career strategies

We begin by analysing data that can reveal predominant attitudes and orientations of men and women in their political activities by means of a question exploring which are the instrumental values and assets that are considered by men and women as important in the political career. Several items presented to the interviewees were grouped for this analysis into three main factors: personal, political and relational resources. In Table 6.3 we present the steps of factor analysis to make this clear.

From Table 6.3 we note that some significant differences emerge between men and women concerning their evaluation of the most important career factors. Women value more than men personal resources (which include skill in public presentation and in interpersonal relations, knowledge and expertise, and geographic mobility) and relational resources (contacts with key people, support from a mentor and from top government leaders). Both give similar importance to political/party resources, such as political achievements and contacts, loyalty to party orientations and leadership and seniority in the field.

This may indicate a more direct and informal approach to politics and a more individually and socially oriented pattern of career progression among women.

Personal contacts and information channels

Taken together, men and women holding elected and appointed offices have very similar frequency contacts with the prime ministers, government

Table 6.3   (a) Important Factors in Political Career Development in General

	Factor 1	Factor 2	Factor 3
Skill in public presentation	0.76549	–0.02877	0.10999
Skill in interpersonal relations	0.74355	0.05256	0.21604
Knowledge and expertise in the field	0.47199	0.02503	–0.07780
Geographic mobility	0.40432	0.21849	0.18066
Loyalty to the party's ideology	0.00072	0.69734	0.01133
Politic achievements	0.44290	0.66353	–0.10460
Political contacts	0.34413	0.56613	0.32466
Loyalty to the top organisation leader	0.04358	0.56196	0.44528
Career seniority	–0.18404	0.37724	0.29407
Support from a mentor	0.22694	–0.19135	0.75725
Contacts with key people	0.30010	0.24567	0.66032
Aid from top government leaders	–0.09305	0.28865	0.54722

	Explained Variance (%)
Factor 1 Personal resources	26.6
Factor 2 Political resources	11.9
Factor 3 Relational resources	9.6
Total	48.1

(b) Gender and Important Factors in Political Career Development

	N		Mean		S. D.		P
	M	**F**	**M**	**F**	**M**	**F**	
Factor 1 Personal resources	342	343	–0.13	0.12	1.01	0.97	0.01*
Factor 2 Political resources	342	343	0.04	–0.04	0.96	1.04	0.33
Factor 3 Relational resources	342	343	–0.11	0.11	0.96	1.03	0.01*

*Significant for $\alpha = 0.05$.

ministers, members of parliament, and with the representatives of interest groups. But men have more contact with presidents of large corporations, party leaders and top-level civil servants, and with military leaders[3] (see chapter 16). On the whole, men seem to be more connected to influential levels of power.

As for the weight they give the various channels of information, in the case of politicians elected to office we found no significant asymmetries by gender, though there were some differences between men and women holding appointed office in government. Women in such positions place greater value on contacts with interest groups and union leaders and on the civil servants within their own ministries. The importance of the media is also more valued by women in government than by men (in a scale from 1 (–) to 5 (+), women 4.0, men 3.7). And regarding the channels of information, women in government tend to favour meetings more than men (p = 0.017). This is consistent with the results on career development, where we noted that women value more personal and relational factors. We can infer that women tend more than men to discuss and receive support from their partners and collaborators (Vianello, 1996). This may occur because they are either more confident or more oriented towards sharing responsibilities.

Life in the political group

In the context of political activity, what differences can we find between men and women? Is it possible that day-to-day group political activity seems particularly aggressive to women? Are they satisfied with the group leadership style, which is usually the responsibility of men? With the knowledge that plenary session work is more visible, though much of parliamentary work is done at the committee level? Where do women prefer to work? Table 6.4 presents the two former aspects; we then discuss the results of the latter.

From Table 6.4, it is clear that both men and women hold a positive opinion of their group. However, women have a more favourable view than men, not only regarding motivation, but also structure, which they, more than men, tend to see as dynamic. As for group leadership – and in some way contrary to what would be expected – women tend to see it as less authoritarian and more participative than do men.

As for daily life in parliament, women dedicate more attention than men to work on committees: 51 women spent more than two-thirds of their time in parliament in them, while only 40 men said they spent a like amount of time. Nearly 200 women, while only nearly 100 men among the MPs interviewed, spent from one-third to two-thirds of their working time in committees.

Table 6.4 Evaluation of the Functioning of Political Group

	N		Mean		S. D.		P
	M	**F**	**M**	**F**	**M**	**F**	
Work environment – stable/turbulent	320	311	3.0	3.1	1.2	1.2	0.96
Group strategy – cautious/aggressive	317	307	3.0	3.1	1.0	1.0	0.10
Work organisation – low/high motivation	309	296	3.8	4.0	0.9	1.0	0.04*
Work structure – rigid/dynamic	319	311	3.3	3.4	1.0	1.2	0.05*
Group leadership – authoritarian/democratic	318	310	3.5	3.7	1.1	1.1	0.02*

*Significant for $\alpha = 0.05$; Scale: 1 (–) 'stable' to 5 (+) 'turbulent'.

Personal style and self-satisfaction

We begin by referring to data on self-evaluation that men and women make of their current political activity, in terms of costs/benefits of some of the most common characteristics of that activity: from media investigations, work overload and lack of time to personal influence, social obligations and personal responsibility.

Table 6.5 gives us a general picture. First of all we see that in equivalent numbers, men and women consider as positive the fact that they have more personal influence and as more negative the lack of anonymity and continual scrutiny by the media. When we look into percentages (not shown), we see that a heavy workload is viewed differently, with one third reacting positively, one third negatively, and one third ambiguously. Men consider it slightly more positively than women. A statistically significant difference is found only when we consider personal responsibility. Women value more than men this characteristic of their work. Other aspects are considered more positively by women than men, such as personal influence, media investigations and lack of time, but are not statistically significant.

The possible explanations for the fact that women in political leadership have a more positive outlook than men on the cost-benefit equation of their activity may have to do with either objective factors (the more socially-oriented areas where they are found) or with more enhanced self-satisfaction due to the very fact of holding such an office. Yet, the analysis of another variable leads us to favour the latter more than the former. When we observe data (not included) concerning appointed positions in their respective ministries (or offices), women demonstrate a slightly greater degree of satisfaction with the overall influence that they have.

Table 6.5   Cost/Benefits in Political Activity

	N		Mean		S. D.		P
	M	**F**	**M**	**F**	**M**	**F**	
Personal influence	235	224	3.9	4.0	1.1	1.0	0.45
Lack of anonymity	229	225	2.7	2.7	1.2	1.2	0.44
Work overload	236	225	3.1	3.0	1.2	1.2	0.66
Social obligations	235	223	3.1	3.1	1.0	1.1	0.87
Continuous media investigations	236	220	2.8	3.0	1.1	1.2	0.16
Personal responsibility	234	225	3.9	4.1	1.1	1.0	0.03*
Lack of time	228	220	2.4	2.5	1.0	1.0	0.46

*Significant for $\alpha = 0.05$.
Scale: from 1 (–) to 5 (+), i.e. cost (–), benefit (+).

And in the context of activity, what differences can we find between men and women?

To gain support for an initiative can be seen as a sign of a convincing performance in the group. Respondents indicated how frequently they had succeeded in winning support for an initiative originally opposed by a majority of their colleagues. No significant asymmetries are found among those who hold elected positions. Nevertheless, men have a slight tendency to confront group opposition more, by taking initiatives that are not initially approved. Those who occupy appointed office show similar behaviour in this area, though in cases of initial opposition women often seem to be more able to move ahead with their proposals (23 cases versus 15), but these figures are not statistically significant.

The interpretation of these data indicates some hypotheses that may be coexistent and not mutually exclusive: women are more easily satisfied than men, due to initially less demanding expectations and a more sympathetic attitude towards others; as they rarely challenge the group leadership they do not enter into as much conflict as some of the men; they project into the group the evaluation of their own work within the same.

Conclusion

The most general conclusion we can draw from our analysis is that in political leadership gender does not make a substantial difference. This is more striking when we consider the main issues that underline most of the discussion on gender and politics: namely personal career strategies and style of power management, where notable differences might be expected.

However, while this can support the idea that politics nowadays is a highly professionalised, i.e. standardised, activity, it does not mean that women and men are equal in the political context. In fact, we note that in general the relationship between political parties and women is more problematic than in the case of men: women perceive less support than men and have less influence within party bodies.

As for the management of power, inequalities are found in the distribution of political areas of responsibility: women are more prevalent in 'social' or 'female' issues. But our data show that their preferences are the same as those of men.

In their activities and careers, women value somewhat more than men personal and relational assets.

Finally, we may say that the attitude of women regarding their political activity is a little more positive than men's: they express a more favourable evaluation of organisation and group leadership and are more satisfied with their situation.

Explanatory hypotheses have been mentioned in the text. But we can briefly stress that interpretation of the gender dissimilarities found does not allow the conclusion that men and women hold and manage power in clearly different ways.

Notes

1. We should note that recent developments in the sense of parity, for instance in electoral lists, have taken place in countries with governments led by more social-oriented parties, but they are not reflected in our data.
2. On categorical and contingency principles, see Dahl (1989: ch. 9).
3. Figures not presented in this book.

Part II
Power: Strategies, Contexts and Uses

Introduction

The issue of the utilisation of power and the rules of power are the key subjects of this part. To what extent do the rules of power seem to conceal the appearance of gender differences among the élites? Do women feel the same as men do in the world of power? What do people do with the power they have, and how are they themselves involved in the reproduction of the rules of power?

Women often have fewer contacts than men with people who will help them advance in their careers. They may also be disadvantaged in male-centred networks and activities which are so important for access to and maintenance of power.

Chapter 7 looks at the way mentors helped women and men to enter top positions as well as how business and political leaders in turn support others, and answers the question whether women and men in similar formal positions are alike in mentoring activities.

Another factor in high-level careers is the use of time. The allocation of time to work and private life and its construction by male and female leaders is explored in chapter 8.

Chapter 9 examines the subjective evaluation of how sufficient access to informal channels of information is and the respondent's estimation of how important various sources of information actually are. Special attention is given to how the percentage of women in national labour market may affect this.

Chapter 10 asks whether women and men in similar élite positions are alike in access to and contacts with other leaders.

The use of power depends on organisational, economic and political structures in which leaders operate. Chapter 11 shows how the structure of business firms affects the leadership style of men and women differently.

Chapter 12, the last in this part, investigates whether women need more privileged conditions in order to exercise the same amount of power men do and tries to determine the factors that differentiate men and women at different levels of power exercise.

7
Top People and Mentors

Michal Palgi

To reach top positions in politics and business entails breaking through many organisational and social barriers, more so for women than for men. This is a result of socialisation, social learning, stigmas and stereotypes. One way of overcoming these difficulties is through the recruitment of a mentor who helps pave the career path. In the literature (Noe, 1988; Burke and McKeen, 1990; Mobley et al., 1994) we find two main types of mentor: formal and informal. In our research we looked only into the function that informal mentors had in the lives of our interviewees.

Mobility paths and obstacles for politicians are different from those for business people. Politicians need more social connections outside their workplace in order to reach their constituencies. Business people need more connections within their own field in order to advance. As women's networks are more limited than men's, especially at the start of their career (see, for example, chapter 10), they are in a greater need of finding access to leaders and lay people in varied sections of society. A mentor who is well connected politically, socially or in business can be very helpful in overcoming network barriers. Therefore, it is hypothesised in this chapter that:

- Politicians in general will have more mentors outside their workplace than business people.
- Women in both sectors will have more mentors than men, as their network is more limited and the mentors can serve as a bridge for important connections (Fagenson and Jackson, 1994).
- In the social democracies and Western countries there will be more awareness of mentors, especially in politics, while in the other countries there will be less.
- Cross-mentoring (men–women and women–men), according to our hypothesis, will prevail more in the economically developed countries. The first reason for this is that in the latter women and men in powerful positions are more aware of the importance of mentoring both

genders. The second reason is that in these countries there is more public debate on this issue.

• Men and women in powerful positions who were aided by mentors will extend more help to junior colleagues than those who did not have mentors.

Our questionnaire included questions about the existence of several types of mentor in the lives of high-positioned politicians and business executives. These were:

1. Mentors within work – (a) peers, (b) supervisors and (c) chief executive officers or other high officers in workplace.
2. Mentors outside work – We had two measures: mentors who were 'educators and family members', and mentors who were 'friends and colleagues from other organisations, and political and religious acquaintances'.

For each type we differentiated between male and female mentors. This was because the literature dealing with the role of mentors in the lives of men and women points to the problematic issue of women not having female mentors and needing to use male mentors. It suggests that men have a different style of coping and a different life situation from that of women, and therefore their mentoring is limited. Men, owing to tradition, stigmas and stereotypes, are more reluctant to have female mentors (Kanter, 1977; Noe, 1988; Burke and McKeen, 1990; Dreher and Ash, 1990; Mobley et al., 1994).

In the first part of the findings presentation, data describing the percentages of men and women in business and in politics who had different types of mentors are given. In the second part, the effect of demographic variables and mentor variables on rank of present position and satisfaction with career progress is shown through regression analysis. The third part looks into the amount of help men and women in powerful positions extend to male and female junior colleagues.

Table 7.1 compares men and women who had mentors within each sector (politics and business) and across sectors.

Is the mentoring pattern of politicians different from that of business people?

We see that more politicians than business people had mentors outside the workplace, especially the women. The business people had more mentors than the politicians among their superiors at work (supervisors, CEOs and other higher officers). Also, at work, women in politics had more mentors from among their peers than women in business. This supports the general hypothesis of this chapter that different patterns of mentoring are needed in each sector owing to their different structure and work environment. To succeed in politics one needs mentors with wide connections

Table 7.1 Percentage of Men and Women who had Mentors, by Sector

Type of Mentor	Politics		Business	
	Women **(N = 419)**	**Men** **(N = 389)**	**Women** **(N = 402)**	**Men** **(N = 348)**
A. Within work				
Male peers at workplace	29.4	27.0	25.4	28.2
Female peers at workplace	27.7*	17.2	19.1	15.4
Male superiors at workplace	21.6	19.9	56.4	58.6
Female superiors at workplace	12.0*	7.7	12.6	9.0
B. Outside work				
Male friends and colleagues	46.7*	36.1	34.6	28.2
Female friends and colleagues	36.8*	25.5	20.7	20.3
Male: family, educators, religious	39.1*	26.9	32.6*	25.4
Female: family, educators, religious	28.3*	21.3	13.7*	20.6
C. All types of mentors				
All men	57.5*	44.1	64.7	65.3
All women	45.9*	30.0	33.2	29.7

*Chi-square test: p < 0.05.

outside the workplace, while in business internal connections are necessary. Recruitment to and staying in business depend much more on supervisors than is the case in politics, where the electorate and general connections have more influence. This is also the reason, apparently, why more women politicians than businesswomen had mentors who were female peers at their workplace and also men and women outside work. Note also that women superiors at work were least mentioned, in both sectors, by both sexes, as past mentors. This might be a reflection of the lower rates of women in powerful positions or a result of the social structuring of gender roles in organisations.

In what ways do women differ from men in politics?

In view of the growing awareness of the need for women to act together in order to change gender gaps, institutional discrimination and under-representation, the findings of Table 7.1 are not surprising. They show that at work more female than male politicians reported they had a female mentor, the difference being especially great regarding female peers at work. In accordance with this theme, no differences were found between men and women politicians in the number of male peers at work and male superiors at work they had as mentors.

Also, more female than male politicians reported they had mentors outside work. They had more male than female mentors who were friends and colleagues outside work. This shows that successful women did not exclude male mentors; on the contrary, they were assisted by them in their careers.

Few differences exist between women and men in business

Only two significant differences were found between men and women in business. Women had more mentors than men who were male family members, educators or religious acquaintances and had fewer female mentors in these categories than men had. This can be explained by the importance that female executives ascribe to entering the 'old boy' network in order to succeed. It also might indicate the practice of family businesses to bring mothers and daughters into the organisation. Women were successful in recruiting male mentors within and outside work who guided them on how to pull strings in the male-dominated business world.

Do countries matter?

Another issue looked at was whether mentoring is different in each type of market economy (to be called type of country: see chapter 2). It was assumed that each type has its own policy, culture, and social norms regarding gender, and these would reflect on the mentoring of highly placed people.

Generally, it can be seen from Table 7.2 that in all types of countries politicians and business people had more male than female mentors. Male mentors were reported more frequently than female especially among business people. This is more noticeable in the free market countries than in the other countries where male mentors were reported much more frequently than female mentors among business people.

Types of country and mentoring of politicians

In the L.D. countries fewer politicians had male or female mentors than in the F.M. countries and the S.D. countries.

No differences were found between men and women in the L.D. countries. Significant differences were found between them in the F.M. and the S.D. countries, where a higher percentage of women reported having had a male or a female mentor, and more reported having had a male mentor. These findings are possible indicators of various phenomena such as a gender equality policy, scarcity of women at the top and women's sisterhood.

Types of country and mentoring of business executives

About two-thirds of men and women in the L.D. and F.M. countries reported that they had male mentors. In the S.D. countries a difference exists between the percentage of women and men who had mentors: significantly more men than women had male mentors. The percentage of men who had male mentors is similar to that in the other types of country, while the percentage of women is much lower.

The picture among business people with regard to female mentors is more complex than with regard to male mentors. More than a third of male and female business executives in the L.D. countries had female mentors, with no difference between genders, while in the F.M. countries the percentages of women and men who had female mentors differ: significantly more women than men had female mentors. The situation in the S.D. countries is the opposite: significantly more men than women had female mentors.

The last finding can be explained in various ways. One may be that female mentors in business are more visible than male mentors because of their scarcity in top positions, so they are better remembered. Another may be that women in the S.D. countries who have managed to reach top

Table 7.2   Percentage of Men and Women from Each Type of Country who Reported They Had Mentors (all types)

Type of Country	**Politicians**		**Business**	
	Women	**Men**	**Women**	**Men**
Economically less developed (L.D.)				
Male mentors	35.5	34.3	65.3	62.2
Female mentors	26.2	26.0	33.8	41.9
	(N = 107)	**(N = 105)**	**(N = 75)**	**(N = 74)**
Free market (F.M.)				
Male mentors	65.1**	45.0	69.8	65.6
Female mentors	50.9**	28.2	34.5**	22.8
	(N = 212)	**(N = 220)**	**(N = 232)**	**(N = 218)**
Social democracies (S.D.)				
Male mentors	68.0	57.8	48.6**	67.2
Female mentors	60.0**	43.8	28.4**	39.3
	(N = 75)	**(N = 64)**	**(N = 74)**	**(N = 61)**

*Numbers in parentheses indicate the total number of respondents in the specific category.
**Chi-square test; $p < 0.05$.

executive positions are more aware of and sensitive to the importance of mentoring both genders for their own career development and for the general status of women. Yet another explanation may be that men in the S.D. countries have been socialised in countries where gender equality has long been on the political agenda, and readily see the advantages of having a female mentor.

Within type of country: politicians and business executives compared

In the L.D. countries only a third of the politicians reported they had male mentors, while about twice as many business people reported this. A similar pattern is found with regard to female mentors in this group of countries, but the differences between the sectors are less extreme. Only a quarter of the politicians in these countries reported having had a female mentor, whereas more than a third of the business people had the same experience. This could be a result of an intentional policy in the L.D. countries to advance the economy and promote people in business through conscious support of mentoring (see Chapter 20).

Table 7.2 shows that in the F.M. countries a similar percentage of women in politics and in business reported they had a male mentor. Fewer men in politics than in business had this experience. As for female mentors, a higher percentage of female politicians than businesswomen reported having had them. On the other hand, a similar percentage of male politicians and businessmen reported having had female mentors. Yet in both sectors women had more female mentors than men did. This could be due to an attempt by women in powerful positions to empower junior women in politics in these countries. It could also point to the reluctance of men to have female mentors.

The S.D. countries are considered to be the most advanced in promoting gender equality, so it was expected that women would have more mentors, especially female mentors. It was also expected that men would have more female mentors than in other countries. The findings support this only in the sphere of politics; in business, matters are more complicated. More women politicians than businesswomen reported they had a male mentor. Even so, twice as many in politics as in business had a female mentor. Among men, fewer in politics than in business reported they had a male mentor, and a similar percentage reported they had a female mentor.

These findings may be a result of the different gender situation in politics from that in business in the S.D. countries. In politics, genders are much closer to equality than in business, but male mentoring is still an important asset on the way to the top.

Mentoring and present position

In this part of the analysis we looked for the predictors of 'rank of present position' (as defined by the respondent) and 'satisfaction with career progress' among the three following sets of variables: (1) demographic variables (respondent's type of country, age and number of years of formal schooling), (2) two variables regarding factors that assisted the career ('having a mentor' and 'knowledge and expertise in the field'), and (3) variables that counted the different types of mentors each respondent had.

Separate analyses were done for men and women respondents from each sector. Table 7.3 sets out only those variables that contributed significantly to the explanation of the variance of the dependent variable. Since in the first analysis there was only one significant predictor (country), the data are not shown. In fact, the politicians' data show that when 'rank of present position' was taken as the dependent variable, none of the demographic and mentor variables was significant, except – as we just stated – the respondent's country. The closer the type of country to a social democracy, the higher was the rank of the present position. For men, an additional variable was significant: namely, the extent to which 'knowledge and expertise in the field assisted career'. Variables representing the number of mentors respondents had, at work and outside work, were not predictors of the rank of the present position.

When 'satisfaction with career progress' was taken as a dependent variable the results were as shown in Table 7.3 (only significant betas are shown).

The regression analysis shows different results for women and for men. For women, the predictors of 'satisfaction with career progress' were:

1. type of country;
2. age: the older the person, the more satisfied she was;

Table 7.3 Regression Analysis for Politicians – Dependent Variable 'Satisfaction with Career Progress' (beta, t, sig.)

Predictors	Women			Men		
Mentors:						
Male supervisors at workplace	0.16	2.67	0.008			
Female friends and colleagues	0.13	2.01	0.046			
Female religious acquaintances	−0.18	−2.76	0.006			
Assisted career:						
Knowledge and expertise in the field	0.15	2.73	0.007	0.12	2.23	0.026
Type of country	0.19	3.42	0.001	0.17	3.09	0.002
Year born	−0.16	−2.87	0.004	−0.24	−4.47	0.000
	$R^2 = 0.13$			$R^2 = 0.11$		

3. assisted career knowledge and expertise in the field;[1]
4. having had mentors – this had different effects: the more mentors who were religious female acquaintances, the less was the respondent's satisfaction with career progress, while the more mentors were male supervisors at work or women friends and colleagues, the greater was the respondent's satisfaction.

The importance of the variable 'type of country' in the regression analysis is evident for both men and women. For women this might point to the importance of the impact of conscious change and affirmative action on their careers. Age and expertise in the field were also important predictors for both genders. But mentors at work and outside work predicted satisfaction with career progress only for women.

In business, these variables explained only 4 per cent or less of the variance of the dependent variables for both men and women. Age was not a predictor, and type of country was only a predictor for women. Again, the political environment is seen to be related to the position of women at work and their satisfaction with it (see also Palgi, 1994).

Do people at the top support others?

People who have reached top positions can empower those on the way to the top in many ways, among them mentoring junior colleagues. In our study we wanted to learn if those at the top did mentor, and if there were differences between men and women and between types of country. We also wanted to find out if experience or lack of experience with mentors was related to the actual behaviour of the leaders. Three main hypotheses were tested. First, women who had to 'break the glass ceiling' would try to assist junior male and female colleagues more than men would, because they were more aware of their situation and empathised with them more. Second, in countries that had made a concerted effort at gender equality, people at the top would mentor more. Third, those who had experienced mentorship would tend to mentor more than those who had not.

Three questions probed this issue. The first asked the leaders to what extent they played an important role in the recruitment and development of junior colleagues for future positions of leadership and responsibility. The second and third asked them to write the number of men and of women they had assisted in this way during the past year.

Most of the leaders in politics and business claimed that they had played an important role in the recruitment and development of junior colleagues. A gender comparison in general showed no significant differences in the two sectors, while according to type of country it shows that only among politicians in F.M. countries there is a difference. A higher percentage (68 per cent) of women than men (49 per cent) stated they played an important role in the recruitment and development of junior colleagues.

As for the number of people assisted, a majority (three-quarters or more) of male and female leaders in politics and business claimed they assisted one or more junior colleagues. Among the politicians, fewer female leaders (65 per cent) than male leaders (71 per cent) had assisted more than one junior male colleague in the previous year, but more (74 per cent of the women leaders and 60 per cent of the men) had assisted junior female colleagues. A slightly different pattern was found in the number of junior males assisted and of junior females assisted, when analysed according to type of country. In the F.M. and in the S.D. countries more female than male political leaders stated that they had not helped men: 30 per cent of the female leaders (compared with 22 per cent male leaders) in the former and 37 per cent (compared with 11 per cent) in the latter countries indicate they had helped no junior male in the previous year. In the L.D. countries no such difference was found, and more or less the same percentage of male and female political leaders stated that they had helped junior male colleagues.

Help for junior female colleagues was significantly more prevalent among female than among male political leaders only in the F.M. countries. In the other types of country there was no difference. A comparison of the percentage of political leaders who assisted junior male colleagues with the percentage of those who assisted junior female colleagues evinces an interesting pattern. In the L.D. countries there was no difference: the same percentage of men and women assisted junior colleagues regardless of their gender. In the F.M. and the S.D. countries female political leaders indicated they had helped more junior female than junior male colleagues, while male leaders had helped both genders equally. This difference points to the conscious efforts of women in those two types of country to empower other women. This is in accordance with a general policy in these countries to advance gender equality, fostered mainly by female leaders and feminist groups (see, for example, chapter 15). Nevertheless, another possible explanation should not be ignored: namely, that junior male colleagues are reluctant to accept assistance from women leaders.

Among the top male business executives interviewed only half had helped more than one junior female colleague, while two-thirds had helped a junior male in the previous year. This difference was not found for female executives. Country differences indicate that male executives in the L.D. and S.D. countries had been significantly more helpful to junior males than to junior females. In the L.D. countries 72 per cent of them had helped more than one male colleague as against 53 per cent who had helped more than one female. In the S.D. countries the figures were 64 per cent as against 41 per cent. Is this yet another sign of the exclusion of women or is it just a reflection of the actual numbers of women in business? Or perhaps a combination of both?

Returning the favour

The third hypothesis was that people who had had mentors would tend to mentor others more than those who had not. Table 7.4 shows the difference between the two groups.

For male politicians, having had a mentor did matter. More of those who themselves had had mentors played an important role in the recruitment and development of junior colleagues to future positions of leadership than did those who had not. No difference was found in the extent of assistance that they gave male or female junior colleagues.

For female politicians, having had a mentor did not affect the role they played in junior colleagues' careers. More of them claimed they had helped junior female than junior male colleagues, but this did not have any direct relationship to their having had a mentor.

Among the business executives no difference was found between those who had had mentors and those who had not: they all helped more or less the same number of junior colleagues.

Only among male politicians was there a relationship between having had a mentor and how greatly the respondents perceived they had supported

Table 7.4 Recruitment and Development of Junior Colleagues by Politicians Who Had and Did Not Have Mentors (%)

	Had Male Mentors		**Had Female Mentors**	
	None	**One or more**	**None**	**One or more**
A. Male Politicians:	**(n = 206)**	**(n = 168)**	**(n = 259)**	**(n = 115)**
Assisted junior male colleagues	80.0	87.6	80.7	89.6
Did not assist junior males	20.0	12.4	19.3	10.4
	100.0*	100.0	100.0*	100.0
Assisted junior female colleagues	77.7	86.9	80.2	87.9
Did not assist junior females	22.3	13.1	19.8	12.1
	100.0*	100.0	100.0*	100.0
B. Female Politicians:	**(n = 150)**	**(n = 223)**	**(n = 194)**	**(n = 179)**
Assisted junior male colleagues	77.0	78.0	77.3	77.7
Did not assist junior males	23.0	22.0	22.7	22.3
	100.0	100.0	100.0	100.0
Assisted junior female colleagues	88.7	86.5	87.6	86.8
Did not assist junior females	11.3	13.5	12.4	13.2
	100.0	100.0	100.0	100.0

*Chi-square test: $p < 0.05$.

junior colleagues. No relationship was found with the number of people assisted.

Conclusion

Three main hypotheses about the mentoring practices of top politicians and business executives were tested. They concerned sector differences, gender differences and type of country differences.

It was found that more politicians than business people had mentors, who usually were not personnel in their own workplace, while business people had more mentors who worked in their own workplace. This was explained by the fact that the characteristics and work conditions of politicians are different from those of business people. Politicians need a vast network of connections in the country to provide communication channels to their constituencies, while business people need more connections within their field. Differences were also found between men and women: among the politicians, more women than men had as mentors female peers at work and male friends and colleagues outside work. Very few respondents, male or female, in business or in politics, had female superiors as mentors. As for type of country, it could be seen that in all types very few women and men from the business sector had female mentors. In the political sector, it was found that in the S.D. and F.M. countries a relatively high percentage of women politicians had female mentors, and in the S.D. countries almost half the male politicians had female mentors. The higher numbers of female politicians who had mentors in the F.M. and S.D. countries can be attributed to the intentional empowerment of women in politics in these countries, and their entry into politics in relatively large numbers. This process and policy were less emphasised in business, mainly because a large number of firms are privately owned and the application of official equality policy to them is limited.

Different explanations can be given for the fact that top people in politics and business had very few women mentors from among superiors at their workplace. The structure of each sector is different. In politics, where only the responses of elected people are analysed, superiors at work are less important for advancement and empowerment. More important as mentors are people who have wide connections within the party, outside the party and with the constituency. In business, a superior is important because the mobility course is very much set by him/her. But in business, women superiors were probably scarce in these positions. Also, it is possible that women superiors were not considered good mentors, owing to their being a minority or to stereotypes about the abilities of women. Another possibility is that, because of the ownership structure of businesses, women executives were not conscious of the need to mentor other women or men. In support of these points, it was shown that in politics, where and when there is a clear policy of advancing and empowering women, as in the S.D. countries, women are present in these positions and also act as mentors for both men and women.

This point was also supported by the regression analysis which showed that the type of country of the respondent is an important variable in predicting satisfaction in career progress. For women, the support of male superiors at work and female friends and colleagues were also good predictors.

Another issue explored in this study was whether people who reached top positions mentored others. To mentor others is also to empower them. Two possibilities were considered. First, women in power positions, because of the history of discrimination and exclusion from these positions, will mentor other women more than they do men. A check of whether female leaders mentored more women than men confirmed this. Second, those who experienced mentoring as they struggled to power positions learnt its importance and mentored others in order to ease their way.

The data in our study can give only an indicative direction of the more prevalent possibility. Generally, a majority of highly placed politicians and business executives claim to have helped recruit and develop junior colleagues. More women political leaders than men state they helped junior female colleagues. Analysis according to type of country shows that in those countries (F.M. and S.D.), where there is a policy of affirmative action and gender equality, more women than men mentored female colleagues. In business, female executives helped the same number of male and female junior colleagues. All in all, the mentoring experience of female leaders did not increase the assistance they gave to young colleagues. It did increase male politicians' tendencies to help.

To sum up, this study points to the extent that informal mentoring is prevalent among politicians and business people in top positions, especially among women. It shows that having a mentor was an almost common practice among women politicians, and in countries where affirmative action laws are enforced more women mentors were mentioned than in countries where no such laws exist.

Also, women politicians have taken upon themselves to mentor junior female colleagues more than junior male colleagues.

It is recommended that a study on mentoring look into the stages at which mentors were most important in business and in politics, because of the different structure of each sector. Such a study should also look more closely into the reasons for empowering others. Is it to gain more control over others, is it to increase equality, or is it some other reason?

Note

1. Note that the variable 'having a mentor assisted my career' was not significant in the regression equation.

8
Gendered Time and Women's Access to Power

Alison Woodward and Dawn Lyon

The challenge of work time and leadership: introduction

Women's workforce participation challenges conceptions of work time for all categories of workers, including top managers and politicians. Across industrialised countries, the combination of work time and family time are at the heart of discussions of the future of work. One of the popular suggested solutions has been a shorter working week. Yet, at the same time, there has been a growing concern that societies are increasingly two-tracked. One track is for those on the fast-time track of the fully employed in highly qualified jobs, and the other for those excluded from the workforce or willing to accept a 'flexible' construction of working time. This second group is the parking place for the 'woman's' problem of combining work and family.

This chapter addresses the extent to which women's entrance into the halls of power will change 'leadership time'. Further, to what extent do present conceptions of time commitment constitute an important barrier for women to top functions? The construction of 'leadership time' is a special variant on the paradoxical time-frame of professionals. 'Leadership time' virtually presupposes a private social support system traditionally provided by female family members. It is a Western and masculine time-frame. The leader's use of time in this way is a model expected by society, but one that is ill supported by the changing social expectations for both men and women.

Both men and women in the business and politics sample find their lives structured by long working weeks, with virtually no time difference between men and women. However, in exploring the findings we will discuss the contradictory nature of what these long working weeks mean in terms of costs for men and women in varying contexts. The leadership time of a politician is different from that of a business leader. Equally the 'sacrifices' in comparison to normal working time are weighted differently, depending on contextual factors including the kind of family life, national welfare system, cultural norms and gender expectations.

Time for men and women at the top – some empirical illustrations

Time for leadership – the amount of time

One of the costs of higher functions is the almost unlimited work engagement. An oft-cited reason for the lack of women in top functions is that they are unable to make the necessary time commitment to their jobs (Parasuraman and Greenhaus, 1993). Because most cultures expect that leaders are totally committed to their jobs, a traditionally gender-roled family life might seem to be a virtual impossibility.[1]

A key hypothesis in this study was that in many ways women who reach top leadership functions have to follow the same 'rules' as men and adapt to the dominant culture. In the case of time use, this hypothesis seems to be supported. Male and female leaders seem in many ways on the surface to be alike in their paths to the top and their evaluation of what got them there. The data show little difference in the length of weeks clocked by male and female leaders (hence the very small proportion of statistically significant male–female differences in the length of working weeks; see Table 8.1). Virtually all the respondents clock what we can call leadership time, which has a very different nature than normal time, as we will discuss below. Respondents in different countries may clock the same number of hours, but the implications are different for men and women, for politicians and business people and for people working in different national business and political climates.

These figures show a dramatic difference between what is considered to be the average working week in the countries studied and the working weeks of top managers and politicians. The average working week for these leaders is nearly 60 hours.[2] Yet, for example, in Belgium, male full-time employees work an average of 38.5 hours/week and female full-time employees 36.9 hours/week (Rubery, Fagan and Smith M., 1995: 145) or even less according to some sources (Elchardus and Glorieux, 1994). This does not reflect the working patterns of a large proportion of our respondents. Elchardus and Glorieux argue that once the combination of housework, childcare and formal work tops 55 hours/week for an individual, 'different mechanisms are called upon to reduce the workload, such as paid household help, a more equitable distribution of the work load between members of the household, and, more importantly, part-time work or even withdrawal from the labour market' (1994: 22). In the sorts of careers represented in our sample this threshold is passed at an early point. Further, the spouses of most of the women, and a significant proportion of the men, are in paid employment.

Table 8.1 Average Hours of Work in Business and Politics in Grouped Countries, by Gender

Country	Male Politician	Female Politician	Male Business	Female Business	Male National	Female National
Austria	65	64*	56	52*	38^2	33^2
Belgium	66	69	55	52	38^1	37^1
Canada	65	76**	51	60*	40^2	
Denmark	63	64**	55	55**	39^1	38^1
Finland	67	70*	55	54	39^2	35^2
France	61	58*	55	53**	40^1	39^1
Germany	69	72	54	57*	40^1	39^1
Greece	64	79	54	56**	43^2	38^2
Nth-land	55	68	57	57*	40^2	39^2
Hungary	69	64	–	–	–	–
Israel	66	70	57	53	42^2	31^2
Italy	64	56	54	51	40^1	37^1
Japan	64	66	54	50	39^2	33^2
Norway	–	57	–	54	$39^{2,3}$	$30^{2,3}$
Poland	–	–	60	62**	$43^{2,3}$	$39^{2,3}$
Portugal	64	51	50	48	41^2	36^2
Slovenia	59	60*	56	62	$41^{2,3}$	$40^{2,3}$
Spain	55	64*	53	55	38^2	33^2
Sweden	71	56	56	55	40^2	33^2
Swiss	59	61*	55	57**	$35^{2,3}$	$25^{2,3}$
Russia	67	60	–	–	–	–
UK	68	76**	59	53*	42^2	38^2
USA	63	76	57	58	–	–
Czech	54	72	65	56	40^2	
Ireland	67	64	54	48	36^2	32^2
New Zealand	75	79**	59	56*	41^2	37^2
Australia	72	69*	60	63*	49^2	30^2
Overall mean	65.10	66.15**	55.85	55.18*	40	36

*Significant at ≤ 0.05; **significant at ≤ 0.01.
1. Source: *Social Portrait of Europe*, 1996, Eurostat, p. 120 (data from 1991).
2. Source: *Yearbook of Labour Statistics*, 1997, International Labour Organisation, Geneva (figures are most recent available ranging from 1994 to 1996).
3. Figure is for employees only.
NB. Figures are based on those who work at least 35 hours/week from a weighted sample.
Significance figures refer to the differences between men and women within the same domain, i.e. business or politics.
For national statistics, where a figure appears on the right-hand side of the column for men, it is the national average of men and women combined.

They must solve the problem of the social support system in non-traditional ways (an issue treated in Part III of this volume).

A second clear difference is the sharp differentiation between business and political life. Leadership time is quantitatively more demanding for politicians. The average working week of the business leaders is about 55 hours, while the politicians claim a mean working week of 63. Further, politicians of both genders have the highest occurrence of a 90+ hour a week. Although exceptional, it is clearly a phenomenon of leadership time worth examining. In fact, there are proportionally more female politicians in the 90+ hours/week group than men. We asked politicians to what extent they saw their workload as problematic: only one third saw it as particularly onerous.[3] Leaders may not see a heavy workload as an extraordinarily high cost of their job for many reasons related to the nature of leadership time itself. As we will discuss below, this may be related to the status value of such workloads as indicative of important responsibilities, or to the belief that long hours are necessary to achieve tasks and retain control. Finally the acceptance of long hours may be a result of successful socialisation into the leadership role.

There are many possible by-ways for discussion, but the questions we are particularly interested in, even if we cannot provide full answers at this point, are the following:

- Why do leaders accept and actually pursue the full workload and how does it relate to the characteristics of leadership time?
- What insights can gender thinking bring to our understanding of the long hours notion of time?
- What contextual factors bring politicians to accept or calculate an extremely heavy workload in many countries, and why does international business seem to have settled at about 55 hours? If the business week is shorter, why is time so often cited as the reason women do not make it through the business glass ceiling?

Characteristics of leadership time

For top functions, any consideration of time will raise paradoxes and contradictions. On the one hand, one of the important attractions of these roles is the idea that one has control over the work situation, including one's own work rhythm. A main benefit of being in a top position is supposedly autonomy in the use of time. Yet, on the other hand, people in professions and leadership functions are assumed to be ever-available, when it counts. The professional is 'always at work', and has a surplus of time and commitment to accomplish a task. They thus supposedly control time, and yet are slaves to the necessarily expanded time-frame of tasks.

Another paradox of time in the upper echelons is that, on the one hand, it is vastly valuable, a costly resource, and yet, on the other hand, the owner of that time must be able to pay it out like water when the situation warrants it. This involves a number of crucial strategic decisions every day. That time management is a central part of leadership and time a costly resource is illustrated by the spate of literature of the One-Minute Manager type

(Blanchard and Johnson, 1981). The leader demonstrates power through the symbolic use of time.

Seron and Ferris (1995: 23) note that professionals are supposed to be always on the job, and thus must be able to ensure themselves of release from private obligations to be able to deal with work crises. These positions require answers to the question of how to find time for social and physical reproduction. One of our interviewees related that her life was well organised to deal with the normal, but that problems would occur when abnormal demands were placed, either from the employer or from her private situation. She characterised her time as 'normal' time and 'crisis' time.

To what extent does the time use of leaders demand a different theoretical understanding? How can gender ideas contribute to seeing that this use of time, which on the surface seems so masculine in the assumptions it makes about what occurs in the private-social sphere, in fact is also 'feminine' in its very 'greedy' nature of demanding commitment of emotional and never-ending energy?[4]

The social construction of time is treated in an expansive literature far beyond the scope of this chapter. It is clear that the study of time is interesting as a way to study a culture (Mercure and Wallemacq, 1988: 7), be it of a profession or a country. Part of the 'capital' that accrues to different positions in the class structure is that of power over time. Some authors suggest that time is not merely power, but that the very forms of usage are associated with the two genders. In this categorisation of time as gendered, they suggest that in some real way there are female and male time systems. Behind this view is the notion of types of time on a continuum, or even in a dichotomy, where there is 'linear/masculine' time at one end countered by a sort of 'process' time of tasks that are feminine, simultaneous, overlapping and flowing in quality. This 'visualisation' or metaphorisation of time has its parallels in Alberto Melucci's (1996) discussion of conceptions of time across history. Linear time is represented by an arrow, a masculine symbol *par exellence*, while cyclical time is a circle. In David Knights and Pamela Odin's review of thinking about time and gender, they describe the notion of feminine, process time as 'relational, continuous, precostal and cyclical...feminine time is shared rather than personal, and relational rather than linear' (Knights and Odin, 1995: 213–14, also citing Adam, 1993).

Underlying this thinking about time is an idea that in the West there is a dichotomy, and sometimes almost polar antipathy between types of time. On the one side of the dichotomy, which is characterised as 'masculine', is the time that is public, for formal work. This time is linear, easily broken into its component units, and single usage. It is the rational time of the Weberian bureaucracy and of Taylorism. Anne Wilson Schaef (1981) calls this the White Male System, characterising it as establishment time, which also reflects an ethnic culture. Linda Hantrais notes that the professional career time of men is linear, whereas for many women their paths are cyclical (Hantrais, 1993: 139). Many authors argue that a linear view of time fails to capture the time of everyday life, which frequently involves carrying out several tasks at various levels of attention simultaneously (Hantrais, 1993: 140, also citing Davies, 1989; Langevin, 1984; Mercure and Wallemacq, 1988). This time is the time that can be characterised as private time, feminine time, in the female system.

Such a dichotomisation of time as happening in separate spheres raises definite problems in a world with household members moving in between spheres dominated by the male, linear time and those ruled by a female process use of time. This is the challenge posed by an increasing participation of women in paid labour. In the virtually all-male working world that persists in top management, the idea that the public linear formal work world is separate from the feminine process world is a virtual cultural pre-requisite. Women entering these roles are a challenge as they make abundantly evident that the linear formal work world is inextricably bound with the process world and in fact is impossible without it.

Leadership time

But in some important ways, the 60+ hour working week of many of our leaders challenge the idea that there is merely linear time at issue here, which can be neatly cut off. Many of the tasks of leaders are in fact of a 'process' nature, requiring that they be, in some real sense, responsibly available in the same way that a mother with dependent children must be. Melucci (1996) argues that these polar conceptions of time are dissolving in modernity, becoming increasingly fragmented. If one thinks of the leader's combination of time spheres, then Melucci's vision renders everyday life as a matter of 'linear time yield[ing] to an experience of transitions without development, to a movement between disconnected points, a sequence of fleeting moments' (1996: 9). Leaders provide examples of what Melucci describes as different ways of living in time, united in a kind of spiral of arrows, cycles and points (1996: 13). The nature of managerial responsibilities is such that unbounded activities of management 'invade' leaders' lives, as one female respondent put it. There is a curious parallel in leadership time and the time characterised as 'feminine' in the private sphere, as they are both perceived as 'process' time, in which the clock is of limited importance, and the task itself is paramount in deciding what expenditure is needed. Hence, the leader needs to have total time autonomy in the workplace to be able to make the investment when appropriate. At work, this means that the time demands of other places where process tasks occur, such as the home (which is also invaded by the linear institutional time of organisations such as schools), must for the leader be kept at bay. Leaders can buy their freedom from societal/institutional clocks through paid/unpaid personnel, and thus use the autonomy they have earned. The temporality of careers and evolution of leadership time as a person goes up the ladder is an important feature of any discussion of the interaction between family and work time for men and women. While the expanded working day is a fact of life throughout the professional career, the meaning of that time differs at different points in the career, ranging from the visible commitment of physical presence at a junior level to the senior use of time in networking or wining and dining (Seron and Feris, 1995: 26).

On their way up the career ladder, the junior manager or politician indicates his or her potential by 'being there' in a quantitative sense, by visible availability. But even in showing this availability it must be for the correct reasons, an availability that also demonstrates discretion, the ability to judge the importance of things. Advice manuals to female managers try to make this difference clear to women climbing the corporate ladder, that managers have a different relation to time. (Harragan, 1977, in Frost et al., 1992: 190–1). The manager needs to demonstrate autonomy, but it is an autonomy that does not result in working shorter hours. They learn to manage being smoothly on time in the early stages of their career. Once at the top, the use of time is no longer an evidence of commitment and ability to be on top of things, but one of power. The leader must be there when it counts, but this is the trap for women.

Yet, leaders accept and even embrace the impossible hours. The special time that is 'leadership time' is one of the strongest parts of the Myth of the Heroic Leader. Top figures in society are characterised in the media as people who never sleep. They are always present, working the 18-hour day endlessly. The true contradiction of leadership time is that time autonomy is paired with a need to be visibly the slave of time. Long hours become a 'badge of status' in many settings (Zerubavel, 1981, cited in Seron and Ferris, 1995).

In our interviews with Belgian leaders we have been struck by the uniform awareness of the high prestige associated with the long working day of the top leader. Virtually invariably, the question 'How many hours do you work in a normal week?' elicits a ritual exercise in sums as the leader figures in the work done in the chauffeur-driven car in the morning and follows the day through to the last business or political dinner. The sum, as we saw above, always far exceeds the legal working week and extends to the weekend. One female executive without children noted that she takes two hours a week out for exercise classes, almost as if asking permission from the interviewer for this frivolous waste of time. This pride and perverse pleasure in the Super-Human Hours is displayed by both the political and business leaders. What is interesting about our findings is what may be occurring in countries where men and women clock less than 55 hours a week, such as the Netherlands, Israel, Slovenia, Spain, Finland, Italy and Portugal. It is not immediately obvious why the demands of politics and even business may be different in these countries, although one might group Italy, Spain and Portugal together as enjoying a Mediterranean life-style, but then why do the Greeks work more? Israel, Finland and the Netherlands may also have had a debate about human working weeks, and be affected by a different kind of social context, but again then why do Denmark, Sweden and Norway not appear?

The 'availability trap': how 'masculine' is leadership time?

In this section we would like to explore further ideas of availability introduced in the last section. The demand of unlimited availability is a paradoxical trap for leaders. They step deep into this trap crucially at the moment of their career when they are being tested for their qualifications and suitability. At present, it seems that women who have arrived at the top positions have totally adapted to the leadership time model in terms of hours of commitment. While leadership time may combine notions of process and linearity, the demands that the model poses for the organisation of private life are more easily compatible with traditional gender roles in which the man makes the work place investments.

As Linda Hantrais (1993: 147) suggests, large organisations such as the ones in this study impose particularly linear and inflexible time requirements for their employees, which are incompatible with family life for both men and women. These organisations take the Weberian bureaucratic ideal modelled on the permanent availability of the serviced worker as the norm for top employees (Ramsey and Parker, 1992). It is often suggested that the inflexibility of large organisations is one reason why so few women are to be found in top positions within them.

Availability takes different forms and is displayed in different ways at different stages in career progression: for example, through shows of visibility, reliability/loyalty and the ability to project intense psychological presence. In the competition for getting the key senior positions in an organisation, our Belgian findings suggest that both women and men have to prove themselves through 'tests of availability'. Visibility is particularly important early on to demonstrate commitment to the organisation and its goals. As a result, women having children at critical stages of their career development are seen as having family priorities and therefore not having senior management potential. Although the women in our sample have successfully passed this stage of their careers, they are only too aware of the importance of managing their availability at these times.

However, other forms of availability remain important. At the senior level, reliability is central. This implies a form of availability to the organisation that transcends physical presence, facilitated by a plethora of technologies to enable immediate location and contact, such as mobile phones and bleepers. Being there in a literal sense is superseded by being perpetually accessible – to superiors only, of course. More generally, one is counted on to make a reliable use of the expanded time devoted to the organisation.

In some organisations the tests of availability may take the form of demanding geographical mobility, making it extremely difficult for those with families or in dual-career partnerships to rise to the challenge. Indeed, this was the case for a number of those in our research. Around one third of our respondents thought that the fact they had been geographically mobile was important to their achievement of success.

It is interesting to compare the career profiles of two male personnel directors, one, who through the availability and support of a full-time housewife was enabled to do his stint abroad, thus securing continued upward mobility in the company; the other, in a dual-career household, perceived that his career ambitions had been thwarted through his lack of availability to fulfil this part of the career track, essential for those seeking even higher positions in his organisation.

Such a feature of career paths operates, amongst other ways, as a 'test of availability'. However, once these 'tests' have been successfully passed, there is greater flexibility for autonomous organisation of working schedules for both men and women. A woman director of personnel describes the process of her own acceptance into the ranks of senior management through the requisite displays of appropriate commitment and values. She commented that she had to be available, or at least *show* that she was available, physically and through what she described as an availability of *esprit*, a kind of psychological presence. In practice, this meant not revealing the complexities of managing the different schedules of her life and those of her partner and children, and never taking time off to look after them. Overall, demonstrating freedom from private obligations is crucial, which again fits the dominant male norm. After a certain period it was as if she had passed the test, she was accepted and the disadvantage that her gender represented faded. Now, she says that she has the autonomy to take the time she needs, albeit in the context of at least a 55-hour week.

In the political context, the forms of availability are different. When business executives have passed the tests, they are allowed somewhat more autonomy in structuring their day, while in the world of politics the electoral process poses the availability test on a cyclical basis. This helps us understand the super-human weeks of the politicians in the sample. Politicians in certain functions are expected to show their availability for the needs of the legislative organisation during the normal linear working week where the hours of the civil servants determine the work rhythm as well as being available for their constituents who need to see the politician in what is their private time, on weekends, in the mornings before the business day, and at night. An interesting feature of the super-hours workers is that they are somewhat disproportionately female. Arlie Hochschild (1997) suggests that the rewards of being able to express creativity and positive feedback in the workplace, which for our leaders seem to be a prime motivation, might be a factor in actually bringing many people to see their workplace as their 'home', and indeed in the stories of political leaders we can see how many do not see their 'work' as work, but rather as life.

But to lead this life, some organisation is necessary. Many leaders rely on someone else to be perpetually available to take care of non-professional demands, particularly at key stages of career progression. This support availability is a mirroring in the private sphere of the availability expected of leaders in the world of formal work. Supporters may be partners, parents or paid helpers. The advantage of family members is that their genuine affective concern shapes their willingness to remain available, and it tends to be men who can count on such family members when they have spouses who fill the 'traditional female gender role expectations'. In the case of paid help, the employment contract rests more on a linear conception of time, clock-time through more or less fixed working hours, with clauses for exceptional circumstances. This is problematic for those whose professional demands may come at short notice.

Thus, at least in this way, even if leadership time combines linear and cyclical or process qualities, it can be characterised as masculine in that it is well served by the traditional role model, and as we will see, the male leaders avail themselves of it by very frequently having an unemployed spouse.

Family moments – the 'cost' of power?

Some of the conflicting demands are simply not resolvable, however much additional help is made available. For those in leadership positions, exceptionally long working hours have implications for the organisation their households and the management of time outside their professional lives more generally, not just for the leaders themselves, but also for those close to them. The conflicting demands take leaders into the thorny territory of compromise. With competing timetables at the level of their career development over the life-cycle, something has to give.

This also is related to the issue of children and the so-called 'quality time' to be spent in educating and caring for one's children. One of the curious consequences of the challenge to deal with the interrelationship of our constructions of time is this notion of 'quality time'. Delegating all childcare to third parties remains culturally unacceptable and is furthermore difficult to delegate, as it demands an emotional input. This sort of 'quality time' is a marriage of 'linear time', as it is definitely finite, with 'process time'. A 'process time' task such as childcare is somehow intensified in its 'quality time' version by the 'presence' of the participants. Process time found in the home in its purest form doesn't involve 'presence'. Leadership time in the world of formal work has the same limitless availability demands as process time, but also requests the reliability of intense psychological presence. The feminine process time found in the home is often characterised by doing several things simultaneously. Feminists have claimed that this female capacity to carry out several tasks simultaneously is valuable, but we can see in the dominant logic of 'presence' in the formal work world that doing several things at the same time is symbolically read as not being present. Modern-day leaders are advised that they can avoid some feelings of guilt if they bring 'leadership time', as we have called it, in terms of its intensity of presence, into the home, and that this can somehow make up for them not being able to fulfil the 'availability' test of process time.

Overall, there is little differentiation by gender in our findings of leaders' perceptions of the sacrifices and time trade-offs they make in the pursuit of their careers. Almost all strongly signal their lack of personal or free time, followed by regrets about the time they have to spend with friends and, of course, with their 'supportive' partners. People seem to sacrifice their own time in favour of using whatever time is left for the family. This is especially true for women. The clearest difference between genders is that women claim they make fewer sacrifices in the time spent with their children, although the differences in the findings amongst male and female politicians are all significant, except regarding a sacrifice in the having or delaying of children. The inverse is true for business leaders (see Table 8.2). Where the sacrifices appear for women, and especially businesswomen, is in family planning, where many more women than men report they made sacrifices in having or delaying children. This is also reflected in family size, as discussed in chapter 13. Businessmen, having slightly shorter working weeks, do not seem to feel that they are significantly sacrificing time with their children, but male politicians seem to feel guilty, as 53 per cent admit to sacrificing child time. Emotionally, however, politicians may receive support

Table 8.2   Sacrifices in Time (%)

	Male Politician	Female Politician	Chi-Sq. (m–f diff)	Male Business	Female Business	Chi-Sq. – (m–f diff)
Personal/ free time	75	83	0.017	71	73	0.482
Friends and social time	54	62	0.020	47	48	0.546
Time with children	54	29	0.000	37	34	0.272
Time with partner	51	40	0.003	43	42	0.619
Delaying children	12	16	0.239	10	26	0.000

NB. Those who work at least 35 hours/week were selected from weighted sample. Percentages are valid percentages, i.e. those without a partner or children are excluded from the third and/or fourth lines.

in their work, as they also are the ones who least strongly claim that they make a sacrifice in terms of social time to be with friends. This may be because the nature of their work involves significant social engagements with like-minded in their political parties.

That female politicians are the ones who claim to make the least sacrifices in terms of time with their children is not too difficult to explain. For women politicians, the management of their roles as mothers is open to public scrutiny in electoral campaigns. This is particularly relevant to those in political parties, where the importance of traditional family values is emphasised, as in Christian Democratic-type parties. One politician told us how she had a leaflet produced, for an electoral campaign, of a day in her life, which focused on her fulfilling traditional feminine roles such as taking her children to school and preparing their meals. Political credibility for women is frequently linked to the 'perfect mother' image. Yet, the overlaps of their political and personal life are double-edged for these women. Symbolically managing their children for an electoral campaign bears little resemblance to the reality of long working hours in politics, which are hard to reconcile with good performance as a 'traditional' mother. For their male counterparts, being a traditional 'family man' who effectively brings home the bacon is often what counts. This is culturally associated with being reliable and trustworthy. This image emphasises the provision of material support rather than physical presence of process time, so long working hours may be interpreted as fulfilling this ideal. The cost for men is high in terms of their participation in family life, and our results suggest men are aware of this.

Conclusion: time crunch for leaders

Leadership time as practised by leaders is constructed on the basis of the availability of a private support system. We can see that women are not 'just like men', even if on the surface they are following the same time scheme, for they make sacrifices in their choices for a personal life to a greater degree than men. It seems that even the ability to pay for private support is not sufficient to allow all women to fulfil their family wishes and leadership role. We need information about how women actually fill their days to see if leadership time is not only quantitatively the same, but also qualitatively. Further, the cross-national data reveal new pathways for research. What developments account for the variation in our time data? A pathway which should be explored is why some countries and some forms of leadership do not require long hours: what are the conditions which allow the leader to work a 50-hour week? We can see clearly across all countries that the working week for business leaders has fewer hours than for politicians. What factors have worked internationally to make businesses slightly more 'people-friendly' than politics? Why has the private sector been more successful at doing it? These questions need to be explored in further international qualitative interviewing and comparison of organisational contexts, as our present data do not really allow us to explore these issues, but only bring them to light.

In terms of findings with implications for increasing the number of women in leadership positions, this variation in hours worked is especially fascinating, for we have seen that women can and do work the inhuman weeks required in politics while maintaining families, and that these weeks do not seem to be required of people of similar responsibility in business. Yet it is in business that the argument that women cannot reach leadership positions because of the time crunch is most frequently used!

This chapter touches only fleetingly on the different sorts of family situations of our leaders in different contexts. Time demands are just one of the reasons which may explain why women leaders may have fewer children than men. The type of welfare regime and expectations about family size seem to enter into the patterns we see as well, and are worthy of further discussion, beyond the scope of this chapter. Women's entry into leadership positions destabilises the implicit gendered arrangements underpinning this construction of leadership careers. Today's women leaders are not leading the same kinds of private lives as their male counterparts, even if they are working the same number of hours. Our findings clearly indicate that leadership time is also becoming a problem in the male leader's world, as the gendered presuppositions on which it is founded are undermined by the increasing work force participation of the well-educated women who are their partners. These women's willingness to support their spouses totally looks shakier.

Notes

1. In élite families, women and men leave much of the process-time chores of caring and housework.
2. Male politicians 65.1 hours per week; businessmen 55.8; female politicians 66.1; businesswomen 55.1.
3. In fact, of the seven factors that could be considered negative about a politician's job, the heavy workload ranked 5, with the most negative factor being the relative lack of room for individual pursuits. Only 125 of the politicians answered this question, however.
4. Rose and Lewis Coser (1974) provided the useful conceptualisation of a number of social instructions such as the 'family' as being 'greedy', a concept that fits well with the commitments demanded of top leaders.

9
Life Choices and Leaders' Informal Networks

Jeannette Bakker

Introduction

This chapter focuses on the extent to which top leaders participate in decision-making, particularly through perceived informal access. It attempts to find the most adequate conceptual framework to explain the extent and ways in which women and men exercise their power.

The approach used refers to the 'double life perspective' (career or children) (Lindenberg, 1991: 32–58; Coleman and Fararo, 1992; Zey, 1992). Whereas women have to deal with an 'or–or' situation, the 'and–and' situation is valid for men, who are expected to be able to combine both careers (career and children), because the female partner is responsible for childcare and housekeeping.

This phenomenon of different choices in the family situation was analysed by Veldman and Wittink (1990), among top officials in the Netherlands. They conducted 60 in-depth interviews with male and female top officials in politics and in business. As in the present study, they used the 'matching method' to select women and men, which in their case was based on educational level, length of service and age.

In politics, according to these authors, the organisation of the family situation is left to the employees themselves. A female leader in politics assumes she has a career for life, possibly with children.

In the organisational culture in Dutch business, however, it is assumed that a career for life and the everyday responsibility for children are incompatible and that family care is the woman's responsibility. For this reason, nearly all female business executives in the Netherlands have opted for careers and not for children (Veldman and Wittink, 1990: 253).

When women have struggled their way to the top, they stand out because there are few other women there. Rosabeth Moss Kanter pointed out this phenomenon in 1977. Women in these positions are faced with increased visibility and far-reaching stereotypes, because they are so few (Kanter, 1977: 207; Adler and Izraeli, 1994).

The pre-existing socio-cultural context and notably the balances of power are given little attentions by Kanter, while Veldman and Wittink have considered these in their study. They found only a small group of female managers in business. These women have to adapt to the mores and (informal) procedures in the firm. This circuit has existed for a long time, is very widespread and men determine the rules and keep the informal network closed to women. It is a male bastion of power.

According to Veldman and Wittink (1990: 258), women in business and politics are extraneous to these informal circuits. Hennig and Jardim likewise described how the informal relations in organisations function: 'The informal system is truly a bastion of the male life-style' (1976: 13). The 'male advantage in leadership positions' includes also access to informal networks, even if formally these are open to anyone with the same qualifications (Epstein and Coser R.L., 1981; Vianello and Siemienska, 1990; see also chapter 10).

Assuming that females in top positions fall more often outside the informal circuit, this chapter deals with the question to what extent the double life perspective poses a dilemma for women leaders and whether it is connected with the percentages of full-time working women in a society. Women's participation in the labour market, indicated here by percentages of women with part-time and full-time jobs, has been given a central place in this chapter, because the Netherlands has the highest percentage of part-time working women among the countries in this study and this probably has an effect on the extent to which women occupy top positions and the sort of work they do. Furthermore, the very popular 'Dutch employment wonder' – the so-called 'Polder model'[1] or 'Tulip model' – can be mainly attributed to the current increase in the percentage of part-time workers in the Netherlands. Whereas in 1979 45 per cent of employed Dutch women had a part-time job, in 1995 this percentage had increased to 67 per cent.

Our question is: is the double life perspective, the above-mentioned or–or dilemma of women, less peremptory when there are more full-time working women? And are these women in leading positions in societies with many full-time working women less extraneous to the informal circuit than women in societies with few full-time working women? The underlying reasoning is that a society with more full-time working women has an increased 'pool' from which to recruit workers, and the number of female top officials may also increase because the 'phenomenon' of a paid, full-time working woman is more normal. In a society with more full-time working women, the cultural climate will be more favourable towards women in top positions and their informal inclusion.

We assume that in many organisations it is impossible to hold a leading position as a part-time job. For this reason the variables to be tested relate to the percentages of full-time working women of all women in the

Table 9.1   Activity Rate of Women as Percentage of Female Employee Population in 1994, aged 15 to 64[a]

	Economically Active Women	Women employed part-time	Female population employed full-time
1. The Netherlands	57.4%	66.0%	19.5%
2. Ireland	46.7%	21.7%	36.6%
Belgium	51.2%	28.3%	36.7%
UK	66.1%	44.4%	36.8%
Italy	42.2%	12.4%	37.0%
Spain	44.2%	15.2%	37.5%
Greece	43.2%	8.0%	40.0%
Germany	61.4%	33.1%	41.1%
France	60.1%	27.8%	43.4%
3. Denmark	73.8%	34.4%	48.4%
Portugal	58.8%	12.1%	51.7%

[a] Luxembourg, the twelfth EU country in 1994, is not part of this study and has therefore not been included.

countries of the European Union. The 'restriction' of the EU has been chosen in order to place the Netherlands, with its low percentage of full-time working women, in a coherent framework, since the characteristics of the EU are largely similar because of the uniform currency, cultural heritage and socio-political integration.

When calculating the percentages of full-time working women as a proportion of women aged 15–64 in the EU countries, three clusters can be distinguished.[2]

That is:

1. EU < 35 per cent (the Netherlands);
2. EU 35–45 per cent (Ireland, Belgium, UK, Italy, Spain, Greece, Germany, France);
3. EU > 45 per cent (Denmark, Portugal).

From now on these three clusters will be used.

We assume, that women's position in the labour market and, therefore, the sexual division of labour is crucial for women's access to leading positions.

Furthermore, the most recent discussion with regard to women in the labour market concerns flexible working hours (so, also part-time work), especially in leading positions. The fact that some men have recently started working flexi-time, notably in government, allows more participation in childcare and housework, which in time may imply a change in the cultural climate (*Yearbook Emancipation*, 1998: 23).

In order not to restrict ourselves to the societal sexual division of labour, this chapter also employs a measure based on the degree of participation of women in decision-making. The countries have been divided into three clusters, according to the Gender Empowerment Measure (GEM). This is a measure reported in the UN *Human Development Report*, 1997, indicating to what extent women are able to participate actively in economic and political life and participate in decision-making. There are 24 top countries (which I divided into clusters of 3×8), in which the Netherlands occupies 10th position and belongs in the second cluster.[3]

We asked whether there is a difference or a similarity between the EU rank (sexual division of labour) and the GEM rank (participation in decision-making).

The reasoning above can be summarised in the following hypotheses:

Hypothesis 1A: The more full-time working women in a society, the better chances they have to work their way up to the top positions,[4] to be less extraneous to the informal circuits in their present function and differ less from their male colleagues.

Hypothesis 1B: The more women in a society participating in decision-making, the less will they be extraneous to the informal circuits in their present function and the less will they differ from their male colleagues.

As a consequence of these hypotheses, the question arises of what life choices the female top officials make in a society with few full-time working women. They might opt for a life career rather than for a family life. It could also be that they have to make difficult sacrifices in their personal lives in order to be able to get high up on the social ladder.

Another question is, what can be said about the lives of female top officials in countries where higher percentages of women can participate in decision-making?

The above-mentioned suppositions can be put in the following hypotheses:

Hypothesis 2A: The fewer full-time working women in a society, the smaller is the number of women who manage to reach a top position,[5] because they have gone through a stricter selection process than their male colleagues.

Hypothesis 2B: The greater the percentage of women participating in decision-making in a society, the greater are the numbers of women who reach top positions,[6] because they have to go through a less strict selection process than their male colleagues.

The structure of this chapter is as follows:

Section 1, *The mum oyster of the world of grey suits*, discusses the opinions of the participating female top officials about their access to informal networks: Do they have as much access as men or possibly more? We assume this is not the case.

The amount of perceived access to informal communication inside and outside the organisation is also studied.

In section 2, *In their after-school hours my children have hindered me in making the necessary informal contacts*, the number of children is discussed in the framework of life choices.

In section 3, *In my environment, women who have both a full-time job and a family are more often the ones who have serious breakdowns*, the general opinions of officials about 'women at the top' are observed. Possibly, these will give a different picture than the leaders' personal experiences show.

1. 'The mum oyster of the world of grey suits'[7]

In 1990 Veldman and Wittink maintained that in the Netherlands female top officials are extraneous to the informal circuits and for this reason they are less successful in accomplishing their jobs compared to male top officials.

We have investigated this by asking the respondents whether they believed they had sufficient access to information through informal channels in order to do their job well.

The t-test in the comparison between men and women in both sectors in all 27 countries shows no significant difference in the expected direction, rather the opposite.

In Table 9.2 the means of this variable for all 27 countries are shown.

Table 9.2 shows that women are slightly more likely than men in all 27 countries to think they have sufficient access to information through informal channels. A number of questions arise.

We might ask whether the Dutch situation is different from that of the other countries or whether it has changed since 1990, the year in which Veldman and Wittink published their study. It could also be that more women have leading functions compared to 1990 so there is a greater chance of not being extraneous to the informal circuits. And if it is true that more Dutch women have leading positions compared to 1990, this may be the result of the increased full-time participation of women in the labour market, with the consequence that there is a larger pool of experienced women.

In Table 9.3 we deal with the same question as in Table 9.2 with regard to the GEM clusters (degree of participation of women in decision-making).

Most leaders report having a high level of access to information through informal channels, notably in countries in which women participate significantly in decision-making and particularly in business. Hypothesis 1B seems to be supported by this finding.

Table 9.2 Opinion about the Degree of Access to Information through Informal Channels (27 countries)

	Politics		Business	
	Men	**Women**	**Men**	**Women**
Mean	3.6	3.7	4.0	4.1
N	429	425	347	371
Std.	1.2	1.2	1.1	1.1

Scale: 1 = insufficient access, 5 = sufficient access.

Table 9.3 Opinion about the Degree of Access to Information through Informal Channels in three GEM Clusters

	Politics		Business	
	Men**	**Women****	**Men**	**Women**
1 GEM High	4.1	4.1	4.2	4.3
2 GEM Middle	3.6	3.9	4.0	4.2
3 GEM Low	3.6	3.2	4.0	4.1

** $p < 0.01$; scale: 1 = insufficient access, 5 = sufficient access.

Testing hypothesis 1A in table 9.4, the three EU clusters were used. It concerns once more the question posed in Tables 9.2 and 9.3.

In Table 9.4 it appears that generally, with an increase in the percentage of full-time working women, the satisfaction with access to informal channels decreases for both men and women. So, the fewer full-time working women there are in an EU country, the more the female (and also male) top officials will have access to informal channels. This result seems to refute hypothesis 1A.

Table 9.5 reports the correlations between the percentage of full-time working women in the EU countries and the degree of participation of women in decision-making in the 24 GEM countries with the opinion about the degree of access to information through informal channels.

As an additional check we will also look at the result of the first 11 EU countries in the GEM ranking.

From Table 9.5 it appears that in the EU countries (row 1) men as well as women are less satisfied about access to information through informal channels when countries have higher percentages of full-time working women. The correlations between the degree of participation of women in decision-

Table 9.4   Opinion about the Degree of Access to Information through Informal Channels in Three EU Clusters

	Politics		**Business**	
	Men**	**Women**	**Men**	**Women**
1 EU < 35%	4.6	4.3	4.1	4.5
2 EU 35% to 45%	3.5	3.7	3.9	4.1
3 EU > 45%	3.5	3.9	3.7	3.9

** p < 0.01; scale: 1 = insufficient access, 5 = sufficient access.

Table 9.5   Correlations of the Percentages of Full-time Working Women in EU Countries, the GEM Ranking of 24 Countries and the First 11 Countries in the GEM Ranking with the Opinion about the Degree of Access to Information through Informal Channels

	Politics		**Business**	
	Men	**Women**	**Men**	**Women**
EU countries (11)	−0.15*	0.00	−0.11	−0.17*
GEM countries	−0.27**	−0.35**	−0.13*	−0.08
GEM ranking for EU countries	−0.16*	−0.32**	−0.12	−0.03

* p < 0.05; ** p < 0.01.

making in 24 GEM countries (row 2) and the opinion about the degree of access to information through informal channels in order to do the job well does not show the same result for women in business compared to women in business in the 11 EU countries (a negative correlation indicating that satisfaction declines in GEM ranking shows greater women's empowerment). But there is a question of significance with men and all respondents in politics. It seems, therefore, that hypothesis 1B is supported by the correlation with the 24 GEM as well as with the 11 EU countries. In other words, the more women (and also men) participate in decision-making, the more access they have to informal channels.

On the contrary, hypothesis 1A cannot be validated by the above results of the EU countries. It seems that the more full-time working women there are in an EU country, the less access male and female top officials believe they have to informal channels. This has come up as an unexpected outcome, worth being studied in greater depth by checking what informal communication top officials use in their jobs, inside and outside the organisation (informal personal communication with officials in their own working environment – e.g., for ministers: in the ministry they are in charge of, the government, the houses – or outside the personal working environment – e.g., for ministers: leaders of interest groups and important companies). This question concerned the actual access to informal communication and not the satisfaction about this access such as shown in Tables 9.2–9.5.

We have found a significant correlation only inside the business sector. The means show a declining score with increasing percentages of full-time working women in an EU country. In cluster 1, the cluster with the fewest full-time working women, the mean is 4.4 (on a scale from 1 to 5), which means that assessment of the access to that communication is high.

Table 9.6 (row 1) shows that, where there are fewer full-time working women, female as well as male top officials in business believe they have more access to informal communications. This shows that, where there is a lower percentage of full-time working women, there is more access to informal channels in business. Thus, hypothesis 1A cannot be confirmed.

The same correlation with the GEM countries (row 2) shows that for men the correlations between the degree of participation in decision-making and the actual amount of informal communication inside the organisation is significant, and negative, while for women it is negative, but weaker. Apparently, there are other factors resulting in the fact that women and men in a country with few full-time working women occupy a top position, considering that the more full-time working women there are in an EU country, the less access top women believe they have to informal channels.

We may wonder whether the fact that hypothesis 1A cannot be validated may have something to do with selectivity regarding these women and men, and whether there is a difference between genders on this.

In the next section we will test this through a review of the lives of the respondents.

Table 9.6 Correlation Between Percentages of Full-time Working Women in 11 EU Countries and the Degree of Participation of Women in 24 Countries with Perceived Amount of Informal Communication Inside Business

	Business	
	Men	**Women**
EU	–0.18*	–0.21**
GEM	–0.12*	–0.08

*p < 0.05; **p < 0.01.

2. 'In their after-school hours my children hindered me in making the necessary informal contacts'

Here we test the hypothesis 2A: 'the fewer full-time working women in a society, the smaller is the number of women who achieve a leadership position, because they have gone through a stricter selection than their male colleagues', and those of the test of hypothesis 2B 'the higher the percentage of women participating in decision-making in a society, the larger is the number of women who could reach leadership positions, because they must have gone through a less strict selection than their male colleagues' are analysed in this section.

We will see that the assumed selectivity of top women in business in a country with few full-time working women has been confirmed, when taking into consideration the number of their children. This variable shows significant gender differences in the three EU clusters in both sectors.

In Table 9.7 the mean number of children per respondent in the EU clusters is presented, and Table 9.8 shows the correlations between the percentages of full-time working women in 11 EU countries and the number of children.

It can be seen that women in the EU countries have fewer children than their male colleagues. And particularly in cluster 1, the EU cluster (one country: the Netherlands) with the least full-time working women, a striking mean is observed: 0.3.

As regards women in business in the EU countries the correlation is positive and significant (Table 9.8), which corresponds to the expectation that the fewer full-time working women there are, the fewer women at the top will have children. The GEM ranking of countries also shows a significant negative correlation with regard to politics (Table 9.7), which means that the greater the participation of women in decision-making is, the more

Table 9.7   Mean Number of Children in Three EU Clusters

	Politics		Business	
	Men	Women	Men*	Women**
1 EU < 35%	2.6	1.8	1.8	0.3
2 EU 35% to 45%	2.2	1.8	2.6	1.4
3 EU > 45%	2.3	1.9	2.3	1.8
1 GEM high	2.4	2.1	2.4	1.4
2 GEM middle	2.3	1.7	2.2	1.1
3 GEM law	2.1	1.7	2.6	1.8

* p < 0.05; ** p < 0.01.

Table 9.8 Correlations between the Percentages of Full-time Working Women in 11 EU Countries and the Number of Children

Politics		Business	
Men	**Women**	**Men**	**Women**
–0.07	–0.00	0.08	0.23**

** $p < 0.01$.

Table 9.9 Correlations between the Degree of Participation of Women (24 GEM Countries) and the Number of Children

Politics		Business	
Men	**Women**	**Men**	**Women**
–0.11*	–0.15**	0.01	0.07

* $p < 0.05$; ** $p < 0.01$.

children these officials have. With regard to business life, a positive correlation was found. This, however, is not statistically significant.

Apparently, female managers in EU countries with lower percentages of full-time working women have gone through a stricter selection process in their personal life choices, opting for a life career, and therefore a full-time leading position, than for having children. The finding of Veldman and Wittink that, especially in business, a life career and the everyday responsibilities of children are incompatible, i.e., the double life perspective or the 'or–or' dilemma, is confirmed by this, especially in cluster 1, the EU country with the lowest percentage of full-time working women (the Netherlands). In the GEM ranking of countries this 'or–or' dilemma is not so apparent.

3. 'In my environment, women who have both a full-time job and a family are the ones who often have serious breakdowns'

In this section the general opinions of top officials about women and leadership are studied, with the expectation that hypotheses 2A and 2B about the suggested selectivity will take on a different aspect. Possibly, these may give a different picture than the opinion regarding the personal situation of the respondent may lead one to assume. In Tables 9.10 and 9.11, we present the scores for two statements: 'Women lack powerful informal contacts' and 'Family life suffers when the woman has a full-time job'.

Table 9.10 Means of the Scores for the Statement: 'Women Lack Powerful Informal Contacts' in Three EU Clusters

Full-time working women	Politics		Business	
	Men	Women	Men	Women
1 EU < 35%	2.9	2.5	3.8	2.3
2 EU 35% to 45%	3.3	2.6	3.6	2.8
3 EU > 45%	3.5	2.7	3.5	2.7

GEM index	Politics			Business	
		Men	Women	Men	Women
1 GEM high	3.2		2.4	3.2	2.6
2 GEM middle	3.3		2.4	3.7	2.8
3 GEM low	3.1		3.1	3.4	3.0

Scale: 1 = highly agree, 5 = highly disagree.

Table 9.11 Means of the Scores for the Statement: 'Family Life Suffers when the Woman Has a Full-time Job' in Three EU Clusters

Full-time working women	Politics		Business	
	Men	Women	Men	Women
1 EU < 35%	3.4	4.2	3.1	4.3
2 EU 35% to 45%	3.1	3.6	2.6	3.3
3 EU > 45%	3.6	3.5	2.8	3.1
Correlation between the above statement and 'number of children' in 11 EU countries.				
*p < 0.05	−0.11	0.02	0.05	−0.14*

GEM index	Politics		Business	
	Men	Women	Men	Women
1 GEM high	3.7	3.7	2.8	3.5
2 GEM middle	3.1	3.6	2.6	3.5
3 GEM low	3.2	3.6	2.8	3.3
Correlation between the above proposition and 'Number of Children' in 24 Gender Empowerment-countries.				
**p < 0.01	−0.14**	0.03	−0.05	−0.01

Scale: 1 = highly agree, 5 = highly disagree.

It is clear that women in EU countries generally 'agree' more with this statement and that men are more inclined towards 'disagree'. In GEM countries we have found the same tendency, although it was less obvious.

We will once again refer to the opinion of the respondents about the degree of access to information through informal channels in order to do the job well as reported in Table 9.4, where the female respondents indicated a 'reasonably sufficient access' (the men's score is lower). From this table, however, it appears that the opinion of the female respondents about the situation of women at the top in general lies around 2.5, which means the women in fact agree with the proposition 'Women lack powerful informal contacts'. Thus, there exists a discrepancy between the opinion about their personal situation and their opinion about the situation of women at the top in general. What does this mean? Should we conclude from this that these women are rather select, because they have been able to gain sufficient access for themselves, although this is not regarded as an everyday reality for female top officials?

The same discrepancy was found in GEM countries (see Table 9.3), although this less obviously. It might therefore be a matter of being a less select group than the respondents from the EU countries.

In the EU countries women generally 'disagree' and men generally 'neither agree nor disagree' with the statement 'Family life suffers when the woman has a full-time job'. Also in the GEM ranking we see that women tend to 'disagree' more often than men, although this appears less obviously than in the EU countries.

The same table shows a significant negative correlation for women in business in the EU countries between this statement and the number of children.

Thus, women disagree with the statement that family life suffers when women have full-time jobs. Their personal experience, however, is that they have few children, especially in business (as shown in Table 9.7) Consequently, once again there seems to be a discrepancy between their opinion of their own situation and their opinion about the situation of women at the top in general.

In the GEM ranking of countries women show a positive correlation, which means that the higher the percentages of women participating in decision-making are, the more often women agree with this statement. This result corresponds with the fact that these women have more children than the EU women (see Table 9.7; in cluster 1 in politics 2.1 children, and in business 1.4 children). A double burden (full-time job and children) appears to be their fate. Thus, there is no discrepancy, and in this sense it is not a matter of selectivity, for EU women with the smallest percentage of full-time working women in their countries.

It looks as if women in business with a few children in cluster 1, the EU country with the lowest percentages of full-time working women (the

Netherlands) are part of a very select top group. The double life perspective is therefore specifically emphasised in this section, concerning the EU women in cluster 1.

Conclusion

Unexpectedly, we discovered in section 1 that women in all 27 countries are reasonably satisfied (more than men) about their degree of access to information through informal channels. We had assumed the opposite.

In this chapter we approached the question of women in leading positions through the sexual division of labour (part-time and full-time working women) and also through the participation of women in decision-making. The access to informal channels, interpreted as part of the exercise of power, turned out to be assessed more favourably by women with both measures, the EU ranking (sexual division of labour) and the GEM ranking (participation of women in decision-making). Thus, women claim to have more access to informal channels than men, which contradicts the findings of Veldman and Wittink (1990) and also Vianello and Siemienska (1990): i.e. that women are insufficiently familiar with 'interconnected male-controlled structures that dominate society through a network of power relations', and for this reason are believed not to be able to take part in this 'game' in their leading position (Vianello and Siemienska, 1990).

In section 1 we tested two hypotheses (1A and 1B).

As far as the GEM ranking of countries is concerned, we found support for hypothesis 1B, that, if the participation of women in decision-making is greater, their satisfaction about the access to informal channels increases.

The EU country clusters show a different picture. With the increase in the percentages of full-time working women, satisfaction with the access to informal channels decreases.

A new insight or an unexpected outcome emerges: namely, that 'the more full-time working women in an EU country, the less access top women believe they have to informal channels'. This was emphasised by the female managers in business, who claim a high amount of actual informal communication inside the organisation in a context with few full-time working women.

We can conclude from this that labour participation cannot simply account for the exercise of power of women.

Section 2 analysed two hypotheses that deal with the number of children.

In EU countries, women in business are more to the fore with regard to this variable. The expectation that 'the lower the percentages of full-time working women, the lower will be the numbers of female top officials with children', stands out clearly, which means that hypothesis 2A is confirmed.

The GEM ranking of countries shows a different picture: the stronger women's participation in decision-making appears to be, the larger is the number of their children, particularly in the world of politics.

The assumed selectivity in hypothesis 2A, particularly regarding women in business life in the EU countries with low percentages of full-time working women, started to take a clearer shape in section 3. In this section, the selectivity found is emphatically underlined by discrepancies. In fact, although women in the EU countries appeared reasonably satisfied with their personal degree of access to informal channels, they are also of the opinion (more so than men) that women at the top in general *lack* powerful informal contacts. Thus, we may conclude that women in EU countries with low percentages of full-time working women are a rather select group, because they have managed to get sufficient access to informal channels, while they do not think this holds true for female top officials in general.

In particular, the discrepancy between the choice of a very low number of children, characteristic especially of female managers, and their opinion concerning the family life of top women in general, which is believed not to suffer from a full-time job, points to validating hypothesis 2A. We can state that the so-called 'or–or' dilemma (career or children), the double life perspective, applies here, which underlines the finding of Veldman and Wittink, and of Lindenberg. This means that top women in business in an EU country with few full-time working women must indeed have gone through a stricter selection process as for their life choices than their female and male colleagues in other EU countries.

The 'or–or' dilemma is not so obvious in the GEM ranking of countries, because women in these countries show the strongest participation in decision-making and have also a certain number of children, and some are of the opinion that, when a woman has a full-time job, her family life will suffer. Thus, these women are confronted with a double burden (full-time job and children). Here it is not a matter of discrepancy as described above with regard to women in EU countries with lower percentages of full-time working women, because these women could apparently choose both a full-time job and children. It might, therefore, be a matter of being a less select group than the respondents from the EU countries. Hypothesis 2B is, therefore, sustained.

In contrast to Hennig and Jardim's statement that 'the informal system is truly a bastion of the male life-style', the females who participated in our study, especially those in business, feel quite comfortable in this 'bastion' in terms of their opinion about and actual access to informal channels; or they have adapted to it by breaking through the glass ceiling, but, then again, only with regard to their own position.

All this arouses curiosity. For, is it indeed the case that female executives actually feel at the 'top' in this male bastion?

We can ask ourselves whether the problem of giving socially desirable answers has an effect here, because the qualitative material from the Netherlands gives a different impression.

A few examples.

The fairly reasonable functioning stated by the female respondents takes on a different aspect when we review the stereotypical views of men, experienced by women, apparently to keep these women in their proper place: 'The female executive is seldom regarded as a colleague. They are regarded as daughter, mistress or mother. And this always happens in secret' (Woman, telecommunication multinational, December 1993). And: 'My boss calls me "emotional", because of my direct approach to people. On this ground, there is now a stagnation in my promotion to the top. I think he feels threatened, because of the fact that I do not conform, and am reputed to be an excellent employee, and all this in the framework of the everlasting tough scramble for the leading functions' (Woman, telecommunication multinational, January 1994).

These quotations, from Dutch women, give a different impression than the results that emerge from the quantitative study, at least for Dutch female managers.

It is crucial to gather more qualitative information about this, not just in the Netherlands, but also in the other countries.

Notes

1. The favourable economic developments resulting from the cabinet policy through pay restraints and job creation (notably by the increase in jobs for women) in the Netherlands.
2. Calculation on the basis of *EUROSTAT Yearbook 1996*. (Calculation of the full-time percentages with reference to the Netherlands: 57.4 per cent is the 'activity rate' of the female population, aged 15 to 64. The percentage of part-time working women is 66.0 per cent. So 34.0 per cent is the percentage of full-time working women against all working women. Accordingly 34.0 per cent of 57.4 per cent = 19.5 per cent full-time working women of all women, aged from 15 to 64, in the Netherlands.)
3. *Human Development Report 1997* of the United Nations, Oxford University Press. The Gender Empowerment Measure (GEM) uses the same variables as the Human Development Index. The HDI sets a minimum and a maximum for each dimension – life-expectancy, educational attainment, income – and then shows where each country stands in relation with each scale, but takes into account gender inequality in achievement between women and men. It examines whether women and men are able to actively participate in economic and political life and take part in decision-making. The country rank is the following (divided in three clusters by the author of this chapter):

   1. Norway, Sweden, Denmark, Finland, New Zealand, Canada, USA, Austria;
   2. Germany, the Netherlands, Australia, Switzerland, Belgium, Italy, Portugal, UK;
   3. Spain, Ireland, Hungary, Israel, Japan, France, Poland, Greece.

(From the 24 top countries, three in our research: Slovenia, Russia, Czech Republic, are missing.)

4. Given this study design with equal size national samples, we cannot test this first part of the hypothesis.
5. See note 3.
6. See note 3.
7. The titles in sections 1, 2 and 3 are quotations from the qualitative material from the Netherlands, respectively: 1. female MP, CDA (Christian Democratic Party), May 1994; 2. female, post and telecommunication multinational, January 1993; 3. male, Minister CDA (Christian Democratic Party), February 1997.

10
Interpersonal Contacts

Gwen Moore and Deborah White

Scholars considering explanations for women's rarity in economic and political élites have identified numerous individual and structural factors (see theoretical chapter). Among these factors are informal mechanisms – such as the importance of mentoring or inclusion in powerful informal networks – working to maintain male advantage in leadership positions, even when these are formally open to all qualified persons (see chapters 7–9 and 12). While only a part of the explanation, informal mechanisms not only help explain men's numerical dominance in élite positions, but may also contribute to an outsider status of the few women occupying senior authority positions in industrialised societies. The basic question we address is: are women and men in similar top positions alike in access to and contacts with other élites? We examine the informal mechanisms of élite networks and interpersonal contacts to see if these mechanisms favour men. We also ask whether any male advantage found is uniform across the business and political sectors and country groupings.

Some research has found that men in authority positions typically enjoy greater resources and opportunity than do equally situated women. Informal networks in and across organisations are among these resources, serving functions such as maintaining communication channels, enforcing informal norms, socialising new members and enhancing mobility opportunities (e.g., Moore, 1988; 1992; Acker, 1991). Epstein and others contend that even when women achieve senior positions, they may not be fully included in male-centred networks of power (Epstein and Coser R.L., 1981; Epstein, 1988). This male advantage might result from men's preference for interaction with one another (homophily), females' small numbers in top posts, or both. Kanter (1977) contends that 'tokens'' small numbers not only result in informal isolation from 'dominants' (those in the majority), but also from one another. These arguments suggest that women élites may be outsiders not only by virtue of their small numbers, but also due to their relative exclusion from male-dominated élite networks.

Previous research

Numerous studies have demonstrated the importance of communication and discussion networks not only in making organisational and national policy, but also in advancing incumbents' careers (e.g., Moore, 1979; Miller, 1986). Indeed, network ties may be seen as social capital (Bourdieu, 1986), with such capital especially accruing to those with connections to powerful persons. Yet, available evidence, while limited, indicates that women are rarely central in informal élite networks. In a study of senior civil servants in Canada, Great Britain and the United States, Meyer found that women were less involved in formal and informal interaction on the job than were their male colleagues in similar positions (1986: 291–3). Men enjoyed greater access to top leaders (who were, of course, overwhelmingly men) than did women.

Further, a late 1970s study of American leaders in business, labour, the media, parties and voluntary associations found that heads of feminist organisations – where most women élites were located – were less acquainted with and had less frequent direct contact with senior government officials than did leaders of any other élite group, except intellectuals (Verba and Orren, 1985: 67–9). The relative exclusion of American feminist leaders from powerful networks indicates that, at least in the 1970s, American political leaders did not view women's concerns as central to society.

Finally, research on network linkages among national élites in politics, business, labour, media and other groups in West Germany (Wildenmann et al., 1982), Australia (Higley, Deacon and Smart, 1979) and the United States (Moore, 1988) in the 1970s and early 1980s confirms that women leaders are somewhat isolated from national élite networks in these three societies. In each national élite, the small numbers of women in top positions were less integrated than their far more numerous men counterparts in policy discussion networks comprised of each nation's most powerful leaders in government, business, mass media, labour and interest groups (Moore, 1988).

These network studies confirm that even women who attained leadership positions in powerful national organisations remained through the mid-1980s less well connected in élite networks than their men colleagues.[1] If this pattern appears in our 1990s data – with wide diversity in economic and cultural conditions in industrialised nations – we will have strong evidence that informal élite contacts operate cross culturally in broadly similar ways to maintain male advantage in leadership positions.

Methods

We investigated frequency of contacts with other leaders as well as service on corporate and non-profit boards of directors – meeting places for the powerful in each nation. We did not collect extensive data on respondents' ego-centred networks, but rather asked how frequently they were in contact with leaders in a variety of specific key positions. This information is used in analyses of leaders' interpersonal contacts. In addition, extensive evidence from Europe and North America indicates that corporate boards of directors and, to a lesser extent, non-profit boards serve as key meeting grounds for influential élites from different organisations and regions (e.g., Useem, 1984; Mizruchi, 1996). We use two measures of network 'range': participation on corporate and on non-profit boards.

Élite contacts are measured by a set of questions asking: 'How frequently in the past year have you had any contact in person or on the telephone with' leaders in a list of other positions and sectors? For business leaders, we use reported frequency of contact with the chief executive officer of their own organisation, members of the board of directors of their firm, chief officers of other major corporations. Frequency of contact is coded 1 (daily), 2 (weekly), 3 (monthly), 4 (less than monthly), 5 (never). A summary index of contact with the three business leader categories (with low numbers reflecting more frequent contact) was calculated. The same question also recorded frequency of contact with members of parliament, the head of government, cabinet members and national party leaders. We use these contact measures primarily for political leaders. A summary index measures frequency of contact with political leaders in those four categories. In network terminology, the frequency of contact with other élites can be seen as a measure of network volume.

Respondents also reported how many directorships of major corporations they had ever held, and the number of memberships on governing bodies of major non-profit organisations they held now or in the past. With increasing numbers of board seats, respondents have networks of greater range, connecting them in ongoing relationships to leaders in other organisations, sectors and regions.

We examine gender effects on these measures to see whether men have more frequent contact with other leaders and serve more frequently on corporate and non-profit boards. Alternatively, women and men in equivalent high-level positions might be equally involved in élite networks within and beyond their organisations.

Because many scholars have found that social background, family status and current position are important individual factors in leadership (see section 1) and informal interaction, we also include measures of these. Generally, we expect leaders with higher status origins and higher level positions to have more frequent contact with other leaders and more service on corporate and non-profit boards of directors. Yet, some of these factors might affect men and women differently. For example, elsewhere in this volume we see that male leaders often have spouses who are not employed outside the home and who manage family tasks. By contrast, the spouses of top women more often have demanding careers that preclude their assuming full household responsibilities (see chapter 16). These gender differences suggest that marital and parental status might affect interpersonal contacts little among men, but more strongly for women. Of course, with the high salaries of élites much household labour can be purchased in most countries, so that even women's work activities are hampered little by family responsibilities. We ask if among top women, but not men, marriage and parenting impede involvement in work-related contacts.

We examined a variety of social background, family and career-related measures and chose those that correlated most strongly with the dependent variables and were not highly correlated among themselves. Social background variables examined were: father's education, mother's education, father's social class, respondent's education. Of these, we use mother's education as the item most strongly correlated with the dependent variables and not highly correlated with other independent variables. In similar fashion, we examined number of children and current marital status as current family measures. We use the number of children the respondent has. Present position is measured by two variables for business leaders: years in the current position, and the number of levels above the respondent in the organisation (for chief executives the number is 0). For politicians' present position, we use two indicators: a four-point scale of office level (with 1 the highest – for head of government, leaders of major parties, cabinet members, parliamentary leaders – to 4, regional and local officials) and years in politics. We expect further that national structural and cultural factors might affect informal contacts and networks. We use country groupings as specified in the methodological chapter to examine this possibility.

We begin with women's and men's mean scores on the dependent variables (Table 10.1), with a t-test of gender differences. Then, for variables in which men report significantly more frequent contacts and higher numbers of board memberships, we test whether gender differences remain net of other independent variables. Regression equations assess whether women and men with similar backgrounds, family status and positions have equivalent élite network connections, or if any male advantages shown in Table 10.1 remain even among leaders who are roughly equivalent in social background and experience. Finally, for significant gender differences found in the t-tests, we report results of regression analyses of gender and other independent variables separately for men and women (Tables 10.2 and 10.3). These results show whether different family, background and career variables are important for women's and men's élite contacts.

Results

Table 10.1 tests our expectation that men leaders have more frequent contacts with other business and political leaders and hold more seats on corporate and non-profit board of directors.

Table 10.1   Means and Standard Deviations of Contact and Board Membership Measures by Gender and Sector

Business Leaders	Women		Men	
	X	S.D.	X	S.D.
Frequency of contacts with:[a]				
chief executive officer own company	1.99	1.20	1.86	1.05
Members of own board of directors	2.64	1.26	2.52	1.29
Officers of other companies	3.29*	1.08	3.15*	1.04
Index business leader contacts	2.67*		2.56*	
Cabinet members	4.45	0.82	4.45	0.78
Board memberships:[b]				
No. corporate boards	1.33**	2.20	1.87**	2.55
No. non-profit boards	1.66	2.57	1.66	2.69

Political Leaders	Women		Men	
	X	S.D.	X	S.D.
Frequency of contacts with:				
business leaders[c]	3.44**	1.15	3.13**	1.16
Members of parliament	1.61	0.87	1.52	0.84
Prime minister/President	3.45	1.29	3.30	1.26
Cabinet members	2.65*	1.14	2.50*	1.09
National party leaders	2.87**	1.17	2.64**	1.14
Index of political contacts	2.63**		2.46**	
Board memberships:				
No. corporate boards	0.37**	0.88	0.67**	1.70
No. non-profit boards	2.35	3.19	2.18	3.17

* p < 0.05; ** p < 0.01 (1-tailed t-test).

[a] Respondents reported how frequently in the past year they had contact in person or by telephone with each of a series of other leaders (e.g., the chief executive officer of their own corporation for business leaders, the executive head of government for political leaders). The frequency of contact scale is from 1 (daily or nearly every day) to 5 (never). The business leader contacts index is the mean frequency of contact with the chief executive officer, members of the company's board of directors and officers of other corporations. The political leader contacts index is the mean frequency of contact with members of Parliament, the executive head of government, members of the cabinet and national party leaders.

[b] The number of corporate boards is the total number of corporate boards the respondent has ever served on. The non-profit boards measure is the corresponding total for non-profit boards of trustees.

[c] For politicians, contacts with business leaders refers to reported contacts with chief officers of corporations.

In general, the results confirm these predictions. For each contact measure examined, with just one exception, business and political men have more frequent contact than their women sectoral colleagues, as well as more corporate board memberships.

Businessmen have higher average frequency of contacts with each of the categories of business leaders, though just two of the five (contact with chief officers of other corporations and the summary measure for business contacts) are statistically significant. Both women and men have ready access to top decision-makers in their firms. They report contacts, on average, with the chief executive of their company slightly more than weekly and at least monthly contact with directors of their own corporation. By contrast, contacts with cabinet members are equally infrequent for both genders. Businessmen have held more seats on corporate boards than have women (a statistically significant difference), but they have not occupied a larger number of seats on major non-profit boards.

Women politicians have less frequent contacts with each category of political leaders examined, as well as with business officials, than do similarly placed men. Both men and women politicians report an average of more than weekly contacts with members of parliament (where many of them hold seats) and more than monthly interaction with cabinet officials and national party leaders. Neither women nor men in politics report frequent interaction with the prime minister or president. With most gender differences statistically significant for political leaders, we conclude that women politicians are less included in élite networks than are their women counterparts in business. As in business, in this sector, male politicians have held more seats on corporate boards of directors, but a similar number of positions on non-profit boards as their women colleagues.

Men business and political leaders enjoy greater access to other élites and to membership on corporate boards of directors. These results suggest that, even when women and men occupy similar senior positions in large corporations or national politics, men hold the edge in contacts with and ties to their (mostly male) peers and superiors in their own and other powerful organisations.

We now examine whether this male advantage is maintained even among élites with similar family and career characteristics.

For contact and board membership variables that showed statistically significant gender differences in Table 10.1 we computed regression equations to see if gender remains significant net of background, family and position variables (results not shown). The findings differ for business and political leaders. Among business leaders, gender is not statistically significant net of other variables in any equation. More important than gender is the level of the leader's position (number of levels above), with higher positions associated with more frequent contacts and memberships. Mother's education is also significant in the two contact frequency equations examined (officers of other companies and index of business leader contacts), with frequency of contacts positively related to mother's level of education.

The results for politicians differ, with male advantage on most measures remaining when other independent variables are included. Among the five contact measures significant in Table 10.1, men's greater frequency of contact declines to insignificance only for cabinet officials. Thus, gender remains an important distinction in situating elected politicians in élite networks. For the contact measures, position level is also strongly associated with how often political leaders report interacting with others.

In contrast to business networks, in which results are similar across country groupings, the findings for political networks vary. Political leaders in the economically less developed countries report less frequent contacts with cabinet members, national party leaders, business officials and in the index of political contacts than their peers in full market economies. Perhaps the patterns of extensive informal consultation among public and private élites that characterise most long-established democratic systems are less typical in the newer democratic polities of Eastern Europe (the majority of countries in the economically less developed group).

We now examine predictors of the contacts and membership measures separately for men and women.

Table 10.2 shows the impact of background, current family and positional variables on frequency of contacts with other corporate leaders and on the summary index of business contacts as well as number of corporate board membership measures. A negative coefficient in the contact equations

Table 10.2   Regression of contact and membership measures for business leaders by gender (unstandardised coefficients)

	No. of Corporate Board Memberships		Frequency of Contact with Officers Other Companies		Index Business Leader Contacts	
	Women	Men	Women	Men	Women	Men
Mother's education	0.07	−0.15	−0.08*	−0.07	−0.21*	−0.18
No. children	0.18*	0.47**	−0.06	0.03	−0.20	−0.06
No. levels above	−0.29*	−0.69**	0.24**	0.29**	0.96**	1.09**
Experience	0.00	0.02	−0.00	0.01	−0.04	0.03
Country groupings:						
Social Democratic	−0.39	−0.09	0.09	−0.12	0.58	−0.08
Econ. less developed	−0.32	0.10	−0.05	0.17	−0.23	0.05
Intercept	1.17**	−1.80**	3.34**	2.88**	7.93**	6.85**
R^2	0.06	0.16	0.08	0.08	0.20	0.18

*$p < 0.05$; **$p < 0.01$.

indicates less frequent interaction (officers of other companies, business leaders summary index). In the corporate board equations, a negative coefficient indicates fewer board positions. Independent variables include one social background variable (mother's education), one family measure (number of children), experience (years in current position), the level of the respondent's position and a set of dummy variables for the country groupings (full market economies is the reference category).

In general, the results are similar for women and men. Frequency of contacts with officers of other corporations and the summary index for business contacts as well as the number of corporate board seats is strongly related to position level for both men and women. Those with higher positions in the organisation have greater access to other business leaders and to seats on corporate boards. Consistent with results in section 1, we find that higher education of business women's mothers (but not business men's mothers) is related to more frequent contacts with other business leaders (though not to board membership). On other independent variables, men and women differ little, and the proportion of variance explained by the set of independent variables is generally comparable for the two groups.

Similar factors, especially level of position, affect the frequency of both businessmen's and businesswomen's contacts with other economic leaders and service on corporate boards of directors. This suggests that, when women leaders have backgrounds and experience equivalent to their male counterparts, the two groups' contacts with other high-ranking business officials are similar. The patterns of contacts and memberships are similar across country groupings.

For business leaders, more important than country grouping or gender is the respondent's position level. Earlier in the book, we saw that women and men do not differ on this measure. Here we see that position level is strongly related to nearly all of the contact/network measures, with fewer levels above respondents in the organisation associated with more frequent contacts and more board memberships among both men and women. Position level contrasts with years in the position, which does not strongly predict the network measures.

In Table 10.3 (political leaders) most independent variables are the same as in Table 10.2.

The measure of experience is the total number of years in politics, and the level of the position is on a scale of 1–4, with 1 the highest level political positions. As in the previous table, the latter variable is most consistently related to frequency of contact measures for women and men. Length of political experience is occasionally significant for men or women, while the number of children is positively associated with corporate board memberships for men only. Again, the economically less developed countries differ somewhat from full market economies on some of the frequency of contact measures. Both men and women – but especially the latter – in the

Table 10.3 Regression of Contact and Membership Measures for Political Leaders by Gender (unstandardised coefficients)

	Frequency of Contact With:									
	Business Leaders		Cabinet Members		National Party Leaders		Political Contacts Index		No. Corporate Board	
	Women	Men	Women	Men	Women	Men	Women	Men	Women	Men
Mother's education	−0.05	−0.02	0.01	−0.03	−0.00	−0.05	−0.09	−0.01	0.02	0.02
No. children	0.01	−0.01	0.06	−0.05	−0.02	−0.06	0.06	−0.11	0.02	0.20*
Title	0.15*	0.20*	0.23**	0.51**	0.07	0.15*	0.59**	−1.03**	−0.04	−0.03
Experience	−0.01*	−0.01	−0.01	0.00	−0.01	−0.01*	−0.03	−0.02	0.00	0.02*
Country groupings:										
Social Democratic	0.22	−0.03	0.12	−0.10	0.17	0.11	0.71	0.09	−0.04	−0.87*
Econ. less developed	0.22	0.04	0.41**	0.29*	0.49**	0.28	1.87**	1.23**	−0.04	0.06
Intercept	3.35**	2.93**	1.95**	1.29**	2.76**	2.72**	9.26**	7.58**	0.32	−0.08
R^2	0.05	0.03	0.07	0.18	0.04	0.06	0.13	0.13	0.01	0.05

* $p < 0.05$; ** $p < 0.01$.

economically less developed country grouping have less frequent contact with cabinet members, national party leaders and the index of political contacts than do their colleagues in the full market economy country grouping. These findings suggest that women politicians in the economically less developed country grouping are disadvantaged in participation in high-level élite networks when compared to both their men colleagues in that country grouping and to women and men in other industrialised countries.

Discussion and conclusion

This cross-national survey of élite women and men offers a unique opportunity to study the rare 'women at the top' who have joined their overwhelmingly male counterparts in political and economic leadership positions in more than two dozen industrialised nations. With men and women in equivalent leading economic or political posts, we can assess similarities and differences in the two groups' backgrounds, career experience and current positions. In this chapter, the focus has been on informal mechanisms, especially the extent to which leaders participate in contacts with officials in their organisations and elsewhere. Since most top leaders are men and male culture is said to dominate the high reaches of the business and political worlds, we expected informal mechanisms to privilege men. Evidence of male privilege in élite ties would be men's more frequent contacts with other leaders and more frequent service on corporate and non-profit boards of directors.

Indeed, on virtually all measures, men do report more frequent contacts with leaders in their organisation and in other élite positions than do their women colleagues. In both business and politics, men also report holding more seats on corporate boards of directors. Men thus appear to be advantaged by more frequent access to top officials within their own organisation and in other influential institutions. As well, men's higher level of service on corporate boards of directors helps integrate them into national economic leadership networks and also increases their broad influence on economic policy. By contrast, women and men have approximately equal experience serving on major non-profit boards of directors. These voluntary sector boards may also be important in joining élites from diverse organisations and sectors, but they are generally less prestigious than corporate boards (McPherson and Smith-Lovin, 1986; Odendahl and Youmans, 1994).

Investigation of the impact of individual and structural factors, as well as gender, on network measures indicates that male advantage is greatly diminished among businesswomen and men with similar personal and organisational traits. However, among politicians, men maintain the network edge even when background, family and career variables are controlled. We thus conclude that élite political networks remain more male-centred than top business networks in the industrialised countries of this research.

In both the business and political sectors a key factor in frequency of élite contacts and in service on corporate boards of directors is the level of the leader's formal position (Tables 10.2 and 10.3). Men and women at the top of the national political or business hierarchy are greatly advantaged in these élite contacts and memberships in comparison to their slightly lower level colleagues. This suggests that, when women hold top economic or, to a lesser extent, political posts and have similar personal and career characteristics to their male counterparts, the women's relative isolation from their over-whelmingly male peers diminishes.

In general, the effects of gender and other variables on network and membership variables are comparable across the three country groupings. A partial exception to this cross-cultural similarity is found in the less economically developed country grouping, where contacts among politicians, especially those reported by women, are less frequent than are those contacts in the full market economy grouping. We speculate that this is due to the newly emerging democratic institutions in the Eastern European nations that comprise the bulk of this category. When these data were collected in the early to mid-1990s, democratically elected parliaments were recent phenomena in Poland, Slovenia, Russia, the Czech Republic and Hungary. In contrast, in the full market economies of Western Europe, North America and elsewhere and the Social Democratic countries of Northern Europe, a long tradition of democratic procedures apparently includes extensive informal discussions among all major élite groups (Higley et al., 1992).

Informal mechanisms within and across political and economic organisations continue to work to men's advantage in these industrialised nations. Social capital, then, appears to accrue not only to privileged classes, but also to the privileged gender. There is some variation across country groupings, but the general pattern holds within such groupings as well.

Yet, there is some reason for optimism about increasing gender equity here. When women business and, to a lesser extent, political leaders have similar personal and organisational characteristics to their male counterparts, their disadvantage in male-centred networks of power – but not in holding corporate directorships – diminishes. These rare 'women at the top' appear to be less disadvantaged in their performance and networking in élite positions than in achieving such a position in the first place.

Note

1. For related arguments on women and élites, see Haavio-Manila et al. (1985); Lovenduski (1986); Hernes (1987); Randall (1987); Adler and Izraeli (1994).

11
Organisational Structure and Gender

Bogdan Kavčič and Marjana Merkač

Introduction

Like other concepts in the professional literature, organisation structure is treated differently by different authors. It is mainly defined as the pattern of relations among constituent parts of an organisation (Kast and Rosenzweig, 1985: 234), although it is also necessary to differentiate between the formal and informal aspects. The organisation structure is the basis for the establishment of relations among positions in an organisation and also the basis for the determination of power relations. Power belongs to a position and not to an individual. The structure of power is the basis for the distribution of tasks among the departments in an organisation and for the development of control mechanisms. In these ways the organisation structure defines the roles performed by individuals in the organisation. It also represents the network linking organisational sub-systems with the environment. Summarising different viewpoints, the organisation structure is determined by the following factors:

- organisation strategy: defines the long-term objectives of the organisation;
- technology used: defines the tasks to be performed by organisation members;
- philosophy (value system) of management (organisation culture): defines the perception of roles and value of workers (employees) in the organisation;
- environment: defines the complexity and flexibility of the organisation structure;
- quality of workforce: defines the level of the capability of the organisation to perform;
- size: defines the level of division of labour, complexity of control, size of management.

In the professional literature very different typologies of the organisation structure can be found. On the basis of different sources (Ivanko, 1980; Kast and Rosenzweig, 1985; Hodge and Anthony, 1988; Morgan, 1986; Lipovec, 1987; Kovač, 1990; Gibson, Ivancevich and Donnelley, 1988; Quinn, Minzberg and James, 1988; Johnson and Scholes, 1997), the following basic types can be differentiated:

1. functional,
2. product (departmental),
3. project; and
4. matrix organisational structure.

There are, of course, numerous other types of organisation structures, which can be found in the literature. A more extensive presentation is available in Kavčič (1991).

In this chapter we investigate organisational structures and gender for business leaders only.

The problem – women's leadership style

Terms like 'sensitive management', 'soft management', 'human management' appear in the professional literature mostly in connection with women in management positions and presume that women have a different approach in managing business or leading people. Twenty years ago only a few researchers were dealing with the influence which gender is supposed to have on the leadership style. It seems that the first women who reached the most responsible positions in management were in principle reasoning, thinking, evaluating and acting like men, because they only had male managers' patterns of behaviour as an example. It similarly still holds true for women in the early stages of their career. They often 'try to behave like male managers' (Brodsky, 1993: 367).

The so-called 'women's leadership style' is characterised by traits which are traditionally assigned to women. Such behaviour is expected from women and is taken for granted. The same holds true for the men's style, but the significant characteristics are of course different.

In research on the influence gender exerts on management style, an important change occurred. Initially, researchers unanimously assumed that the male management style is the norm. In recent decades, researchers more and more frequently stress that what is understood under the stereotype 'women's characteristics' is potentially valuable for efficient management (Vianello, 1996). Rosener established that women managers use transformational leadership (Rosener, 1990: 119–25). According to Calas and Smircich (1993: 71–81), in higher-level management the predominant opinion was that women's harmonious style of management is only useful at the lower levels, while at the top levels the male style is needed. L.P. Smith and J.S. Smith (1994) concluded that in the 1980s the opinion prevailed that men's style is a successful management style: aggressive, competitive and ruthless. But in the 1990s a different approach prevailed: women's management style is effective, when connected with characteristics typical of early socialisation of women including: partnership with colleagues, helping subordinates, sensibility for family needs while at work and also adaptability to team work.

The general tendency in management style development is its democratisation. But an efficient style depends on circumstances: the position of the organisation, the quality of employees and the organisational culture. Each condition requires its own management style. If a man manager is not successful in a company, there is no guarantee that a woman manager will be efficient due to her female management style.

Hypotheses

The following set of hypotheses is tested here.

The organisation structure practised in a company is strongly influenced by the predominant management philosophy in the country. The management philosophy basically creates the organisational culture and the organisation structure to a large extent reflects this philosophy. Therefore, the organisation structure is expected to be strongly influenced by the differences typical of the country (in firms where women were found at the top in the various countries of our studies). This influence is expected to be stronger than the influence of the gender of our respondents.

The level of the influence on decision-making within organisations is supposed to be mainly related to positions, and not persons in these positions. Therefore, it is expected that our male and female respondents in top management positions would have the same amount of influence on decisions in their organisations.

The organisation structure also has some influence on the way the managers exercise their power in organisations. Therefore, it is expected that different types of organisation structures help male and female managers differently in using their power.

The women's management style is more in favour of the participation of workers. Therefore, it is expected that women managers' ratings of the level of participation practised in their enterprises would be higher than the ratings of men managers.

The type of organisation structure practised in a company influences the level of workers' participation. It is expected that the functional structure would be less favourable to workers' participation, while the matrix structure would be the most favourable.

Analysis and interpretation of results

Women in top management and organisation structure

The data showing the organisation structures practised in companies from our sample are summarised in Table 11.1.

Table 11.1   Organisation Structure of Companies Compared by the Gender of Top Managers (%)[a]

Type of organisation structure	Men	Women	Together
Functional	46.4	47.7	47.1
Product	19.2	16.1	17.7
Project	2.6	6.2	4.3
Matrix	26.6	19.6	23.2
Other	5.2	10.4	7.7
N =	271	260	531

[a] Due to a misunderstanding, about 40 per cent of the organisations men were chosen from are the same as where women were found. The results based only on the data of the first-level managers, 115 men and 85 women, who obviously could not belong to the same company, confirm the results presented in this, as well as in the following tables.

The data show that the functional organisation structure is by far predominant. It is followed by the matrix organisation structure. The product organisation is reported to be used in one fifth of all organisations. The project organisation structure is used in a very small proportion of companies. Also other forms of organisation structures are adopted.

The differences between organisations headed by men or women (or women being among top managerial personnel) are in general small and not significant. This is clearly a result of the way the sample was constructed.

Country and organisation structure

The comparison of data concerning the organisation structure by country in firms where women were found at the top shows substantial differences. In some countries certain types of organisation structures do not appear at all, but in others they are quite frequent. It was expected, e.g., that the project organisation structure would not appear in every country, because it is used only rarely. In our sample, it does not appear in Austria, Belgium, Finland, France, Germany, Netherlands, Sweden, Switzerland, the USA or Czech Republic. The product (divisional) organisation does not appear in Austria, Belgium or the USA. Our sample of firms is too small (15–37 firms per country) to enable a general conclusion, but it seems sufficiently supported by data that practically every country has a type of its own. This finding supports the hypothesis that national culture has an important, if not decisive influence on organisation culture and through it on the organisation structure.

Altogether, our data support the hypothesis that differences in the national culture strongly influence the organisation culture and through it also the organisation structure. This influence is stronger than the influence of gender of top managerial personnel. Our data do not offer sufficient support for the formation of clusters of countries. For example, differences among participating Scandinavian countries are larger than usually reported. But it has to be taken into account that our sample of companies is not a probabilistic one.

Influence and organisation structure

Influence is one of the crucial variables in understanding organisations. Related terms are power, control and authority. Theoretical elaboration of these terms in the professional literature is very extensive and a lot of empirical material has been analysed, especially in the 1950s and 1960s (Likert, 1961, 1967; Tannenbaum, 1968; Kavčič and Antončič, 1978; etc.).

In our study also respondents' perception of themselves in taking important decisions in their organisations was measured. The amount of influence was measured on a five-point scale from 1 = not at all, to 5 = very much. Table 11.2 summarises the results.

The results are clear: women top managers perceive themselves as having somewhat less power than men top managers. The difference is not large, but systematic, except in one case: staff selection. But it is important to note that both men and women top managers perceive themselves as having quite a lot of power.

Consequently, the hypothesis that men and women managers perceive themselves as having the same amount of influence on selected decision-making in their organisations is not confirmed.

As stated above, the organisation structure defines the level of influence (power, authority) and its distribution in organisations. The association between types of organisation structure and perceived amount of influence is summarised in Table 11.3.

The data for the project organisation are omitted, due to the small numbers of this type of organisation.

Table 11.2 Average Ratings of Perceived Influence on Selected Decisions in Their Organisations, by Gender

Selected Decisions	Average Influence: male	Average Influence: female
Work arrangements and decisions of who will do what	4.1	4.0
Financial and budget decisions	4.0	3.8
Hiring new employees	4.0	3.8
Promotion and transfer	4.1	3.9
Selecting your own staff	4.5	4.5
Policy and strategy decisions	4.3	4.0
Average	*4.1*	*4.0*

Table 11.3   Average Ratings of Influence of Men and Women Managers on Selected Decisions by the Type of Organisation Structure

Type of Organisation Structure	Average Influence: men	Average Influence: women
Functional	4.2	4.1
Product (divisional)	4.3	4.0
Matrix	4.0	3.9
Other	4.1	3.8
Average	*4.1*	*4.0*

Scale: 1 = not at all, 5 = very much.

The following main conclusions can be drawn from the data shown:

1. Theoretically, it can be expected that the functional organisation structure assigns the highest level of power to the top managerial positions. According to our data, this expectation is confirmed only for women top managers, while men top managers gave the highest rank to the product organisation structure. But this can be due to the sample of respondents or the sample of decisions. It is surprising that the matrix organisation structure is ranked so low. Obviously, the conflict between functional and project managers in a matrix organisation diminishes their power (as perceived by our respondents).

2. The general pattern that women managers perceive themselves as less powerful than men managers stated in the previous section is also confirmed by data in Table 11.3. In all types of organisation structure women top managers perceive their positions as being weaker than those of men managers.

At the same time, the picture emerging from our analysis tends to show that different types of organisation structure fit women better than men in the exercise of power.

The analysis of data by country adds important insight into these problems. Differences among countries concerning the perceived influence of top managerial personnel on selected issues are much greater than gender differences. The average influence on all six selected issues varies from the lowest 3.7 in the Czech Republic to the highest 4.6 in Sweden. Even larger are differences in ratings of average influence on individual selected issues, as can be seen in Table 11.4.

These differences are essentially larger than differences between men and women managers.

The conclusion is that the influence of the country on the perceived pattern of power distribution is much larger than the influence of gender or type of the organisation structure adopted.

Table 11.4   The Lowest and the Highest Average Ratings of Influence of Respondents on Selected Decisions, by Country

Selected Decision	The Lowest Average Influence	The Highest Average Influence
Work arrangements and decisions who will do what	3.4 New Zealand	4.8 Sweden
Financial and budget decisions	3.0 Italy	4.6 Sweden
Hiring new employees	3.2 Italy	4.5 Sweden
Promotion and transfer	3.3 New Zealand	4.6 Czech Republic
Selecting your own staff	3.1 Germany	4.9 Spain
Policy and strategy decisions	3.3 Austria	4.9 Czech Republic

Participation

Relations between work and capital as well as employers and employees are the most important work relations. We measured perceptions of the following forms of participation:

- Informal consultation: it consists of irregular, non-obligatory and non-formalised forms of exchange of points of view of managers with employees.
- Participation through trade unions: in some countries the whole mechanism of participation is under the control of trade unions (not only due to collective bargaining, which is regularly in the hands of trade unions).
- Joint consultation: it is implemented through specially elected bodies (works councils, work committees) representing all employees and workers; employers (managers) regularly perform consultation with this body about formally and informally agreed issues.
- Co-determination: it is effected through workers representatives in decision-making bodies of the company.
- Self-management: it means that workers by themselves decide about particular issues or about the management of the firm as a whole.

The practice of different forms of participation in the firms where respondents are employed was measured, as summarised in Table 11.5.

The differences between the ratings of men and women are very small and not systematic in one direction. The hypothesis that participation would be higher in organisations with women managers is not supported by these findings.

Our research also provides data needed to test the hypothesis about the influence of the organisation structure on the participation of workers (Table 11.6).

The data show some differences in the directions expected. The ratings in the case of the functional structure, in fact, show the lowest level and in the

Table 11.5   Average Ratings of Participation Practised in Firms Studied

Form of Participation	Average Rating: Men	Average Rating: Women
Informal consultation	2.0	1.9
Through trade unions	2.0	2.1
Joint consultation bodies	2.1	2.1
Co-determination	2.4	2.4
Self-management	2.7	2.6
Average	*2.2*	*2.2*

Scale: 1 = to a large extent, 2.0 = to some extent and 3 = not at all.

Table 11.6   Average Ratings of All Forms of Participation Practised in Different Organisation Structures, by Gender

Type of Organisation Structure	Average Rating of Participation: Men	Average Rating of Participation: Women
Functional	2.4	2.3
Product	2.2	2.1
Project	2.3	2.1
Matrix	2.0	2.0
Other	2.2	2.3
Average	*2.2*	*2.1*

On a three-point scale: see Table 11.5.

case of the matrix structure the highest level of participation. The same pattern appears in the case of women as well as men respondents. Therefore, the hypothesis is supported by our data. But the differences in the level of participation in different organisation structures are small.

The comparison of data on participation has shown that the differences among countries are much larger than the gender differences or between different forms of organisation structures used. Some data are shown in Table 11.7.

On the basis of the average ratings of all respondents and of all forms of participation, the highest level of participation is reported from Sweden (1.5) and the lowest from the USA (2.8). This difference is substantially larger than the differences between organisation forms or gender of respondents. In some countries, some forms of participation are not practised at all, at least in the companies in our sample.

The gender comparison of average ratings by country shows that in some countries these differences are very small or even non-existent, while in other countries they are quite substantial. Selecture data are shown in Table 11.8.

Table 11.7 The Lowest and the Highest Average Ratings of All Forms of Participation

Form of Participation	The Lowest Rating	The Highest Rating
Informal participation	3.0 Canada	1.2 Ireland
Through trade unions	2.7 Greece	1.0 Finland
Joint consultation	3.0 USA	1.1 Netherlands
Co-determination	0.0 Finland, Portugal, USA	1.4 Netherlands
Self-management	0.0 Denmark, Finland, Greece, Italy, Portugal, USA	1.9 Australia

Data for Israel, Norway, Poland and UK are missing.

Table 11.8 The Lowest and the Highest Difference in the Average Rating of the Selected Forms of Participation between Male and Female Respondents

Form of Participation	The Lowest Difference	The Highest Difference
Informal consultation	0.00 Canada, Finland, Netherlands, Spain	0.77 Japan
Through trade unions	0.00 Canada, Finland, Franc, Netherlands, USA	0.57 Sweden
Joint consultation	0.00 Canada, Finland, Netherlands, USA	0.74 Spain
Co-determination	0.00 Finland, Germany, Portugal, Sweden, USA	0.33 Austria
Self-management	0.00 Canada, Denmark, Finland, Greece, Italy, Portugal, USA	0.60 Switzerland

Maximal possible difference is 2.00.

These data illustrate that the variable 'country' produces a lot of very substantial differences, which are as a rule much larger than differences in answers of respondents of different gender. Again, our data do not confirm the hypothesis that gender has an important effect on the participation practised in the organisation.

Conclusion

Issues regarding organisation structure and gender were tested with several hypotheses. The relevant findings are the following.

The hypothesis that national culture has an important, if not decisive influence on organisation culture and through it on organisation structure appears confirmed. This influence is stronger than the influence of gender of top managerial personnel.

The hypothesis that men and women managers perceive themselves as having the same amount of influence on selected decision-making in their organisations is not confirmed.

Our data support the hypothesis that different types of organisation structure suit women better than men managers in achieving power.

The influence of the country on the pattern of power distribution is greater than the influence of the gender of respondents or the type of the organisation structure adopted.

The hypothesis that participation would be higher in organisations with women managers is not supported.

The hypothesis that type of organisation structure practised in a company influences the level of workers participation is supported by the data in our study.

It is evident that the variable 'country' produces a lot of very substantial differences, which are as a rule much larger than differences in answers of respondents of different gender.

12
The Exercise of Power

Mino Vianello

The problem

In Chapter 3 Liddle and Michielsens investigated gender differences regarding *access to power*. This chapter deals with a different, although closely related, issue, widely debated theoretically (Dahl, 1989; 1991), but much less explored empirically, and almost not at all from the point of view of gender: *the exercise of power* (Frey, 1993; Nagel, 1975, 1995; Wright, 1997). In analysing this phenomenon, the variable considered is not the formal hierarchy of offices endowed with different degrees of power, but *the impact office-holders feel they have in carrying out their functions*.

Given the specific object of this research, gender difference, the question is whether women perceive a lower degree of power exercise than men, and whether any such perceived difference is due to structural barriers or not.

Method

Within the category of political leaders we distinguish three groups: *government members*; *representatives in legislative offices* (like chairs or vice-chairs of parliament or senate committees and of one's own party's group in the parliament or senate, etc.); and *party leaders*. These groups are treated separately from each other and, of course, from business leaders.

The indices used, based on a factor analysis carried out on all variables[1] concerning the exercise of power as perceived by the respondents[2] based on a Likert scale (1–5), consist of the following items:

1 – Political leaders
1a – Government members (118 cases)
'If in the last year you, as a member of the cabinet, have taken an initiative which was initially opposed by the majority of the members of it, how often did you eventually succeed in winning their support?'
'How much influence do you have as a member of the government on matters of national importance?'

'On matters in your sphere of responsibility?'

'On what goes on in the ministry under your jurisdiction?'

1b – Holders of legislative offices (476 cases)

'If in the last year you took initiatives that were originally opposed by the majority of the members of your own party's group in the parliament or senate, how often did you eventually succeed in winning their support?'

'If in the last year you took initiatives that were originally opposed by the majority of the members of parliament or senate committee you are a member of, how often did you eventually succeed in winning their support?'

c – Party leaders (157 cases)

' If in the last year you took initiatives that were originally opposed by the majority of the members of your own party's executive committee, how often did you succeed in winning their support?'

'How much influence do you have on the decisions adopted by your party?

'On the party apparatus?'

'On the strategies which are necessary to implement the decisions of the executive committee?'

2 – Business leaders (862 cases)

'How much influence do you have in your organisation concerning work arrangements and decisions of who will do what?'

'Financial and budget decisions?'

'Hiring new employees?'

'Promotion and transfer?'

'Selecting your own staff?'

'Policy and strategy decisions?'

For a comparison between women and men that takes into account broad socio-cultural contexts, the countries, as explained in Chapter 2, are grouped in three categories.

Analysis of data

The average of the factor scores is shown in Table 12.1.

As expected, the level of the perception of power exercise is, in the first two groups of countries, higher for business leaders[3] who enjoy an almost autocratic authority within their corporations, above all in the countries of the first group (the averages are 0.42 for men and 0.28 for women).

Besides, for both women and men members of the government and party leaders, the index increases passing from the first grouping of countries to the second and from the second to the third, while it shapes up as a parabola as far as the other two categories (holders of legislative offices and business

Table 12.1 Factor scores[a] of the Perception of Power Exercised, by Gender and Groups of Countries[b]

Countries	Political Leaders						Business Leaders	
	Government		**Legislative Offices**		**Party**			
	M	**F**			**M**	**F**	**M**	**F**
			M	**F**				
Group 1								
	Mn −4.2, Mx 1.5		Mn −1.8, Mx 2.4		Mn −2.7, Mx 2.5		Mn −2.8, Mx 1.2	
Means	−0.92	−0.08	0.33	0.24	−0.31	−0.35	0.42	0.28
N	12	10	55	59	20	22	74	75
t-test	ns		ns		ns		ns	
Group 2								
	Mn −2.4, Mx 1.8		Mn −3.2, Mx 2.4		Mn −2.8, Mx 2.5		Mn −4.2, Mx 1.2	
Means	−0.30	−0.07	−0.15	−0.07	0.00	0.11	−0.04	−0.25
N	24	38	166	132	36	17	217	233
t-test	ns		ns		ns		p = 0.03	
Group 3								
	Mn −0.93, Mx 1.8		Mn −3.2, Mx 2.4		Mn −1.1, Mx 2.4		Mn −2.6, Mx 1.2	
means	0.72	0.64	0.24	0.04	0.35	0.42	0.17	0.21
N	16	12	32	46	10	13	61	74
t-test	ns		ns		ns		ns	

[a] These are the scores obtained on the first factor with the analysis of principal components. Only one case was found, in which a second factor with an eigen value higher than 1 was discovered: in the case of the cabinet members, with a contribution of 25.6 per cent to the explanation of variance. The contributions of the factors to the explanation of the variance are the following: *political leaders*: government 49.5 per cent, legislative offices 72.7 per cent, party leaders 60.2 per cent, *business leaders* 50.1 per cent.

[b] The countries are grouped as indicated in the methodological chapter: group 1 identifies the less economically developed countries where democracy has been established recently; group 2 the free market old democratic countries; group 3 the serial democracies typical of Northern Europe.

leaders) are concerned: a possible sign that a step forward in socio-economic development is matched for both genders by a more marked perception of exercise of power on the part of members of the government and party leaders, while for the other categories operating in the countries of the second group it brings about a reduction of the level of perception of the exercise of power, probably as a consequence of the conspicuous increase in the need to mediate between the various interest groups which characterise full market societies.

Gender differences tend to be minuscule. The t-test indicates only one statistically significant score in favour of males: the one concerning business leaders in the second group. In all other cases, differences are non-relevant. In fact, in five cases women's scores are higher than men's.

Interpretation of results

The question then is: if the perception of the exercise of power on the part of women is not lower than men's, are the factors that promote it respectively for women and for men the same?

Given the gap between men and women as far as access to the public sphere is concerned, as documented exhaustively by both literature and daily experience, it is reasonable to suppose that, at an equal level of perception of exercise of power, women are backed by more favourable conditions than men (Verba, Nie and Kim, 1978; Vianello and Siemienska, 1990). More specifically, it is plausible to assume that, although it is true for all people that families of origin and of orientation have a strong impact on participation in public life (Bourdieu, 1987; 1989; Crompton, 1993), parents' and partner's status count more for women than for men.

At the society level, if Inglehart's thesis is correct, we should find that countries rank from less developed to free market, to social democracies as far as gender differences in terms of social advantages are concerned (Inglehart, 1997).

Finally, again with reference to Inglehart's thesis concerning the transformation from modern to postmodern society (Inglehart, 1997), we may surmise that in less developed countries the factors that explain the amount of power women perceive they exercise tend to be more of an external nature (parents' and partner's status), while in the others – and above all in the socio-democratic countries – of an internal nature (values). Besides, in general, father's and partner's status count for women more than interpersonal, factors (like informal flow of information, economic and political contacts, etc.).

In order to test these hypotheses, female and male members of the political and business élites were compared with respect to the following individual socio-economic variables, keeping under control the level of the perception of power exercise:

a – Career
a1 – number of months during which the present office has been held;
a2 – increment of the prestige inherent to the office held by the respondent from the first occupation to the last before last, the last and the present;[4]
a3 – whether the respondents held top offices in big organisations;
a4 – and how many.
For political leaders:
a5 – number of months of affiliation to a party

a6 – and of the years, during which the respondent held one or more offices in it;

a7 – number of years, during which the respondent held offices in the government;

a8 – number of years, during which the respondent held offices at the legislative level (like chair of a parliament or senate committee and of one's own party group in the parliament or senate; etc.).

For business leaders only:

a9 – number of years, during which the respondent held an elective political office (in the party or the public apparatus) at the three levels: local, intermediate, national (var. 601).

b – *Ways of access to power*

b1 – access to information via informal channels;

b2 – evaluation of this information from the point of view of the possibility it grants to do well one's job;

b3 – frequency of political contacts with (index):[5]

   1 – members of legislature;

   2 – prime minister;

   3 – government members;

   4 – national party leaders;

b4 – frequency of contacts of economic nature with:

   1 – top managers of major corporations;

   2 – representatives of national or international interest groups;

   3 – trade union leaders.

c – *Parents' and spouse's status*[6]

c1 – mother's

c2 – father's

c3 – spouse's

d – *Help in the career*

d1 – degree of political involvement of the family of origin;[7]

d2 – loyalty towards and contacts with key people in political and non-political organisations, to have worked as an assistant of a high dignitary

d3 – number of patrons who protected the respondent's career.

e – *Education*

e1 – highest degree achieved;

e2 – number of years of school completed;

e3 – whether the respondent attended mainly a private or a public school;

e4 – discipline in which the respondent achieved university degree.

f – *Visibility*

f1 – this index reflects the frequency with which the respondent in the last year:

   1 – took the floor at public meetings

   2 – on radio or television

   3 – published articles in periodicals

4 – was interviewed by the media
g – Affiliation with associations
This index is the sum of the affiliation to the following associations:
1 – professional
2 – social or sport clubs
3 – religious organisations
4 – Rotary, Lions, etc.
5 – military circles
6 – trade unions
7 – women's organisations.
For business leaders only:
h – Hierarchical position
h1 – number of direct subordinates;
h2 – number of hierarchical levels above the respondent.

We can now verify the hypothesis that, at an equal level of perception of the exercise of power, women have more favourable background conditions than men.
The results are the following:

1 As far as the government members are concerned
The hypothesis is only very partially confirmed.
At the low and medium levels of the perception of the exercise of power,[8] out of 26 possible comparisons (that is, as many as the variables considered) between men and women who are alike in terms of perception of the exercise of power, 20 do not show any significant difference between male and female leaders. Out of these 20, only seven show higher scores for women. There is only one significant difference (none highly significant) pointing in the direction that women enjoy better conditions, and a suggestive one, that points though in the direction that women, in higher percentages than men, attended public high school (contrary to the stereotype that considers private school as a privileged channel of access to power).
At the high level of perception of the exercise of power, while, if the hypothesis were true, an increase in the number of significant differences should have been found, the picture does not substantially change: 19 non-significant comparisons, with women showing a more privileged condition in only seven cases. Yet, in support of the hypothesis two highly significant differences appear relative to variables that are traditionally most heavily discriminant for women: the father's and the spouse's status.
Comparing the picture concerning the two levels of perception of the exercise of power, it appears clearly that the three variables that to a relevant extent tend to diverge between men and women are: the mother's status, from non-significant to suggestive; the father's, from significant to highly significant; and the spouse's, from non-significant to highly signifi-

cant. In the same direction evolves the difference concerning the variable about associationism, which from non-significant becomes suggestive.

As far as the members of the government are concerned, consequently, it is justified to uphold the view that women and men do not belong to two distinct universes, with women privileged by a constellation of more favourable conditions than men. Yet, in general and especially moving from the lower to the higher levels of the perception of the exercise of power, women appear to come from a superior social background than men.

2 As far as holders of legislative offices are concerned

The hypothesis appears to be even less valid for this category, which, being numerous, allows for a three-way split in terms of the perception of power exercise: low, medium, high.

At the low level, no comparison is significant, and in only eight cases do women enjoy better conditions.

At the medium level, 13 comparisons are non-significant, of which seven reveal better conditions for women. One comparison supports suggestively the hypothesis (mother's status); four are significant, but of them only one (concerning the spouse's status) supports the hypothesis; and four are highly significant, but show that men enjoy a privileged condition![9]

The contingency coefficient concerning university studies shows a highly significant difference between men and women: men outperform women with regard to degrees in law and economics; women outperform men with regard to those who do not hold a university degree, achieved a degree in engineering (contrary to a common stereotype, a significant association with this discipline will be found also for other categories) and in 'other'.

At the high level, 21 non-significant comparisons are found, out of which only eight point in the direction of better conditions for women. To have had the support of a patron is the only significant comparison, which reveals a more advantageous condition for women.

The hypothesis, therefore, is tendentially rejected, especially when the high level of perception of the exercise of power is considered. It is at the medium level that women benefit to a highly significant extent in enjoying a more favourable condition as far as the affiliation with associations and, at a more modest extent, social origin are concerned.

It looks as if for this category, the more women feel they exercise power, the less they benefit from advantageous conditions. The stereotype that maintains that successful women are backed up by privileged conditions does not hold. In fact, it looks as if it fits men better.

It is reasonable to argue that, since the fortune of this category depends to a great extent on electoral mechanisms, personal qualities may count more than contextual advantages: people at the top, as is the case with our respondents, are highly motivated, and women especially are spurred to emerge as individuals.

3 As far as party leaders are concerned

At the low and medium levels, out of 23 comparisons, 19 are not significant, and ten of them point in the direction of a more advantageous condition for women. Barely four comparisons are significant, of which only two (spouse's status and number of mentors) support the hypothesis.

With regard to education, a suggestively greater number of women who graduated in engineering and, vice versa, of men who graduated in law emerges.

Comparing the low and medium with the high level of perception of power exercise, only one – easily explainable – difference, concerning the length of party affiliation, appears, which changes from a non-significant (in the same direction of a more advantageous condition for women) to a significant comparison.

4 As far as business leaders are concerned

At the low level of the perception of power exercise, no statistically relevant, not even suggestive, comparison (yet 14 indicate a better condition for women) emerges out of 24 comparisons.

At the medium level, the non-significant comparisons are 22, of which 11 point in the direction of a better condition for women. The only (highly) significant comparison in support of the hypothesis concerns the spouse's status.

Although the contingency coefficient is highly significant, it is not justified to state that women enjoyed a privileged condition in terms of education: in fact, they achieved to a larger extent than males a vocational degree and a baccalaureate or a master, degree; while men tend to concentrate to a higher proportion at the extremes – junior and senior high school, on one side, and doctorate, on the other.

At the high level of perception of the exercise of power, 14 non-significant comparisons are found, of which seven support the hypothesis of a better condition for women. Out of the four significant comparisons, only one shows a better condition for women (access, via informal channels, to information that grants the possibility to do one's job well) and out of the five highly significant ones three (mother's, father's and spouse's status).

With regard to university curriculum, a suggestive association between the number of men who graduated in economics and the number of women in engineering is found.

The hypothesis does not appear to be strongly upheld for this category, above all for the low and medium levels of perception of power exercise (it is noteworthy remarking that, comparing one level with the other, the only difference that emerges concerns the spouse's status), while it looks more probable for the high level (access, via informal channels, to information that grants the possibility to do one's job well, and mother's, father's and spouse's status).

In conclusion, the hypothesis that élite women need a constellation of conditions more favourable than élite men in order to feel that they exert the same amount of power appears to respond to a stereotype more than to reality – with the exception, to a considerable extent, for the support deriving from the father's and, above all, the spouse's status.

But even if the traditional factors concerning the status of the family of origin and of orientation appear to have an impact of some relevance on distinguishing men and women in their perceptions of their ability to exert power, for both women and men in none of the three groupings of countries does this ability depend heavily on it. Even suggestive correlations for the different categories within the three groupings of countries are very rare, and do not evidence any difference in the direction of the hypothesis put forth. Nor are significant differences (Fisher transformation) found between the correlation coefficients referring to males and those referring to females within the same categories by groupings of countries. Status, therefore, whether ascribed or acquired, at the top-level counts only to a modest extent (Wright, 1997: 350–1).

We may wonder, at this point, which of the most relevant variables examined so far has more predictive power in explaining the phenomenon under consideration.

The multiple classification analysis by category of respondents, done on the following variables used as predictors:

- *father's and spouse's status*
- *stance as to women's decisional autonomy*[10]
- *access to informal channels of information that enable the possibility to do one's job well*
- *economic and political contacts*[11]

shows that they have only a moderate impact (the R ranges from 0.19 for female business leaders to 0.29 for male political leaders, with an average of 0.23).

For both male and female political leaders structural facts inherent in informal networks of communications come in the foreground, followed by the father's status for males and the value of decisional autonomy for females.

Also for male business leaders informal communications and contacts (in this case, as it was obvious to expect, of an economic nature) come in the foreground, followed this time by the spouse's status. For female business leaders, the spouse's status comes in the foreground together with economic contacts and informal communications.

There is no coincidence between male and female top leaders. In fact, Spearman's ρ between the rank orders, on one side, of the β weights of the male political leaders and of those of women and, on the other side, of the β weights of male business leaders and of those of women are in both cases 0.06: that is, of almost absolute indifference, which means that the rank order with which the items affect the phenomenon under consideration is not the same for both genders.

The results obtained support only very weakly the hypothesis that factors of personal nature – social conditions and values – explain for top women more than for top men the level of the perception of power exercise in comparison with interactive factors like the flow of informal communications and economic and political contacts.

A more detailed analysis, with control for the sub-categories of the political respondents as well as the groupings of countries, supports the hypothesis better than the global analysis does. In the first place, the explained variance of the perception of power exercise increases (from a minimum of 0.27 for the male business leaders of the less developed countries and of the full free market countries to a maximum of 0.90 for the male and female party leaders of the less developed countries [the average raises to 0.49]); and, in the second place, the impact of the predictors changes with gender. The rank orders of the β weights relative to the variables under consideration computed on all sub-categories by groupings of countries shows that the father's status, which comes in second place for women, has a negligible impact for men. Also the spouse's status has a larger impact for women than for men. Conversely, the 'external' (structural) variables, concerning political and economic contacts, which play a minor role for women, come in first place for males. The value of decisional autonomy for women, finally, has, as expected, a larger impact for women than for men; besides, for the latter agreement with the opinion that women prefer not to be autonomous as far as decision-making is concerned prevails!

It is interesting to observe that access to informal channels of information comes third for both, but in a different context: for males after contacts with the economic and political world, for women after status.

As far as differences between groupings of countries are concerned, the rank order of the variables considered shows that in the economically less developed countries the value of decisional autonomy for women, totally absent among men, appears to play a very modest role also among women, while the status of the father and of the spouse count more for women than men; in the full market countries status, especially of the spouse, matters also – and even more – for women than men, while for men the major impact comes from contacts; in the social democracies, in line with Inglehart's thesis, for women the value of decisional autonomy switches to the first place.

In general, the father's and even more so the spouse's status, important for women more than for men in the power élite, shows up among the relevant factors in all situations. For males, though, it ranks after contacts, especially of a political nature.

The analysis done controlling the functions performed (that is, the three categories of political leaders, and business leaders) validates that the factors that influence the perception of power exercise tend to shape up in a slightly different way for top women and for top men: for the latter, it stems above all from a network of contacts established throughout the life course, while for the former it appears to be more the effect of inherited resources that facilitate getting access to the centres and channels of power.

A note concerning Kanter's 'critical mass theory'

Kanter's theory that the relative number of the representatives of minorities has an impact on their reactions to the organisational context is widely known.

While this theory might be true as far as women's success in top offices is concerned, we may ask whether it applies also to women who are already in power. This chapter has shown that the input to the perception of the exercise of power differs from the factors that determine access to power. If Kanter's thesis held true also in the case of the exercise of power, we should find a higher perception of it in more balanced organisations as well as in organisations that have moved from a skewed to a more egalitarian presence of women.

In our sample, top women are found in organisations that vary, in terms of the relative number of females, from highly unbalanced, most often in business, to moderately balanced to few equalitarian organisations, like, at times, in politics.

The picture is shown in Table 12.2.

The correlations of, on one side, the percentage of women at the top of the party and the increment of their presence in the last ten years with, on the other, the perception of the exercise of power are close to zero and show, therefore, indifference between the two phenomena, the same holds true for women managers.

Also the correlations of the perception of the exercise of power with:

- *for the members of the government*, the number of women at the top of political life and the relative increment in the last ten years;
- *for the members of parliament and senate*, the percentage of women in parliament and senate and the relative increments in the last ten years;
- *for the party leaders*, the percentage of women at the top of the party and the relative increment in the last ten years

show the lack of connection between the two phenomena.[12] These findings lead to the conclusion that, *for women who have already succeeded in entering the power élite*, the number of females who are present in the same organi-

Table 12.2 Presence of Women in Different Organisations

	Means	**S.D.**	**Mn**	**Mx%**
% of Women at Top *Respondent's Party*				
1991	25.7	196.0	1.0	58.0
1981	22.6	149.3	0.0	50.0
increment	3.1		−12.3	60.0
% of women in political top executive power, 1991	18.3	19.5	3.0	80.0
idem, 1981	11.6	17.4	2.0	68.0
increment	6.7		−2.0	2.1
% of Women in Parliament				
1991	15.7	97.0	0.0	35.8
1981	14.0	109.1	3.5	34.5
increment	1.7		−23.1	16.0
% of Women in Senate				
1991	11.0	77.0	2.5	19.0
1981	8.6	12.9	3.1	12.0
Increment	2.4		−83.2	10.1
% of Women Top Managers	16–25	3.3	0.0	>50

sations and even at the top does not count from the point of view of the perception of the exercise of power.

Conclusion

Contrary to what Liddle and Michielsens found with respect to access to power, no relevant differences in terms of the perception of the exercise of power appear to exist between women and men who hold top positions in public life, although for men, more than for women, it seems to be structural factors that have an impact on the phenomenon considered here. Yet this is only a tendency, which does not alter a substantially homogeneous picture.

It seems that, while in order to enter the élite of power women need more advantageous conditions than men, once they are in the factors required to feel that they exert power to the same extent as their male counterparts do not include more favourable requisites than are found among men (Vianello and Siemienska, 1990).

In fact, as we have seen, it is even possible to detect in some cases the opposite tendency: men need to enjoy a better background than women in order to feel that they exert as much power as women do.

This holds true in general and within each of the three groups of countries as well as comparing groups of countries.

Notes

1. For reasons of space, the variables that entered the factor analysis, and the comments on as well as the statistical results, cannot be reported in detail. They vary from category to category: six variables for government members, five for holders of legislative offices, 11 for party leaders, 13 for business leaders.
2. For a general treatment of the issue, see Frey (1993). The literature concerning the gender gap in power concentrates more on business than on political organisations: see Wolf, 1979; Woly and Fligstein, 1979; Rosenbaum, 1984; Jaffee, 1989; Jacobs, 1992; Reskin and Ross, 1992.
3. No inter-category comparison, strictly speaking, is possible on the ground of these scores, since indices are built on different items. Yet, since these items are homogeneous in the sense that they are all based on Likert scales, the reader can get an approximate indication from them: for instance, the range of greatest variation is found among members of the government, the smallest among business leaders – which looks realistic.
4. Three indices were used:

   1. the algebraic difference of the prestige index provided by Treiman between the *actual* and the first occupation;

   2. $$\frac{1}{S-n}\left(\frac{2\sum_{i=1}^{n-1}(n-1)x^i}{n-1}-S\right)$$

   where S is the sum of the prestige indices of the four offices held by the respondent; n the number of levels (4); x the values of the prestige indices. The resulting coefficient varies from −1 to +1.

   3. $a+b^2/a+c^2/b+d^2/c$.

5. This index, as well as the following ones, was built as averages of factor scores.
6. The status indices are the standardised averages of the level of education and of the prestige of the position held.
7. This index is the average of the factor scores for the following two items:

   a. To what extent your family was politically active?
   b. Has some of the members of your family ever held a political office?

8. The scores of the index of the exercise of power were split. Where, as in the case of the members of government, the low number did not allow for a three-way split into low/medium/high, 'low-medium' was used for scores below the average and 'high' for scores above the average. Since these are factor scores, the average is 0. In the other cases a three-way split in percentiles was done.
9. These items are: having held top offices in big organisations, and how many; seniority in the present office; frequency of political contacts (see b3 above).

10. This is a five-score indicator of agreement–disagreement with the explanation 'This is what women prefer' with reference to the statement 'There are more men than women holding top positions in society'.
11. See, respectively, b3 and b4 above.
12. There is only one almost suggestive correlation for women members of government. It is perhaps useful to specify that in these correlations the units of analysis are individual respondents in the respective organisations.

Part III
Hindrance or Asset? Combining Everyday Life and Élite Careers

Introduction

At the top leadership level there are special difficulties in combining everyday life and career. The total time availability required in a top position implies that a career not only take up most of one's time, but takes precedence over everything else. This mode of operating in top positions has been organised by men for men, because traditionally it was a male sphere of influence.

As a consequence, there has always been a clear separation between public and private life, where one was excluded from the other. Thus, the successful involvement of men in public life depended on women organising everyday life. However, as women entered the paid labour force in increasing numbers, the separation between public and private life had to change. The previous arrangement where women's work in the private sphere was invisible was bound to be re-examined.

Where once it could be assumed that marriage and having children was the norm, now there are more variations on the theme. People make choices about whether they will get married, stay married and have children. At times, it is difficult to say that these are real choices, as circumstances dictate the course of action to be taken. But, in general, men are more likely today to have partners with careers of their own, and women will not necessarily be available to run their private life. Therefore, some men now adopt different ways of operating in order to take into consideration the demands of family life as well as their careers.

However, where élite careers have been premised on traditional ways of life, it is difficult to combine the old and new work and family cultures. Women may also be trying to balance tasks of everyday living with their demanding careers and require the support of their partners. A realistic option for women may well be not to have a partner or children. However, this raises the question of whether this is a real and genuine choice.

The chapters in Part III suggest that, while traditional models of the family still exist, for top leaders, especially men, there are other ways of combining career and family life which do offer a choice. It is not necessary to forgo a partner or children, if these new models are adopted.

Each of the four chapters takes a different focus in exploring the ways in which this happens.

Chapter 13 looks at the differences and similarities between leaders, comparing both political and businesswomen and men, both within and between groups of countries.

Chapter 14 addresses the question of whether there have been changes in the way of living between the two cohorts of leaders (i.e., those born before and those born after 1945) and whether they show new trends in managing their private lives.

Chapter 15 focuses on a comparison between the ways in which leaders from Northern and Southern Europe arrange their career and everyday existence.

Chapter 16 compares different country groupings from the point of view of career life forms.

13
Family Characteristics

Jenny Neale

Introduction

The male and female leaders in our study have already attained positions of power and influence. Although they had a great many characteristics in common as far as their families of origin are concerned (detailed in Part I), there are marked gender differences in the way they now organise their private lives to fit with their public duties (see the chapters 14–16).

It is hypothesised that, as well as gender differences, different patterns will also be manifested by female and male business leaders and female and male political leaders in the way they manage their family life and responsibilities in conjunction with their demanding, high-status careers. As a result, the extent to which the leaders reproduce their family of origin will vary.

This chapter examines the ways in which the international leaders organise their lives in terms of the extent to which they conform with stereotypical roles for women and men, whether or not they have a partner, children or other caring or domestic responsibilities that might impact on their career, and draw conclusions about why political or business leadership has a differential effect on women and men.

A traditional role?

There has long been recognition of the difficulties, particularly for women, in trying to reconcile the responsibilities of family and paid employment. The 1979 UN Convention on the Elimination of All Forms of Discrimination against Women stressed the importance of equal responsibilities in the context of family life (European Commission, 1997). This theme of equal responsibility in the domestic sphere was highlighted again in 1985, in the *Nairobi Forward Looking Strategies*. Paragraphs 18 and 59 reminded member states that, in spite of advances in a number of countries, women were still facing a 'double burden', often because of a lack of support services, and stressed the importance of all family members sharing domestic responsibilities (European Commission, 1997).

At the end of the United Nation's Decade for Women, a report (Taylor et al., 1985) summarised available information on the status of women, women's and men's place in the workforce and related issues around the family. The discussion then and now revolves around the amount of unpaid work expected of women in the home because they are the childbearers: 'And instead of defining just one difference between men and women, women's ability to bear children is used to define their entire lives' (Taylor et al., 1985: 3).

The theme of reconciling work and family responsibilities continued into the 1990s. The *Programme of Action* of the International Conference on Population and Development held in Cairo in 1994 urged countries to make it possible for women to combine their professional and family roles. The *Beijing Platform for Action*, 1995, adopted by 181 states, suggested the development of policies to change attitudes in order to promote the concept of shared family responsibilities in the home as one way in which family and work could be combined. Finally, the emphasis on the need for women and men to work together to enable an equitable integration of work and family life was reinforced in the EC proposal for a Council *Recommendation on the Balanced Participation of Men and Women in Decision-Making* presented to the Council of Ministers in December 1995. Under the heading of education and training, article 2(a) states that 'equal access to decision-making is dependent on school textbooks and education and training not representing public responsibilities as being reserved for men and private responsibilities for women, but as being shared between the two' (European Commission, 1997: 29).

Given this general background of concern about the way in which access to power is constrained, how do political and business leaders deal with the dual responsibilities of work and family life? Each group has made different choices in the way that they have structured their family life and the toll that a powerful position has taken on personal life.

People usually are or have been married and this was the case for the majority of our sample. However, Davidson and Cooper (1992) indicate there is ample evidence cross-culturally to suggest that women in leadership positions are much less likely to be married than their male counterparts. This was the case in our research where a significant[1] minority of the women leaders had never been married (17.6 per cent compared with 7.7 per cent of male leaders). Women leaders were also less likely to be currently married or living with a partner (75.5 per cent compared with 93.7 per cent of male leaders). Business leaders were more likely to have cohabited at some stage than their political counterparts. Female business leaders, in particular, were likely to have cohabited at some stage (33.6 per cent compared with 21.0 per cent for their male counterparts, 24.3 per cent for female political leaders and 19.3 per cent for male political leaders). There were some country differences as well. Female business leaders in Canada, Denmark, Germany, New Zealand and Australia and male business leaders in Denmark and Sweden were as likely as not to have cohabited.

The differences between business and political leaders could be a result of the latter being more open to public scrutiny than business leaders and under more pressure to uphold social mores if they wished to retain their powerful positions. Women business leaders in the sample are a slightly younger group and thus may reflect prevailing trends, which have seen a decline in marriage in a number of countries.

Although the women business leaders are younger, on the whole, than the other leaders, they are likely to be of a similar age to the partners of the male leaders, as most men have partners who are younger. Therefore, the fact that the women business leaders are less likely to have children, on average when women of the same age (who are married to their male counterparts) have two children, means that the women business leaders are not 'typical' of women of their age.

Therefore, there were both gender differences and sectoral differences between business and political leaders in terms of their relationships. A significant minority of women leaders (1 in 4) was not currently married or cohabiting. Clearly, there were very real problems for some leaders in trying to balance their career and give time to an ongoing relationship. These difficulties are reflected in the number of leaders who have been divorced.

The countries represented in this study have a range of divorce rates extending from Ireland (where divorce has only recently become legal) and Italy, Sweden and Japan with just over 10 per cent of marriages ending in divorce to the United States of America where about 50 per cent do. Again, in our sample gender differences were apparent with women leaders more likely to have been divorced than men ($p = 0.00$). Over a quarter of female business leaders had been divorced (26.3 per cent compared with 21.3 per cent for female political leaders and 16.4 per cent for male leaders). Thus, while the male leaders had similar or slightly lower rates of divorce than average, the women leaders had a higher rate. This may indicate the personal difficulties that arise for women in highly pressured situations which do not conform to a stereotypical role. This may be particularly the case for the women business leaders in that political life could be seen to be an extension of women's traditional social service role, while business has definitely been viewed as a male sphere of influence.

Also, as Diem-Wille and Ziegler suggest, only after divorce can women pursue their careers and concentrate their entire energy on their profession since they are not held back by marital obligations. In fact, Bischoff (1990: 136) notices an interesting gender-specific difference in the experience of single living after a marriage breakdown. Women see divorce as liberating and advantageous for their career, whereas men often suffer, as result, and feel guilty towards their ex-wives.

Having a partner

As Davidson and Cooper (1992) point out, leaders need the approval and support of their partners to succeed. On the whole, over three-quarters of partners were perceived to be supportive of the leaders' careers. More female leaders than males saw their partners as being positive (82.1 per cent compared with 71.6 per cent) about their present position. It could be hypothesised that the male leaders saw their partners being less positively supportive of their careers, because of the way their life-style and work commitments impacted on the family. On the other hand, this might reflect a feeling of guilt on the part of these men who may not be achieving the type of balance in their lives that they had anticipated. Changing mores around an expectation that men will be involved in the life of their families is also a consideration here. For the women to stay in a relationship, it was clear that the support of their partner was essential and some compromises for both partners were necessary. A small percentage of the leaders indicated that their partner's negative attitudes to their work had affected their career: around 8 per cent of the political leaders and the male business leaders, but only 4.2 per cent of the female business leaders.

The female leaders had more highly educated partners than the male leaders (80 per cent with tertiary qualifications compared to 66.7 per cent of the male political leaders and 57.2 per cent of the male business leaders). This supports the contention that the occupational attainment of men and women is mutually enhanced by their partner's educational attainment (Airsman and Bam, 1993). It also suggests that female leaders and their partners represent a different type of partnership, with the biggest contrast being between the female business leaders and the male business leaders.

Fewer than half of the male political leaders' partners (48.9 per cent) who were in the paid workforce were in supervisory positions compared with over half of the female business leaders' partners (53.9). Male business leaders were more likely than male politicians to have partners working part-time rather than full-time if they were in paid employment (41.5 per cent compared with 30.2 per cent for male political leaders). On the whole, the partners of the female leaders tended to be in top management (53.7 per cent for partners of political leaders and 62.1 per cent for partners of business leaders), while employed partners of male political leaders tended to be at the middle management level (42.1 per cent). However, women leaders were more likely to say that pursuing their career had disadvantaged their partner's career (32.6 per cent compared to 20.5 per cent for the male leaders).

As chapters 15 and 16 indicate, structural imperatives and the dominant family ideology in different countries affect the ways in which family life and career are combined. There is a difference between traditional patterns and other career life-forms. Trying to deal with the issues arising around maximising the potential for two careers is an area that can be contentious and, where this was the case, the leaders considered that being in a partnership did have some effect on their career. If they moved because of their partners' employment, for example, their own employment opportunities could alter. This had an almost negligible effect on the male leaders. Only one male political leader, from Portugal, reported working part-time for three years because he had to move for his partner's job and he indicated that this change of residence had affected his career. Partners' jobs had some effects on a small number of the female leaders. A few female political leaders (3.2 per cent) and female business leaders (2.6 per cent) worked part-time for varying periods, because they needed to move for their partners' jobs. Changing residence for their partners' job had interrupted the careers of 1.9 per cent of the female business leaders and 5.5 per cent of the female political leaders. It is interesting to speculate whether more women would be involved in leadership positions if they were not susceptible to the influences of their partner's careers. As we looked at only those who have achieved powerful positions, this is not a question we are able to answer here.

Having children

In most countries, there has been a steady decline in fertility since the beginning of the twentieth century. Over half the countries in this study showed a sharp decrease in the 1990s. Where there was an increase, it tended to be fairly small (except for Germany, where the rate nearly doubled over the decade: this is likely to be an artefact of the reunification of East and West Germany over this period.) Apart from Canada and Germany, the study countries are now below replacement rate in the number of children born. Fertility decline is associated with economic development in both capitalist and socialist countries as is women's entrance into the paid workforce.

Economic development and fertility decline go together, not just with the lowering of infant mortality, but 'also by modifying economic relationships among family members' (Folbre, 1994: 104). As noted earlier, it has been assumed that, because women are the childbearers, they will take the major responsibility for childcare. This has a detrimental effect on their subsequent career opportunities and thus women pay more of the costs of having children (Headlee and Elfin, 1996). Access to contraceptive advice and the availability of abortion in the majority of countries in this study ensured that most of the leaders would have been able to exercise some choice as to whether or not they had children. Some clearly decided that having children was not a viable option for them. Female leaders were proportionately less likely to have children than men, with a particularly marked contrast among business leaders, where a third of the women did not have children compared to 5.9 per cent of the men.

Interesting differences are noticeable also between the countries:[2] in Germany, Israel, Great Britain and Russia all male top leaders have children, while in Switzerland 23.3 per cent and Portugal 20.7 per cent have no children.

What is the distribution among the women interviewed? For the top female leaders, parenthood is not at all self-evidently compatible with a career. The number of women without children is 28 per cent. In several countries, every second woman in a top position decided against parenthood. The Netherlands has the highest number of childless top female leaders with 53.3 per cent, followed by Switzerland, Austria, Germany and Italy. In Russia, Israel and Sweden it seems that a career for women in leading positions does not exclude parenthood. In Russia, none of the women in top positions is childless, in Israel only 4 per cent and in Sweden only 6.7 per cent are childless.

A quarter of the female business leaders indicated that they had sacrificed much or very much by either deciding not to have children or delaying having them because of their career. This compares with 9.3 per cent of the male business leaders and 14.3 per cent of the political leaders. This is supported by earlier research (Davidson and Cooper, 1992), which suggests that women managers are less likely to have children or more likely to delay having them than are their male counterparts.

The male leaders were likely to have two or three children. This family size accounted for 63.4 per cent of the political leaders and 70.1 per cent of the business leader among men, but only 50.9 per cent of the female political leaders and 40.2 per cent of the female business leaders. There is a direct relationship between number of children and occupational attainment: females are negatively affected by having more children, while a larger family has a positive effect for males (Airsman and Bam, 1993).

Most of those with children had some currently living with them (72.6 per cent of political leaders with children and 78.6 per cent of the business leaders). While there were gender differences in the number of children leaders had and whether or not these children were living with them, being a female or male business leader or a female or male political leader also made a difference. Male political leaders in the Netherlands were least likely to have children living with them. While the majority of the leaders did not have children aged under six years, business leaders were most likely to have a pre-school child living with them (17.2 per cent compared with 10.3 per cent for the political leaders). Male business leaders were most likely to have at least one child aged 6–12 years living with them (32.2 per cent compared with 20.6 per cent for female business leaders and 27.1 per cent for male political leaders with children). Female political leaders were least likely to have children in this age group (16.4 per cent) or in the age group 13–18 years living with them (26 per cent compared to 33 per cent male political leaders, 36.2 per cent male business leaders and 31 per cent female business leaders). The one aspect that nearly half of the leaders with children (48.4 per cent political and 44 per cent business) had in common was at least one child aged over 18 years living with them. Having older children at home reflects the age and life-stage of the leaders.

Caring for children

Care of children showed some interesting and significant gender and sectoral differences.[3] Children of male leaders – especially in business – were most often cared for by their mother. However, where the mother was not doing the childcare, different alternatives were chosen.

Quite different patterns emerged for the women leaders and there was more diversity both within and between categories.

Female political leaders clearly take most responsibility for childcare with 28.7 per cent involved, far more than the female business leaders.

Care of children or other relatives had more impact on the women. The female political leaders, in particular, considered this had interfered much or even very much with their careers (17.8 per cent compared with 10.8 per cent for female business leaders, 6.6 per cent for male political leaders and 3.4 per cent for male business leaders). Female political leaders were most

Table 13.1 Choices of Childcare by Male Leaders

Male Political Leaders		**Male Business Leaders**	
Other parent	48.7	Other parent	64.4
Public childcare	11.6	Private childcare	8.8
Private childcare	9.3	Public childcare	6.1

p = 0.005.

Table 13.2 Choices of Childcare by Female Leaders

Female Political Leaders		**Female Business Leaders**	
Self	28.7	Private childcare	28.8
Private childcare	20.3	Public childcare	16.3
Public childcare	12.6	Other family	12.5

p = 0.005.

likely to consider that after-school care for their children had often inter-fered with their career (32.4 per cent compared with 22.4 per cent for their male counterparts and 16.7 per cent for business leaders).

Given the generally small amount of personal involvement leaders had with caring for their young children, we were not surprised to find that male political leaders considered they had not sacrificed much or very much time with their children (53.8 per cent compared with 31.3 per cent of the female political leaders and 35 per cent of the business leaders). Overall, this acknowledgement of sacrifice of time spent with children is clearly a realis-tic appraisal of one of the personal costs paid by those in positions of power that demand a great deal of time and attention.

Female political leaders had worked part-time at some stage because of responsibilities associated with childrearing than had other groups (22.4 per cent compared with 14 per cent for female business leaders and 1.6 per cent for the male leaders). This was the case for the majority of Australian women political leaders. Fine (1992) indicates that women managers are likely to continue working with shorter breaks for childbearing and rearing in order to stay in their positions of authority. Only three male leaders (0.04 per cent) interrupted their careers for childrearing or care of other relatives, compared with 19.4 per cent of the female political leaders and 14.7 per cent of the female business leaders. Given these patterns it is not, then, surprising that business leaders are less likely than politicians to see a conflict occurring often or very often between work and life outside work (31.6 per cent com-pared with 43.7 per cent for political leaders).

Household tasks

While women have moved into employment, men have scarcely moved into childrearing and housework (Vianello and Siemienska, 1990). Research indi-cates that, even where both partners are in full-time paid employment, the woman does a disproportionate amount of both the housework and child-care (Ellis and Wheeler, 1991; Headlee and Elfin, 1996). Rantallaiho (1993) suggests that a gender contract operates, based on the traditional division of family responsibilities, along male breadwinner/female homemaker lines. In some countries, then, the individual right of women to paid work and a certain amount of independence is exchanged for women's continuing responsibility for human care in both the public sphere and the family. Women in leadership positions, though, have tended not to take respon-sibility for housework, instead paying someone else to do it (Ellis and Wheeler, 1991). In fact, most leaders – men and women – report doing less than or about half the housework. However, female leaders did more domes-tic work than males: 31 per cent of the women did more than half of the domestic work in their household (this is true both for political and business leaders) and 13 per cent of the female business leaders did it all. On the other hand, 19.7 per cent of the male political leaders and 25.9 per cent of the male business leaders did none of the domestic work and only 3.6 per cent of men interviewed reported performing more than half of the housework. Presumably, as Diem-Wille and Ziegler suggest, the career might be used to legitimise doing nothing in the household or men delegate to paid help and thus 'buy' themselves free.[4]

It is not surprising, then, that a third of the women leaders report frequent experience of symptoms of overwork, compared with under a quarter of the men, with 9.3 per cent of women indicating that this happened very often compared with 4.5 per cent of men (see also chapter 15).

Taking responsibility for household tasks had interfered very much or much in the careers of political women leaders: 13.2 per cent reported this in comparison with female business leaders (8.1 per cent), male political leaders (4.1 per cent) and male business leaders (1.5 per cent), as had other family commitments (11.5 per cent compared to 6.6 per cent for female business leaders, 5.2 per cent for male political leaders and 2.2 per cent for male business leaders).

The female political leaders reported that the traditional responsibilities as part of a 'women's role', such as childcare and household tasks, had a negative effect on their careers. As with other aspects of family life in high-profile positions, being constantly in the public eye may mean that female political leaders feel they have to fulfil the traditional women's role successfully as well as having a career because they are expected to 'do it all'. Any perceived neglect of responsibilities may detract from their overall perceived competence and suitability as a 'woman in politics'.

The traditional pattern where the woman partner is busy solely in the household varies between countries.[5] Japan stands out noticeably, where nearly all men (89.3 per cent) have a partner who does only unpaid work at home. In Ireland this traditional role distribution is also very strong for male leaders (66.7 per cent). Next come several countries where half of all male leaders are relieved of daily chores by their partners: Germany, Spain, Switzerland, USA, New Zealand and Australia. In sharp contrast to this stands Israel, where the traditional division of labour does not apply to a single (!) career man. Men in Eastern European countries also rarely have non-employed partners (7–14 per cent), as do Denmark and Sweden, which have a long tradition of women's movements, employment and activism.

The effects of combining career and family

Trying to balance a public and private life has its costs. Political leaders were more likely to indicate that they have 'very much' sacrificed personal or free time for their career (47.3 per cent compared with 35.6 per cent for business leaders). Only 18.6 per cent of the female political leaders felt that they had not sacrificed 'very much' or 'much' of their personal or free time. A similar pattern emerged in sacrifice of social time and friendships because of careers. In fact, 61.5 per cent of the female political leaders felt that they had made very much or much of a sacrifice compared to 46.9 per cent of the male political leaders and 48 per cent of the business leaders. Male political leaders were most likely to indicate sacrificing time with their partners (52.3 per cent compared with 42.4 per cent for male business leaders and 40.5 per cent for female leaders). The majority of Austrian and Finnish male political leaders reported sacrificing time with their partner. As Moss (in Lewis, Susan and Lewis, Jeremy, 1996) points out, one of the current policy challenges is to redistribute the use of time spent by women and men in paid and unpaid work so that women do more of the former and men more of the latter.

Reproducing the family of origin

Given the family-related differences between the female and male leaders, to what extent are they reproducing their family of origin in their present situation? There were some aspects that were similar. For leaders who currently had partners, the partners' educational qualifications reproduced the situation found in their family of origin. This was particularly so for the women business leaders, who often had highly educated parents, were well-educated themselves and had partners who were also. Over 80 per cent of the leaders overall had a university qualification, making them a very well-educated population. On the other hand, male business leaders were most often reproducing their family of origin, by having partners who were more likely to be in unpaid work (42.9 per cent compared with 24.9 per cent for male political leaders) and looking after their children, particularly before they started school.

Conclusion

While this research concentrates on an élite group of women and men who have a lot in common in comparison to the general population, the ways in which they combine their careers and domestic responsibilities differentiate the male and female leaders from each other. The greatest gender contrasts are among business leaders, while women and men political leaders are more similar.

In some respects, the male business leaders and the female political leaders are following more traditional and established patterns in balancing career and family. Male business leaders often have a partner at home who keeps the family running smoothly and, thus, they see no conflict between work and family life. If their partners are in paid employment, it is frequently part-time. Female political leaders, on the other hand, are trying to do it all.

They are endeavouring to carry out two full-time jobs by adding a high-profile career on top of a traditional female family role. Having attained a position of power, it appears that they are trying to combine a demanding career with responsibility for the majority of the household tasks and childcare. Female business leaders differ markedly from their political counterparts. They appear to have made more compromises in their personal lives. In the attainment of a high-status position, they have moved away from a traditional female role. They are less likely to have partners or children and have made other arrangements for dealing with household tasks or childcare, where this applies. Male political leaders differ from their business counterparts in indicating that they would perhaps have liked more involvement in the life of their children.

The business and political leaders in this study (see methodological chapter) were not representative of the national populations from which they came. Generally, they originate from families where education was valued and their parents, as well as being well educated, provided strong role models in terms of attainment of positions of power. The leaders themselves were very well qualified educationally, as were their partners. For the majority of the leaders, being in a powerful position meant that they had had to make compromises in their personal lives. This was particularly the case for the women who, because of their position, did not conform to the stereotypical role expected of women. Being a woman political leader had different personal consequences from being a woman business leader. For many women business leaders their career was the first priority and other aspects of their lives were shaped by it. Women political leaders were trying to juggle the competing demands of 'woman' and 'political leader', in part because this was what the electorate expected. Male leaders also did not seem to have a choice other than to fit into a stereotypical role, where family concerns and responsibilities automatically come second to a career. Whereas male business leaders generally did not appear to see this as an issue, male political leaders were more concerned about this division.

With the increased participation of women in paid employment, the greater involvement of men in childrearing and declining birth rates, the situation for both men and women in positions of power is likely to be one of change. As chapters 14 and 15 point out, there are ways in which policy and circumstance can work towards supporting a more balanced way of combining careers and other responsibilities to ensure that there is the possibility of choice for both women and men, regardless of whether they are business or political leaders.

Notes

1. The comparative figures have been tested using chi-squares and all reach a level of significance between $p = 0.05$ and $p = 0.005$.

2. The comparison between countries was done by Gertraud Diem-Wille and Judith Ziegler.
3. This issue, as well as the following one, will be examined especially from the point of view of the career life-forms in chapter 16, where country groupings are also given special attention.
4. See also the hypothesis expressed by Kuusipalo and Kauppinen in chapter 15 (see also chapter 14).
5. The comparison between countries was calculated by Gertraud Diem-Wille and Judith Ziegler.

14
Traditional or New Ways of Living

Gertraud Diem-Wille and Judith Ziegler

Instead of the traditional marriage and family, we see today a multiplicity of arrangements in private life. Whereas the traditional norm was to get married and have children, the method by which a couple organise their living together is no longer self-evident and has to be negotiated. New possibilities are opening up. Nothing is taken for granted any longer, everything has to be treated anew, all of which induced Beck-Gernsheim and Beck to speak of the 'chaos of love' (1995). As a result of the 100-year discourses of the women's movement, it is no longer taken for granted that the wife will give up her career in favour of running a household and caring for children. The transformation of these values is also expressed in language. Less is spoken about marriage than of partnerships or relationships (Kotthoff and Wodak, 1997). To live as a 'single' is one of several options. 'Patchwork families' are those where one or both partners bring children from previous partnerships into the family. The individual seems to be a stronger architect of his or her own private life and takes the risk of building it.

In this chapter we ask how men and women leaders combine their demanding career with the task of everyday life, with a focus on the two cohorts of leaders born up to and after 1945.[1] Will we find traditional or partnership-like forms of living? We assume that since the end of World War II, changes have taken place in the traditional role models, due to better education, increasing income for women and their higher professional positions which may distinguish the two cohorts' everyday lives. The different current living situation of the top leaders will be analysed regarding their choice of partner as well as in reference to their professional position, in order to explore their orientation to traditional or new ways of living.

Current living situation and partnership

Professional work as exclusively a man's field has been increasingly challenged over the last century. We can consider the women in our study as pioneers in this process of change, as they have been successful in rising to the male-dominated top positions, participating in power and decision-making processes. It is, therefore, especially interesting to see whether they have also developed new models in the private sphere. No less interesting is how much men in top positions have changed.

The present living situation of the leaders shows clear gender differences. The first main difference is the number of partnerships in a household, as shown in the previous chapter. This result corresponds with many others, in which a similar distribution of partnerships of top leaders has been found (cf. Bernadoni and Werner, 1987; Bischoff, 1990; Diem-Wille, 1996; Liebig, 1997). No differences regarding living situation with/without a partner can be seen between the two generations. That is, nearly all older as well as younger men live with a partner. Surprisingly, the proportion of women living alone neither increased nor decreased. As a partner is a strong support, who can have an important influence on the course of a career, we find that the men can more frequently count on such support than top women.

However, the diverse forms of living together increasingly blur the sociological categories. The objective information, how much of the week is actually spent together or apart, is often less important than the emotional experience and the subjective appraisal of belonging together as a couple. Some of the partnerships of interviewed leaders only exist at weekends. This can be described as a new living style, an intermediate form between living alone and marriage.

A further gender-specific difference is observable in the proportion of divorces, as reported in the previous chapter, though there are no significant differences between the two age groups.

There are large gender differences in the professional status leaders' partners (p = 0.00). Just under 47.3 per cent of the spouses of the male and 60.8 per cent of the spouses of the female leaders are employed as white-collar workers. In partnerships where the woman devotes her work solely to the support of her partner, he can rely on freedom from household responsibilities, thereby pursuing his work without hindrance. In these partnerships the experience of work is very different: communication and exchange of experiences about professional activities is often one-sided or limited. Beck-Gernsheim (1993: 89) speaks about the danger of alienation in those partnerships where the man has a career providing new experiences, and the woman remains trapped in a recurring cyrcle of experiences. Women as 'career companions', who relieve their man of daily tasks and support 'his' cultural and business life, are no longer predominant, as this study clearly shows.

Are there differences between the two generations?

With male leaders, a decrease from 37.3 per cent (born up to 1945) to 28.8 per cent (born after 1945) of partners who do unpaid work at home is found. The proportion of female partners who pursue an independent occupation is 10 per cent higher in the younger cohort. A further 15.2 per cent of female spouses in both cohorts are self-employed or own firms. The number of self-employed and firm owners among male spouses in both cohorts is twice as high (29.9 per cent). We posit that it as an indication that these couples place a great importance on career.

Furthermore, a decrease in non-employed male partners (for other reasons) from 13.1 per cent (older ones) to 3.2 per cent (younger ones) can be seen. The reason could be that the number of already retired partners is higher among the career women born before 1945. The number of male partners who exclusively do unpaid work at home decreased from 3.3 per cent in the older group to 1.0 per cent in the younger group. This means that there is no role-reversal in the households. The new trend is to enable both partners to pursue a professional career. Fitting with this image are the nearly 80 per cent of male partners who have a positive attitude to the careers of their spouses.

A further difference in professional status of spouses is in hours worked. As outlined in chapter 13, more female than male partners work part-time. These women seem to practise a model of compatibility, according to which they pursue an occupation, which can be easily combined with household labour. In this model, the men's role has not changed: they concentrate on their career and contribute little to responsibilities at home. This solution, that a partner (usually the woman) works part-time, is generally considered to be both satisfactory and fair by both partners. Whether the sharing of work is felt to be fair depends on the amount of income. With a smaller income, (i.e. a smaller percentage of the family income) women tend to feel obliged to take on a larger part of the domestic work. We see this pattern of a wife working part-time as a transitory form between the traditional marriage with gender-specific allocation of work and the new forms of relationships. The woman's paid work can be combined with her function as housewife without coming into conflict with the dominance structure of the married couple: the husband's work is deemed to be more important and represents the financial base.

The majority (73 per cent) of employed partners of career women have supervisory managerial functions. This is also true of half of all female partners who are employed. If we look at all partnerships, the difference is even clearer: 9.9 per cent of the female partners can be found in top management, while 37.9 per cent of male partners are at the top. These partnerships are classified as 'dual-career couples'.

These relationships with both partners employed in high-status positions are pioneers of social change. They have broken through the conventional model of the man as the sole earner and the woman as solely responsible for household and family tasks. Dual-career couples are often characterised by more uniformity and equality of rights. Mutual understanding through one's own work experiences can lead to greater satisfaction for both partners. Men may experience relief at not being solely responsible for the family income. Both partners are financially independent and thereby enjoy more freedom. An advantage of partnerships where both partners pursue careers is that men can better appreciate the needs of their partner for independence and professional success, and therefore can be more supportive than hindering of their partner's career. Besides a mutual challenge in professional life, the competition between partners can be seen as an advantage, one that spurs them on to greater achievements. According to Beck-Gernsheim (1993: 185ff), a critical point in these relationships arrives if the woman achieves more recognition, income and higher status, because in doing so she violates the norms of male superiority. Conflicts can arise, says the author, as soon as she earns more and thus threatens the traditional family power structure. With dual-career couples, both have equal rights and learn to 'negotiate' different wishes and needs, which is why Hood (1983) speaks of the 'bargaining power' of successful women. 'Bargaining power' is the ability to get another person to 'cooperate in or to allow the achievement of one's goals' (Hood, 1983: 7). Negotiating power is dependent on self-confidence and personal autonomy as well as the experience of making one's own ideas and conceptions comprehensible to others, a skill which can be developed through motivating co-workers. Couples who devote a lot of energy to their careers can stand by each other, advising, discussing questions of strategy and timing of action, thinking together about important decisions and inspiring each other. All these positive aspects in a partnership are possible, if envy and competition act as no more than a stimulus. If these emotions are excessive, they change into destructiveness, mutual devaluation and power struggles, although they may be mitigated by compensating factors of tenderness and love (Joseph, 1994).

The top leaders show divergent expectations, which lead to fundamental contradictions between the occupations and family tasks of women. On the one hand, the occupation is considered as a path to emancipation; on the other, traditional roles meet with high approval. Thus, 65.3 per cent of the male and 45.4 per cent of the female leaders agree that family life suffers if the woman has a full-time job. The different acceptance of the professional work of women and men is clear: the man works 'for' the family, but, when the woman works, the family is neglected. More than half the female leaders no longer agree with these traditional values, and feel enriched by being active in both spheres. However, there is a general agreement with the statement: 'having a paid job is the best way for a woman to be an independent person', with 78 per cent of the men and 85.3 per cent of the women agreeing. Thereby, the patriarchal obstacle to women's education and employment is robustly refuted. The coexistence of old and new role models breeds conflicts; feelings of uncertainty and insecurity can thus arise, especially for women. That nearly half of the women in high positions agree with the statement that family life suffers with full-time employment suggests a hidden potential for conflict and a possible emergence of guilt regarding one's own family. At the same time, it also shows the high price that must be paid for a career, which perhaps women are more consciously aware of. The role expectations concerning men are, by comparison, more uniform. The traditional image is that the man should take care of the family economically. What is new is the demand that he also takes on family responsibilities. However, the statement 'when jobs are scarce, men should have more rights to a job than women' gets 25.7 per cent agreement from men, but 18.5 per cent from the female leaders.

Responsibility for children and household

The central question examined in this chapter is if, by comparing generations, we can observe changes in decisions about parenthood and the number of children desired. The comparison shows highly significant age-specific differences concerning the number of children/childlessness among the career men as well as among the career women. Only 18.4 per cent of the women born before 1945 had no children, whereas 34.3 per cent of the younger ones are living without children. There is also a decrease in the number of children each has. Only 14.7 per cent of the younger women have more than two, while one-third of those born before 1945 have three or more. One third of women of the second cohort are (still)[2] childless, while among the women of the first cohort the two-child family predominates, with 35.6 per cent. It seems that among younger women parenthood and career are increasingly mutually exclusive. Or are they less ready to accept both areas of responsibility and decide in favour of career when they become aware of career options? No reason for their childlessness can be deduced from our data. It is often interpreted as a decision against children in order to pursue their professional work unhampered. Such a decision, however, is not to be understood as simple egoism (Beck-Gernsheim, 1993), but much more as a protection against possible claims by others, against additional demands and duties. Next to this possibility, avoiding the social sanctions of being a 'bad mother' remain open (Bernadoni and Werner, 1987).

As we saw in the previous chapter, top male leaders overwhelmingly (91.6 per cent) are fathers of one or more children. This does not represent any difficulty in planning their lives, nor in establishing a family with children, nor in pursuing a career.

But there is also a significant decrease in the number of children of the younger career men. The percentage of top male leaders without children is 11.7 per cent, significantly higher than the 5.3 per cent of those born before 1945.[3] The two-child family clearly predominates: 41.8 per cent in the first cohort and 45.5 per cent in the second. But almost half of the men born before 1945 have several children (3–7), whereas only 27 per cent of the leaders born after 1945 are fathers of three or more children. Few have just one child.

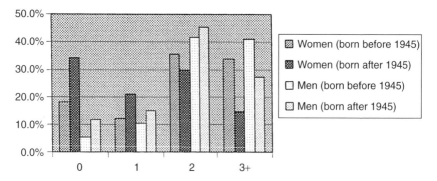

Figure 14.1   Number of Children, Generation Comparison (N = 1,632)

Childcare

Can trends be distinguished between how the first and second cohort top leaders who have children organise their care?

Up to school age (the most intensive period of childcare) only a small minority of the male leaders (4.7 per cent of the older and 5.5 per cent of the younger ones) cared for the children themselves. However, there has been a generational change in terms of partners taking care of them. Whereas 62.6 per cent of the first group could rely on partners, this figure dropped to 48.1 per cent for the younger group, partly no doubt due to the increased participation of women in the paid workforce. Thus, younger male leaders are less likely to be able to hand over responsibilities for daily tasks to their partners.

There has been a small increase in privately paid care (8.3 per cent to 12.2 per cent) as well as in publicly financed care (6.5 per cent to 12.2 per cent) in the younger male cohort. The various other combinations of organised childcare (oneself and other family members, or the other parent together with state nurseries) also shows an increase for men of 4 per cent.

Among the top female leaders a decrease of 10 per cent in personally caring for their children can be observed. Support and relief by the other partner remain unusual. For career women the importance of private (from 18.6 per cent to 29.4 per cent) and state nurseries (from 7.7 per cent to 19.3 per cent) has clearly increased. The younger cohort of the two did half the domestic work and childcare. The career women reported little help from their partners, but sought and found childcare in state nurseries or external, often private sources. The question remains open whether they felt there was sufficient institutional help.

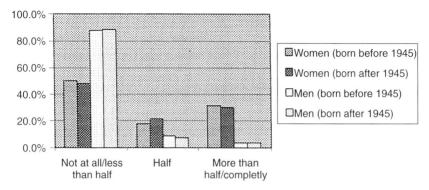

Figure 14.2 Participation in Domestic Work, Generation Comparison (n = 1,585)

Participation in domestic work

There are clear gender differences in the amount of household work under-taken, with only minor differences in household participation between the two age groups. Contrary to expectations, no declining tendency in the amount of housework undertaken can be observed between the career women in both age groups.

Almost half of all women in a top position (50.3 per cent in the first, 48.3 per cent in the second group) report performing less than half or no house-work. This shows that for many women in top positions the traditional role model is changing and has declined in importance. They have at least partly detached themselves from a (possible) double burden and put the priority clearly on their professional roles. The 'half–half' model has increased insignificantly from 17.9 per cent of the first group of career women to 21.4 per cent of the younger ones. This applies to 20 per cent of female leaders. Among the male leaders there are significant differences in the two age groups, but the direction is towards a decline in participation in housework. Only the number who admit to doing no household work at all has clearly diminished.

A model of shared responsibility for the household has not yet been estab-lished. The percentage of male leaders who report doing more than half of the housework has not increased. In both age groups it is merely between 3 and 4 per cent.

As these are self-evaluations, there may be some distortion. Increasing participation by men in domestic work is considered socially desirable and admitting little or no involvement is, then, seen to be less 'politically correct'. It is important for leaders with a public profile to show the 'right image' (see also chapter 15).

Conclusion

The expectation that leading figures in politics and business shape their private lives in an innovative way has only been partly confirmed through our results. There were relevant gender differences, but fewer in generation comparisons.

Notes

1. In the following chapter we speak about the first cohort (born up to 1945) and the second (born after 1945).
2. Some women in the younger cohort might become parents since they are still of childbearing age.
3. As for the younger women, some of these men may have more children. Indeed, even men in the older cohort might father more children.

15
Life and Career in North and South Europe
Jaana Kuusipalo, Kaisa Kauppinen and Iira Nuutinen

Introduction

This chapter discusses the differences between Northern and Southern Europe in combining everyday life and a top-level career. Our hypothesis is that the dominant family model has a strong impact on this relationship. Southern Europe represents a male breadwinner model, whereas in Northern Europe a dual-earner family is more dominant. By Northern Europe we mean Finland, Sweden, Denmark and the Netherlands.[1] Italy, Spain, Greece and Portugal are considered the countries of Southern Europe in our study.

There are, however, some problems with this country clustering. While the Nordic countries are regarded as representing a dual-earner model, the Netherlands has been cited as an example of a strong male breadwinner model (Lewis, Jane and Ostner, 1991: 32). On the other hand, the Netherlands resembles the Nordic countries in terms of women's political representation and women's employment rate.[2]

According to these indicators, the Northern European countries are at a higher level of women employment and the Southern European countries at a lower level than the member states of the EU on average (European Commission, 1996; 1997) However, women's access to managerial posts is equally limited in the North. Most businesswomen get stuck in middle management (Adler and Izraeli, 1994: 7; Kauppinen, 1994). In Sweden (1990) and Finland (1991) only 1 per cent and 4 per cent respectively of the top managers or capital owners of the largest corporations are women (SOU, 1990; Kuusipalo, 1994: 53–4).

The absence of women in top-level positions was not an issue until the late 1970s (Adler and Izraeli, 1994: 3). When studied, it was only to demonstrate how women deviated from the male career pattern. Women's primary role in a family was seen as a 'natural' hindrance to their political or professional career because of feminine socialisation (Diamond, 1987; Randall, 1987: 122–30). Consequently, women's under-representation in top-level positions was explained by their making a 'choice' between work and family – a choice which only women have to make (Harriman, 1985: 262).

The daily and weekly working time of a leader does not fit in with the time schedule of parents who want to look after their children. The masculine code of a leader presumes that he is willing to sacrifice most of his time (see chapters 8 and 16).

In recent decades, more and more women have refused to make this choice, which excludes them from either a working life or a family. This refusal is most prominent in the Nordic countries, where the dual-earner family model has replaced the male breadwinner model (Lewis, Jane, 1993: 15). Parental leave, flexible working hours and state childcare support women's right to work and men's right to fatherhood. Shared parenthood and normalisation of mothers' work challenges the masculine concept of career, which does not take into account the demands of the family responsibilities of both parents.

In Southern European countries women's employment rate is lower than elsewhere in Europe. But this is changing as more and more women enter the labour market. This causes problems with combining family and work, particularly since these countries cannot afford such extensive and efficient state services as the Nordic countries.

While Nordic welfare states are moving away from a gender order based on difference by making it possible to combine work and family for both genders, the Southern welfare states still maintain a more traditional gender order. Have these different family models explanatory power when studying top leaders? Is it easier for the Northern European women than the Southern European women to combine family duties and a top-level career? And what about the men?

Having a partner is 'easier' for Northern women – more mothers of young children in the South

As reported in chapter 13, it is the female leaders who are most likely to be single or divorced (Table 15.1). The male top leaders are more likely to be married than the male population on an average. This is the case in Denmark, Finland and Sweden where the proportion of married or cohabiting men in the total population is 76 per cent. This implies that a family is an important asset for male top leaders (Valdez and Gutek, 1987: 158).

In Northern Europe the difference between male and female leaders in terms of marriage/cohabiting was not statistically significant. The Northern female leaders, on average, are more likely to be married or cohabiting than the other female leaders (p < 0.05) and Northern women in general (the proportion of married or cohabiting women between 35–64 years in three Nordic countries is 74 per cent). Marriage/cohabiting seems to have become, if not an asset, a typical choice for the Northern female leaders. The

Table 15.1   Family Status and Children (%)

Family Status	NM	NW	SM	SW	TM	TW
Married/cohabiting	92	85	89***	71	94***	75
Married/cohabiting and children	86***	65	80***	55	88***	60
Young children (0–12) of those leaders who have children	49***	25	50	41	40**	32
Single/divorced	8	15	11***	29	6***	25
No children	7***	29	16**	31	8***	28
Divorced at least once	27	20	15	26	16***	28

Chi-square: *** = p < 0.001; ** = p < 0.01; * = p < 0.05.
NM = Northern men, NW = Northern women, SM = Southern men, SW = Southern women, TM = total men, and TW = total women.
The same use of the asterisks is adopted in the following tables. Statistical tests refer to the differences between the sexes.

Northern women were also more likely to be cohabiting (16 per cent) than the top leaders in general (6 per cent) (p < 0.001).

Combining family and career should not be a more difficult choice for women than for men (Hernes, 1987: 15). The Northern women have started to 'fit' in with the masculine career pattern in terms of having a partner, but not in terms of having children. The great proportion of childless female leaders indicates that children, rather than marriage, pose a problem for career women (Andrew, Coderre and Denis, 1994: 380–1).[3]

Not everybody wants children or is able to have them. But according to our results, 39 per cent of the childless leaders reported forgoing children because of their career. Even though the absolute number of the childless men is much smaller, some of them also acknowledge the problem of combining children and a career.

The decreasing birth rates in Southern Europe reflect the problems for women of combining children and work. Spain and Italy, for example, have the lowest birth rates in the European Union (European Commission, 1997). Keeping in mind the modest childcare facilities in these countries, women may give up having children in order to continue working. This may also be one reason for the greater proportion of single/divorced female top leaders in the South than in the North (p < 0.01).

However, in Southern Europe there was no significant difference between female and male leaders in having young children as there was amongst the Northern leaders, even if the women were on average of the same age as the men. The Southern female leaders who have just started to enter top positions are obviously refusing to make a 'woman's choice'. This 'silent revolution' may predict future changes in women's career patterns.

Male leaders may have to change their expectations for family life as well. The Southern men seem to report slightly more difficulties in combining family and career than other male leaders. This may reflect the contradictions between the dominant male breadwinner model and the choices women actually make.

The unusually high divorce rates among the Northern male leaders compared with all male leaders (p < 0.001) suggest difficulties in combining family and career, at least at the first attempt. The proportion of divorced men (also of those currently married or cohabiting) in the North was of the same magnitude as for the female leaders. However, fewer of these women were currently married, while the Northern men were more likely to have remarried.

The high proportion of married or cohabiting female leaders in Northern Europe indicates that combining family and career is easier there, but a vision of the family as an asset for women is still distant. The 'choice' of not having children was typical among the Northern women too. In conclusion, the relationship between family and career is changing and should be reformulated, not least because the male leaders are facing the problems caused by the changing role of the women both as colleagues and as wives.

An equal partnership for the women and an asymmetrical one for the men – the Northern model differs from the others

What kind of families are top leaders likely to live in, in Northern and Southern Europe? Even if there are now more alternatives in the way the family life of top leaders can be organised (see chapter 14), the most typical are the one-career family and the dual-career family. The one-career family may include a housewife or a spouse working outside the home, but having no career. In dual-career families a spouse has a career, which in our typology means that she or he has supervisory functions (see chapters 14 and 16).

The one-career family is most typical of the male leaders and the dual-career family for the female leaders (Table 15.2). The Northern men (p < 0.01) and the Southern men (p < 0.05) were, however, more likely to live in a dual-career family than the male leaders in general. Differences among the Southern and Northern men reflected the dominant family model in these regions.

One third of the Southern men live in accordance with the male breadwinner model and have an economically dependent partner, compared with 17 per cent of the Northern men (p < 0.01). Consequently, the great

Table 15.2   The Career Families in Southern and Northern Europe (%)

	NM	NW	SM	SW	TM	TW
The spouse is economically active (in paid employment, self-employed, owner of firm) Dual-Career Family	83***	98	67***	100	66***	98
The spouse has supervisory functions	39***	66	38***	79	29***	65
is a top leader One-Career Family	19**	35	24**	62	33***	58
The spouse is working but has no supervisory functions, is a	43	32	30	21	37	33
Housewife or househusband	17***	2	33***	0	34***	2
Together – one career family	60***	34	63***	21	71***	35

N = only those currently married/cohabiting.

majority of the partners of the Northern men are economically active compared with 67 per cent in the South. But since a considerable number of the economically active partners of the Northern men did not have supervisory functions in their work, the proportion of one-career families amongst the Northern and the Southern men is almost the same.

The Southern women were most likely to live in dual-career families and have a spouse in a top position compared with the other female leaders ($p < 0.05$). But the Southern men were also more likely to live in a dual-career family compared with all the male leaders ($p < 0.01$). This did not, however, reflect the privileged background of the Southern leaders as we expected, assuming that a person prefers a partner who belongs to the same social class as her/himself. There were no such differences between the Southern and the Northern leaders.

On the other hand, a high-status family of origin, which was most typical for the Southern female leaders, may be an important condition for a career in terms of economic and cultural capital (Bourdieu, 1984). But it may also imply that it is difficult to break the norm of the male breadwinner model according to which a husband should be the main breadwinner in the families of the Southern women.

There are no differences between the Northern women and all the female leaders in terms of the family model. But, because the Northern men were more likely to live in a dual-career family than the male leaders in general (p < 0.01), there seems to be a convergence of the partnership models of the male and female leaders in Northern Europe. The Northern example shows that it is also the changing family models of the *male* leaders which can diminish the inequality between female and male leaders in terms of family life.

Housework: the Northern men do more and the Southern women less than the other leaders of the same gender

The results concerning housework reinforce the impression that the dominant family model – and the level of equality policy – has a strong impact on the everyday life of top leaders. Even at the top level, men do more housework in the countries with a weak male breadwinner model than in those where the male breadwinner family is dominant. The Northern men were the most likely (p < 0.01) and the Southern men least likely (p < 0.05) to do domestic work compared with all the male leaders (Table 15.3). Men's more positive attitudes towards doing the housework in the Nordic countries seem to apply also to the male top leaders (cf. Lewis, Jane, 1993: 6–7; and this volume Chapter 20).

Most of the leaders, as we saw in chapter 13, do less than half or about half of the housework. But the women much more often than the men do most of the housework, and the men more often than women report doing no housework at all. The question was asked also of single leaders, who were more likely to do housework. Amongst them there were no gender differences.

Because there are many more single women than single men in the sample, this may also increase the number of those female leaders who do most of the housework. However, this alone cannot explain the gender differences. Among the married or cohabiting leaders, the female leaders did more housework than the male leaders. Even if the spouse is working, 18 per cent of the male leaders do nothing, while 27 per cent of the female leaders do more than a half (p < 0.01).

Table 15.3   Who Does the Housework? (%)

Doing domestic work	NM	NW	SM	SW	TM	TW
Not at all	13	6	37	13	24	9
Less than half or about half	82	64	62	76	73	60
More than half or completely	6	30	1	11	4	31

The significance of the gender differences in all cells is p < 0.01 (NM/NW, SM/SW and TM/TW).

The differences between the South and the North were clear. Almost one third of the Northern women do the majority of the housework, compared with only 11 per cent of the Southern women ($p < 0.001$). The figures are even more impressive, since 29 per cent of the Southern female leaders were single or divorced women, who, according to our results, do more housework. Besides, 13 per cent of the Southern women did not do any housework at all. This was exactly the same proportion as that of the Northern men. The Northern men do less housework than the Northern female leaders ($p < 0.01$), but much more than the male leaders in the South ($p < 0.001$).

In dual-career families at least some of the housework is done by housekeepers or maids. This may partly explain why the Southern women differed so much from the other women. The married/cohabiting Southern women live mostly in dual-career families where neither of the spouses has time for domestic duties. This makes it more likely that they will hire domestic help.

On the other hand, it is probable that in one-career families with a female partner not in paid employment, most of the domestic duties are done by her. This would explain why the proportion of male leaders who do no housework at all is more or less the same as that of the male leaders who have a non-working wife. This was true both in the South and in the North.

The Southern men seem to leave most of the housework to their wives even if they are working, while the Northern women are doing more than their part even if their partners do not have as demanding a career as they have. Unlike in Southern Europe, in Nordic countries it is not so common to pay for extra help and the double burden of work and household accompanies women in top positions. On the other hand, Southern women are either 'forced' to live alone or to find a wealthy husband, who can and will employ extra help and does not need her services as a housewife.

Childcare arrangements: wives for male leaders, day care for female leaders

Keeping in mind that having children is a more difficult choice for female leaders, the childcare arrangements of top leaders should illustrate this situation. In some respects, Northern and Southern European childcare arrangements differ from those of the top leaders in general (Table 15.4).

First, the great majority of all the male leaders in the whole sample have solved the problem by leaving the children to their mothers, but much less so in Northern and Southern Europe ($p < 0.001$). Secondly, only a few of the Southern and Northern women had taken care of their children themselves compared with one fifth of all the female leaders in the whole sample ($p < 0.001$).

Table 15.4 Typical Forms of Childcare among Top Leaders

Northern Men	%	Northern Women	%
wife/partner	28	public day care	31
public day care	24	Other	16
private day care	12	Domestic help	15
himself + partner	8	private day care	14
Southern men	**%**	**Southern women**	**%**
wife/partner	37	private day care	32
private day care	22	relatives	20
relatives	16	domestic help	9
domestic help	7		
Total men	**%**	**Total women**	**%**
wife/partner	57	private day care	26
private day care	11	herself	20
public day care	8	public day care	14
		relatives	11
		domestic help	8

The significance of the gender differences in all cells is p < 0.001 (NM/NW, SM/SW and TM/TW).

The regional differences reflected the respective dominant family ideologies and social policies, and consequently the availability of the different forms of childcare. Excluding the spouses of the male leaders, private childcare and the relatives were the most common forms of childcare for both male and female leaders in Southern Europe. Hardly any of the Northern leaders mentioned 'relatives', as did 20 per cent of the Southern women and 16 per cent of the men in the Southern countries.

The principle of subsidiarity in Southern Europe, largely connected with the Catholic idea of the family, implies that it is the family – in a broader sense – which should primarily take care of its own members (Lewis, Jane, 1993: 13). For example, grandmothers take care of their grandchildren, while grandmothers are cared for by their adult children.

This is not the case in Northern Europe. The principle of individual citizenship embedded in Nordic social policy presupposes that adults should take care of themselves and, if not possible, society, not the family, is responsible for their well-being. In Northern Europe, most of the grandmothers are in paid employment themselves and, even if retired, usually do not live in the same household with their adult children. This makes it more difficult for the Northern leaders to use their relatives as babysitters.

Most of the partners of the Northern male leaders were working, and a quarter of them had left their children in state childcare, which in the Nordic countries has been, in principle, available for all parents. This is not the case in Southern Europe, where hardly anybody mentioned it. Both male and female leaders (31 per cent) in Northern Europe had benefited from the state childcare system. However, without state day care, the Northern women had been forced to find other solutions, such as nannies and private nurseries, while 28 per cent of the Northern male leaders relied on the unpaid work of their spouses.

The state childcare policy of the Nordic countries embodies the principle of gender equality: both parents must have an opportunity to leave their children in good care, while they are working. In Nordic countries, approximately 50–80 per cent of all children aged 3–6 years are in state day care.

The principle of social equality is also important, as the quality of childcare should not vary according to the incomes of the parents. In practice, this has not been so easy. Ten years ago it was quite difficult to get children into state day care due to lack of provision and even private day care was hard to find. Perhaps this is why 16 per cent of the Northern women chose the alternative 'other', when asked about childcare.

Conflicts between family and career

Because leaders are supposed to devote themselves to their work, they have to minimise the time spent on other activities. Both women and men had reported most often that among career–related sacrifices was their personal free time (Table 15.5). The Southern women and men had sacrificed slightly more of their time to be with their children than with their partners.

Compared with all leaders, the Northern men had sacrificed slightly more of their time to be with their children ($p < 0.05$), whereas the Northern

Table 15.5 Sacrifices Made for the Career (%)

Sacrificed Much or Very Much	**NM**	**NW**	**SM**	**SW**	**TM**	**TW**
Personal time/leisure	65	78	71	77	72	77
Social time/friends	51	52	45	60	50	55
Time with partner	54	42	41	36	47*	40
Time with children (only those who have children)	55**	23	47	39	47**	33

women had sacrificed least of their time for their children (p < 0.01). The Northern women, who, according to our results, do more housework than other leaders and thus may spend more time with their children, feel least guilty about the time sacrificed for their children. On the other hand, the Northern male leaders were most worried about the time they had not spent with their children. Cultural differences in terms of the father's role probably had some influence on these results.

Career sacrifices were also analysed in another context, which measured reported conflicts between work and private life. More than 40 per cent of the Southern leaders (men and women) as well as the Northern men had recognised these problems often or very often; whereas only 29 per cent of Northern women, had experienced these conflicts often or very often (p < 0.01).

The conflicts between work and private life were related to reports of burn-out and mental fatigue (p < 0.001). The women were particularly susceptible. As shown in chapter 13, 47 per cent of those often experienced such conflicts, but only 27 per cent of those who seldom had these conflicts experienced great deal of burn-out and mental fatigue.

These symptoms seem unrelated to the number of working hours as such, but to the contradictory demands of private life and working life. The partners' support brought some relief. Of those women whose partners' attitudes were very positive, only 29 per cent reported burn-out, while 45 per cent of women whose partners had less supportive attitudes experienced a great deal of burn-out and mental fatigue (p < 0.05).

While most (78 per cent) of the leaders reported a lot of support from their partners, 57 per cent of the female leaders chose the alternative 'very positive', when asked how their partners felt about their jobs, compared with 34 per cent of the male respondents (p < 0.001). As the results concerning burn-out and mental fatigue indicate, the partner's support is more important for the well-being of the female leaders.

This could be explained by the different social status of men and women. Even if the woman is in a higher position than her partner, she needs extra support because, as a woman, she is lower in the gender hierarchy and faces more problems in a male-dominated environment.

The Northern women did not experience conflicts between private life and work as often as the others, and consequently are less likely to feel symptoms of burn-out.

Conclusion

In this chapter we have analysed the differences in the everyday life of the male and female top leaders in Northern and Southern Europe. The results support our hypothesis that the dominant family model influences the ways in which top leaders combine family and career.

In Nordic countries with the dual-earner family model, where mothers' waged work is accepted as a normal way of living and strongly supported by government policy, it is easier for female leaders to combine family and career. This is more difficult in Southern Europe, which has a strong male breadwinner tradition and where social policy is less supportive of working mothers.

It is not only mothers' waged work, but also the changing role of fathers which has challenged the relationship between work and private life, and consequently the concept of career. This has had some influence on the attitudes of the Northern male leaders, such as the concern they felt about not being able to spend more time with their children as well as their higher participation in housework compared with other male leaders.

The male leaders in the Northern European countries can no longer rely on the help of their partners, or at least not as much as the other male leaders. Almost a half of them live in a dual-career family, with partners who are not willing to take on all domestic work. This makes male top leaders pay more attention to the duties and joys of everyday life, but not without conflicts, as indicated by the high divorce rates among the Northern male leaders.

The problems related to combining family and career amongst the Southern women were reflected by the high proportion of single/divorced female leaders. When married, the Southern women – mostly living in a high-status family – could depend on the help of private child day care and relatives. Helpful relatives and the availability of domestic services may also explain why they (when married) were more likely to have young children and did less housework than their female colleagues in the North.

The popularity of state childcare among the Northern élite women indicates that it may be one concrete way to remove at least one obstacle to women's careers. But state child day care does not guarantee equality within the family. Small children who need constant care seem to be a problem for the Northern women too. In fact, they do more housework than the Northern men, which must prevent them from devoting as much time to their work as do their male colleagues.

One question remains: whether leaders should sacrifice their personal life for their career or whether the political and business culture should be changed so that both male and female leaders are able – as partners and parents – to take full responsibility for their work, but also enjoy their daily life. This would also give them an opportunity to use their experiences from 'ordinary' everyday life in their work.

Notes

1. Norway was excluded because there were no men in the data from that country. Moreover, the Norwegian welfare state which treats women primarily as wives and

mothers is said to be closer to Britain than it is to Sweden (Leira, 1994; Lewis, Jane, 1993: 14–15).
2. Most of the Dutch women are working part-time (see chapter 9).
3. The highest proportion of childless female leaders was found in the Netherlands (53 per cent), which increased the average number of the childless women in Northern Europe.

16
Career Life-forms
Johanna Esseveld and Gunnar Andersson

Introduction

This chapter focuses on the interrelations between work, career and family. It emphasises the gendered and contextual nature of these interrelations. At a theoretical level, the concept of career is scrutinised and an alternative concept of career life-form is introduced. At an empirical level, the differences between male and female top leaders in relation to four types of career life-forms within different regional contexts are examined. The theoretical perspective in this chapter is constructivist and similar to the one presented in chapter 15. Gender is seen as a cultural discourse that is created, renewed and reproduced through individual actions in social space. The cultural discourse of gender consists of universes of meaning that structure masculinity and femininity as a binary opposition at the same time that they help maintain a hegemonic masculinity. The emphasis in this chapter differs somewhat from that of Højgaard and Esseveld in that a central place is given to hegemonic masculinity and the construction of careers as masculine as well as how this construction affects the social practices of top leaders in different ways.

On individual careers and career life-forms

The concept of career has been used in different ways in the social sciences: e.g., to refer to social mobility in a work organisation or society, individual work choices and work careers (Hall, 1976; Ahrne, 1985; Burton and Higley, 1987). Common to all of them, however, is reference to movements of one individual or a group of individuals in relation to a particular field of politics, business or administration.[1] These movements can be vertical, radial and circular (Hansson, 1996). Of these three, vertical movement, where individuals' mobility in a particular organisation and/or society is placed at the centre, is the most frequently used in common language. Lately, attempts have been made to broaden the concept to refer to an individual's work career in the context of the totality his/her life – family, social networks and community – or to an individual's movement through different familial life stages.[2]

Even in these newer uses, however, the career concept contains elements of the context out of which it originally evolved: the public sphere of politics, organisations and public bureaucracy. A sphere that historically was – and to a large extent still is – dominated by men. Despite its suggested gender neutrality, there are certain masculine assumptions assigned to it. It reflects men's traditional relation to working life: with a particular timetable and separation between the spheres of family and paid work. This timetable is taken for granted (and almost seen as natural). Characteristic of it is that a work career starts and takes off during the same stage in an individual's life-cycle when s/he is starting a family. Another characteristic is that continuous efforts are needed to ensure success, meaning advancement and/or upward mobility. The latter presupposes a loyalty to a particular organisation.[3] Loyalty can be defined in different ways, but the assumption is made that the organisation is to be given priority over life outside of it.[4] Loyalty is also defined through continuous, life-long, full-time work (where working weeks of 50–65 hours are usual – see chapter 8), but also through an adherence to the assumption that stability in life outside the organisation helps an individual's work career. Stability in private life is, in this traditional career, given a particular meaning: namely, as life in a family with a supportive wife, who does not work for pay and who helps to see that her partner's work career is given priority over her activities in the family.

Briefly, we maintain that careers are embedded in traditional divisions between public and private spheres, and workplace and family, as well as on the assumption that the public sphere and paid work are prioritised over the private sphere. Besides, even today, careers carry with them masculine inscriptions. Together with the gender division of labour, these constructions provide a frame in which men and women reflect on and make choices about work, family and leisure activities.

Career life-forms in the empirical material

In our usage of the concept of career, we emphasise the interactional and contextual nature of careers and place the interrelation between work and family careers at the centre of our analysis.[5] The concept of *career life-form* is introduced for this purpose. It was elaborated by Thomas Højrup in the early 1980s to study the ways in which individuals organised the totality of their daily activities and has since been used in a number of Scandinavian studies (see Højrup and Christensen, 1988; Friberg, 1990; Andersson, 1993). Højrup suggests that different activities – such as paid work, housework and leisure activities – influence each other and also that they partly receive their meaning from this totality of daily activities. Højrup distinguishes different life-forms depending on the role played by husband and wife in the spheres of production and reproduction: family as business, paid work and career life-forms. In all three, the family is taken as a central unit, men are primarily seen as breadwinners, while women's roles differ depending on whether they work for pay or not, and whether or not they have a career. Primacy is given to men's roles in the sphere of production. It is difficult to make use of Højrup's typology for our sample: both men and women have top positions and many do not live in nuclear families. Still, we found the concept of life-form and its assumption of the interactional nature of work, career and family useful and constructed four career life-forms out of the empirical material:

a. traditional career life-form;
b. mixed-career life-form;
c. dual-career life-form;
d. single-career life-form.

The 'traditional career life-form' refers to a top leader with a partner as a non-working spouse; the 'mixed-career life-form' refers to a top leader with a partner who works for pay or runs a business with fewer than ten employees; and in the 'dual-career life-form' both partners have careers and leadership positions or, alternatively, the top leader has a partner who runs a business with more than ten employees; fourth is the 'single-career life-form', where a top leader is living without a partner.

Besides this emphasis on the interactional nature of the top leaders' professional and family careers, we wish to stress their contextual nature. One such contextuality is provided by the overall social conditions in which male and female leaders are placed, another is provided through the different fields – politics and business[6] – in which male and female leaders find themselves. In the following we make use of the former only, and do this by placing the countries included in the study into five different regions: Scandinavia, North/Western Europe, Southern Europe, Eastern Europe and Other Countries.[7]

Countries Included in the Five Regions

Scandinavia	North/Western Europe	Southern Europe	Eastern Europe	Other Countries
Denmark	Austria	France	Hungary	Australia
Finland	Belgium	Greece	Poland	Canada
Norway	UK	Italy	Russia	Japan
Sweden	Germany	Portugal	Slovenia	New Zealand
	Netherlands	Spain	Czech Republic	USA
	Ireland			
	Switzerland			

Below we present the four career life-forms. This presentation consists of three sections. In the first the distribution amongst the top leaders is shown. The second centres on the presence/absence of children and on the partner's employment status amongst the leaders by the four career life-forms. The third section focuses on the division of labour – with childcare and house-work – in them. In each of these three sections, a presentation of the total population is followed by one where regional differences are placed at the centre of the analysis. On the basis of the literature on gender equality, we expect slight differences between the male and female top leaders in regions with a weak breadwinner model (Lewis, Jane, 1992) and a more equal divi-sion of labour between men and women (Orloff, 1992) in Scandinavia and partly Eastern Europe both in relation to family arrangements, status and type of partners' work and division of labour in the family. In other words, we expect large differences between the male and female leaders in regions with more traditional division of labour and a strong breadwinner model such as Southern Europe (see also the previous chapter), where the Catholic Church plays a role in the maintenance of gender differences (Siaroff, 1994). Northwestern Europe, Eastern Europe and countries outside Europe are expected to be between these two extremes. The patterns within these regions, however, will differ. In Eastern Europe we expect a high level of gender equality in work careers and a break with traditional life-forms, but large differences between men and women in relation to housework and childcare.[8]

Career life-forms amongst the top leaders

The division of the total population of top leaders according to the four career forms is as follows: most top leaders (36 per cent) live in a dual-career life-form, 31 per cent in a mixed, 16 per cent in a traditional and 17 per cent in a single-career life-form. There are, however, significant differences between the male and female leaders: whereas 33 per cent of the men live in traditional career life-forms, none of the women do. There are other dif-ferences as well: 49 per cent of the women live in dual-career life-forms versus only 23 per cent of the men; and whereas 38 per cent of the men live in mixed-career life-forms, only 25 per cent of the women do; 26 per cent of women live in single-career life-forms and only 6 per cent of the men.[9]

As Table 16.1 shows, there are significant differences, when the career life-forms for the male leaders in the five regions are compared to each other. The traditional career life-form predominates amongst men in North/ Western Europe as well as in the grouping of countries we put together in the category 'other'. Few men in these two groupings live in dual-career life-forms. In Eastern Europe and Scandinavia, on the other hand, few men live in traditional career life-form, and in Southern Europe the men are nearly equally divided between the three types. There are fewer differences amongst

Tables 16.1 Career Life-form, by Region and Gender (%)

	Other Men	South European Men	North European Men	East European Men	Scandinavia Men	Total
Traditional	51.9	29.2	43.5	11.3	10.2	33.2
Mixed	31.1	32.7	33.7	52.7	45.5	37.2
Dual	12.0	27.5	17.9	29.6	34.1	22.5
Single	4.9	10.6	4.9	6.4	10.2	7.0
Total	21.3	21.2	29.8	14.3	13.3	100.0 (660)

	Women	Women	Women	Women	Women	Total
Mixed	23.2	18.8	27.9	29.1	31.0	25.7
Dual	41.2	53.4	47.0	45.9	48.8	47.3
Single	35.6	27.9	25.1	24.9	20.2	27.0
Total	20.2	21.0	28.8	13.9	16.0	100.0 (670)

Chi-square p = 0.11.

the women than the men. The proportion of women living in dual-career life-forms exceeds 41 per cent in all regions and is highest in Southern Europe (53 per cent). Slightly over a third of the women from the countries outside of Europe live in single-career life-forms, while the proportion of women living in that form in Scandinavia is 20 per cent.

At first sight the data do not support the expectation that these top leaders embrace traditional careers. All forms are represented amongst the leaders and a minority of them live in the traditional one. But the fact that more men than women live in mixed-career life-forms and the high percentage of women who live in a single-career life-form can be interpreted as an adaptation to traditional career norms. Living alone, then, is these women's strategy to cope with the high demands of a career. Differences between the regions are large. The gender differences as far as living arrangements are concerned are highest in the countries belonging to the other regions, closely followed by North/Western Europe. Differences are slightest in Scandinavia, followed by – rather surprisingly – Southern Europe.

We shall continue our analysis with a comparison of partners' occupations, whether partners work for pay and whether full-time or part-time. We shall also see whether or not partners' occupations include leadership responsibilities. After that we take a closer look at the presence/absence of children and their impact on the phenomenon under investigation.

Partner's employment patterns

Partners' paid work, partners' full-time and part-time work

Slightly over three-quarters of the partners of top leaders work for pay; of the others, 5 per cent are unemployed or retired, and 19 per cent carry out unpaid work in the home. Again, there are significant differences between men and women. Whereas 93 per cent of the partners of female top leaders work for pay, only 63 per cent of the partners of male leaders are employed, and whereas 1 per cent of the partners of female leaders carry out unpaid work, a third (34 per cent) of the partners of male leaders do the same. There are also large gender differences in relation to whether partners work full-time or part-time: of the female leaders' employed partners, 89 per cent work full-time and 11 per cent part-time, whereas 65 per cent of the partners of male leaders work full-time and 35 per cent part-time. The proportion of partners working full-time or part-time differs greatly, when the career life-forms are compared by gender.

A comparison by regions shows that there are significant differences between the mixed and dual-career life-forms amongst men and women in Southern Europe, 'other countries' and Northern/Western Europe. The gender differences in Scandinavia are large, but not significant, and there are hardly any differences amongst men and women from Eastern European countries when part-time/full-time employment is considered. In the

Eastern European countries included in the study, around three-quarters of the partners of both male and female top leaders work full-time. In the Scandinavian countries, the percentage of partners of male top leaders who work full-time is also around 75 per cent. However, more than 90 per cent of the partners of female top leaders work full-time. In the other three country groupings, the patterns of the men who live in mixed-career life-forms differ most radically from the other patterns: in Southern Europe, 33 per cent of these men's partners work part-time, in the countries belonging to the 'other' grouping, this percentage rises to 54 per cent and in North/Western Europe to 64 per cent.

Partners' employment includes leadership responsibilities

In our sample, 64 per cent of the top leaders' partners employment includes leadership functions. The proportion differs again, as we saw in chapter 13, between the partners of male and female leaders (78 per cent of partners of female leaders versus 48 per cent of partners of male leaders). There are also large differences between men and women, when the levels of these leadership functions are compared: 59 per cent of women's partners are top leaders and 30 per cent are found in middle leadership positions, while only 33 per cent of the men's partners are top leaders and 37 per cent are in middle leadership positions. These gender differences become particularly clear when top leaders in dual-career life-forms are compared. For men in the dual-career life-form the division is as follows: 26 per cent of their partners have leadership functions at lower, 46 per cent at middle and 28 per cent at top levels. Whereas 55 per cent of the partners of the women in the dual-career life-forms are top leaders, 10 per cent and 35 per cent have partners at lower and middle leadership levels. The pattern that the partners of the women have leadership positions of higher levels than the partners of the men is confirmed.

The top leaders were also asked to indicate whether their partners' careers interfered with their own work career: 80 per cent of the men and 67 per cent of the women indicated that this was not the case. There are not surprisingly significant differences between the different career life-forms: whereas the proportion who suggested that the spouses' career had not interfered with their own career was 90 per cent for the men who live in traditional career life-forms (and for Scandinavia as high as 100 per cent), only 60 per cent of the men who live in dual-career life-forms felt the same way about their spouse's career (again, Scandinavian men are an exception here, with their 87 per cent). There are no significant differences between the women in the three career life-forms, and the percentage of women who answered that their spouse's careers did not interfere with theirs was between 60 and 70 per cent for Southern Europe, North/Western Europe and other countries, while the percentages for Scandinavia and Eastern Europe were slightly higher.

Presence and number of children

We saw in chapter 13 that very few male leaders have no children, while she opposite holds true for female leaders.

The following ranking presents the different career life-forms by sex according to number of children: men living in traditional career life-forms have most children, followed by men living in dual-career life-forms, men living in mixed-career life-forms; women in dual-career life-forms and women living in mixed-career life-forms. Single women have fewest children.

When the different country groupings are considered, the statistics for men who do not have children are as follows: 2.5 per cent in Scandinavia, 4.7 per cent in Eastern Europe, 6 per cent in other countries, 7.1 per cent in Southern Europe and 7.5 per cent in North/Western Europe. For women, the proportion is at least quadruple that of men: 20.5 per cent in Scandinavia, 21.1 per cent in Eastern Europe, 27.5 per cent in Southern Europe, 27.8 per cent in other countries and 38.7 per cent in North/Western Europe. This high proportion is mainly due to women living in single-career life-forms, although there are extremely large differences between them. Whereas 73.1 per cent of single women in North/Western Europe do not have children, in Eastern Europe the proportion of single women without children is similar to the proportion of women living in mixed-career life-forms (29.1 per cent v. 25.4 per cent).

Men in Southern Europe have most children, closely followed by men in North/Western Europe: 41 per cent of Southern European men have three or more children and 34.5 per cent have two children. The percentage of children is higher amongst the men in traditional career life-forms; here, 55.5 per cent have three or more children. However, the percentage of men with three or more children is high also in the 'other country' groupings. With the exception of Eastern Europe, where only 19.6 per cent of men have three or more children, the percentage lies around 40 per cent.

Two children is most common amongst women in all countries groupings, and the percentage of women in mixed-career life-forms with two children is higher than the percentage of women in dual-career life-forms with two children. Again, Eastern Europe is an exception. Here, a higher percentage of women in dual-career life-forms have two children than women in mixed-career life-forms. Interesting also are the differences between the country groupings when women with three or more children are compared to women with one child. In North/Western Europe and Scandinavia more women have three children than one child, while in Eastern Europe the percentage of women with one child is much higher than the percentage of women with three or more children.

The results lend support to some of our expectations. More women then men are childless and there are fewer children in dual- and single- than in traditional and mixed-career life-forms. In country groupings with more equal division of labour, fewer men and women have children. The highest percentage of women without children was found in North/Western Europe. Again, these findings are interpreted as strategies by women to cope with the traditional career demands and also suggest that careers in this region – as well as the ones closely followed by it in 'other countries' – are more masculine identified than in other regions.

Divisions of tasks in the family

We now continue with a presentation of the division of labour in the family from the point of view of the different career life-forms. Two aspects are examined: childcare and housework.

Childcare

The top leaders were also asked (as we saw in chapter 13) what type of childcare they used most often when the children were of pre-school age.[10] The results indicate that a high proportion of the men lived more traditionally: work careers took priority over care for their children, while this was not the case for the women. Many of the women, however, did not take care of the children themselves. In their answers, as we saw, a variety of forms of childcare is mentioned.

There are significant differences when the answers of the male and female leaders are placed in the different career life-forms. Again, the most striking differences can be found: 86 per cent of men in the traditional, 55 per cent in the mixed and 40 per cent of men in dual-career life-forms mentioned that the children were cared for by their partners. Only 8 per cent of women in the mixed and 7 per cent women in the double-career life-form gave a similar answer. Again, there are many different forms of childcare mentioned by the women.

There are also significant gender differences, when the types of childcare are compared by country groupings. Table 16.2 provides an overview of the types of childcare adopted by the leaders.

As we have seen, for the men the most common type of childcare was provided by their partners. In Southern Europe, however, this is combined with private childcare (52 per cent in 'other country' grouping and North/Western Europe; 25 per cent in Southern Europe). The Eastern European and Scandinavian countries differ again from the other three regions: here, slightly over a third of childcare is provided by partners. There are some differences, however. Whereas nearly a third of the childcare is provided by public institutions in the Scandinavian countries, the Eastern European men mention a mix of patterns, including publicly funded day care (21%), own care (18%) as well as other types of childcare (17%).

Table 16.2 Childcare

	Others Men	South Europe Men	North Europe Men	East Europe Men	Scandinavia Men	Total
Self	4.2	8.7	11.4	22.2	14.0	11.3
Partner	83.0	46.8	76.1	35.0	36.0	59.9
Private	6.4	22.3	6.0	3.2	11.6	9.7
Public	2.2	2.5	1.4	22.1	29.1	8.8
Other	4.3	19.7	5.0	17.5	9.3	10.3
Total	21.8	19.7	29.2	15.4	13.9	100.0 (619)

	Women	Women	Women	Women	Women	Row Total
Self	38.0	16.1	30.3	48.4	25.7	31.4
Partner	3.8	12.3	10.8	4.0	3.0	7.1
Private	27.2	38.0	29.4	4.5	11.5	23.2
Public	9.6	6.0	3.4	28.8	28.6	14.1
Other	21.4	27.6	26.1	14.3	31.2	24.2
Total	20.6	20.4	23.9	17.8	17.3	100.0 (505)

Chi-square p < 0.000.

The patchwork where different types of childcare are chosen by the women leaders is also visible in the Table 16.2. Interestingly enough, the content differs by country groupings. In Eastern Europe and countries belonging to the 'other' group, the women themselves provided most of the childcare, but, whereas this is combined with state childcare in Eastern Europe, it is combined with private childcare in 'other countries', where 24 per cent of women mention other solutions. In Southern Europe, 45 per cent of women had made use of private childcare and 25 per cent made use of childcare placed in the 'other' category. In Scandinavia and Eastern Europe, the combination of 'self', 'state childcare' and 'other' received most answers. Table 16.2 shows that the patterns of the types of childcare used differed amongst these regions.

Housework

As we have seen, three-quarters of the leaders say that they do less than half the housework (this includes the 18 per cent who do not carry out any housework at all). Again, however, there are significant gender differences when different career life-forms are compared.

As can be expected, the proportion of men who do not do any housework at all or very little is even higher amongst the men in the traditional career life-form, namely 97 per cent. Interestingly, 86 per cent in dual-career life-forms do less than half the housework. For women, 51 per cent in the mixed-career life-form do less than half the housework, 20 per cent do half and 29 per cent do more than half. The proportions are about the same for the women who live in the dual-career life-forms.

In Table 16.3 we compare the amount of housework carried out by men and women by country groupings. It is clear that there are significant gender

Table 16.3 Amount of Housework Carried out, by Country Grouping and by Gender (%)

Country Grouping	Men			Women		
	Less than 50%	50%	More than 50%	Less than 50%	50%	More than 50%
Southern Europe	95%	4%	1%	74%	12%	14%
North/Western Europe	91%	6%	3%	57%	21%	22%
Eastern Europe	94%	4%	2%	30%	24%	46%
Scandinavia	80%	16%	4%	36%	27%	37%
Other Countries	87%	8%	5%	50%	22%	28%

differences in the five regions. It also shows that there are large differences between women, while the differences between men are quite small. In all regions, at least 80 per cent of men do less than half the housework. In Southern Europe, North/Western Europe and even Eastern Europe the proportion of men who do less than half the housework is around 95 per cent. The percentage of women who do less than half the housework is also high in Southern and North/Western European countries: 72 per cent of women in Southern Europe and 66 per cent of women in North/Western Europe do less than half the housework. These statistics suggest that housework in these countries is often carried out by others.

In the countries outside Europe the gender differences in relation to housework are as follows: 88 per cent of men and 53 per cent of women do less than half the housework and 13 per cent of men and 47 per cent of women do half or more of the housework.

In the Scandinavian countries men do more housework than the men in the 'other country' groupings: 17 per cent of men in Scandinavia do 50 per cent of the housework. Still, the gender differences in the Scandinavian countries are significant. Whereas 20 per cent of men do half or more of the housework, the percentage of women who do the same is 64 per cent. Most significant, however, are the gender differences in Eastern Europe. Here, 46 per cent of women do more than half and 24 per cent half the housework, whereas for men the percentages who do more than half the housework is 2 per cent and half of it 4 per cent.

The data on childcare and housework among top leaders support earlier research which suggests that, while more and more women have moved into paid employment, thus sharing the provider role in the household, most men do not share the unpaid work such as childcare and housework (see e.g., Friberg, 1990; as well as chapters 13–15).

Conclusion

Social science research has over and over again shown that men's and women's relation to and embeddings in the worlds of paid work, career and family differ. Compared to men, women are more family-oriented, while men more work-oriented. This work v. family orientation makes itself felt in choices about types of work and career, working hours, part-time/full-time employment and even whether or not attachment to the sphere of work is continuous or not. Through these social practices, women and men help maintain a gender labour market (Walby, 1988; Allen, 1997). Much of the research in which these gendered patterns are found is based on Census data, where women and men in certain cohorts are compared, and/or data where women and men with different occupational and social backgrounds are compared (Billing and Alvesson, 1994). It is, in other words, unusual that men and women in similar occupations and positions are compared. Our study offers a unique opportunity to investigate how women and men who are at the same levels in top positions relate to the dominant career discourse with its masculine inscription.

We found that male and female top leaders chose different career life-styles as solutions to the demands this discourse places on them, and identified four forms: traditional, mixed, dual and single-career life-forms. These different career life-styles and their distribution amongst the male and female top leaders, the presence/absence of children as well as the work situation of the partners to the top leaders were analysed in this chapter together with the gender division of labour regarding childcare and household tasks. The data show that there are clear differences between female and male top leaders, when the different life-forms for the sample as a whole are considered. One such difference is the frequent presence of the traditional career life-form amongst men and the high proportion of women living in single career life-forms. Another is that more men than women have partners who work part-time and do not have a career. Thirdly, in the dual career life-forms, the partners of the male leaders have lower leadership positions, while the partners of the women more often have leadership positions at higher levels. A fourth difference is that even those men who live in career life-forms with partners who also have a work career do little of the housework and undertook little of the childcare when the children were small. Women as a whole do more of the housework and childcare.

This chapter has also shown the importance of a contextualisation of these different life-forms. The five regional groupings provided such a contextualisation. Some of the above-mentioned gender differences were also found when the whole sample was divided into the five regional groupings. It is worth noting in this respect that gender differences were particularly great amongst the top leaders from the 'other' grouping, in which we placed countries outside of Europe (Japan and those formerly belonging to the British Empire). Gender differences were also large in North/Western Europe and Southern Europe, while, these were smaller in Scandinavia and Eastern Europe. In the Eastern European countries, however, housework tasks provided an exception. Only a few of the men and a very high proportion of the women carried out more than half the housework. These findings where North/Western Europe can be placed together with Southern Europe and 'other countries', while Scandinavia can be placed together with Eastern Europe, is also supported in a comparison of the different career life-forms. More top leaders in Scandinavia and Eastern Europe have moved away from the expectations traditionally connected to work careers, and this is – not surprisingly – particularly true for the women. This result can be attributed to the long history of paid work for women in these countries, but also to active attempts to bring about gender equality in these countries. Most of the male top leaders in North/Western Europe, Southern

Europe and 'other countries' live in either a traditional or a mixed career life-form. Traditional divisions of labour dominate in these regions. The relatively high percentage of women living in single-career life-forms may also indicate how difficult it is to create alternative career life-forms in these regions. Despite attempts to the contrary, we would argue that these different strategies to combine family and work career are still framed through the existence of a hegemonic career discourse. It is difficult to say whether this discourse will be challenged or maintained in the future. Developments, such as processes of globalisation, increased competition for control of world markets as well as the dismantling of welfare state, seem to suggest that strategies in the future will more closely resemble the economies that at present dominate the world market.

Notes

1. See Bourdieu (1977; 1988) for an explanation of the concept of field.
2. See Andersson (1993, 1996) and Hansson (1996) for further elaborations of these newer usages of the concept of career, and Esseveld (1988) for an analysis of familial and work roles as a totality.
3. We use organisation in a broad sense to refer to political parties, unions, organisations and bureaucracies, etc., and thus as a concept that is used interchangeably with the concept of field.
4. That does not mean, however, that an individual cannot place loyalty towards his own profession or career before a loyalty to the organisation. A change of organisations happens frequently and is part of this work career. But such a change does not affect the relation between family and organisation; even today, it is nearly impossible to motivate a change of profession and/or organisation by referring to a loyalty to one's family, for example by arguing that work.
5. See Andersson (1993) for a further discussion.
6. An analysis of the empirical material shows that there are large gender differences in career life-styles in the fields of politics and business as well as when the five regions are compared. Space does not allow us to present the results of this analysis.
7. Scandinavia usually refers to Denmark, Norway and Sweden, but here includes Finland. Israel is excluded from the analysis, since we were unable to construct life-forms out of the existing data. It is also important to point out that the countries included in Scandinavia and Southern Europe differ from the countries included in the previous chapter.
8. These expectations are based on the long history of attempts by governments in these countries to bring about class equality and paid work for everyone, including women, while on the other hand helping maintain a traditional division of labour in the home (Vianello and Siemienska, 1990).
9. In the rest of this chapter, we will present only six of the above categories for career life-forms: traditional career life-forms for men, mixed for men and women, dual for women and men, and single for women. The few women in the traditional career life-forms (two out of 698 women) and the few men in the single-career life-forms (46 out of 720 or 6.4 per cent) are not included in the following analysis. Percentages excluded differ by country groupings since the single

men can be placed on a continuum with a high of 10 per cent in the Scandinavian countries and a low of 4.5 per cent in North/Western Europe, with the other groupings in between.

10. Even though the top leaders were asked to give the type of childcare that was most prevalent during the children's pre-school years, many of them answered by placing a cross in a number of boxes where different alternatives were given. We suggest that there are primarily three explanations for this. First, different types of childcare were used for different children and/or the same child. Secondly, different types of childcare may have been used at the same time, e.g., one parent plus state day care, public and private day care together with care by other family members. In this alternative the top leaders may have wished to emphasise that they shared responsibility for childcare for the child(ren) with other forms of childcare. In our presentation the category 'self' is used when the top leader indicated that s/he was primary caretaker or shared childcare with other types of childcare. Similarly, 'other' means that childcare was carried out by a partner, or by a partner together with other forms of childcare. Private and public childcare are also extended to include other types of childcare, such as au pair/nanny, other family members. The category of 'other' includes all types of childcare not mentioned above, such as care by other family members, by au pair/nanny, by both parents.

Part IV
The Cultural Dimensions of Gender (In)equality in Élites

Introduction

Cultural forms of gender segregation symbolically legitimate and support historically shaped gender inequalities, by which in turn they are continuously reproduced. They engender public and professional tasks and functions, defining normatively how they should be achieved and performed. They reserve careers leading to the most powerful positions in society to men, describing them as intimately connected with dominance and rationality, seen in opposition to constructions of femininity. They constitute part of the 'invisible barriers', which exclude women from positions of power. And they partly explain why gender legislation and its implementation to date show such limited success.

This part approaches culture as a crucial factor in the realisation of gender equality. Recognising the complexity of cultural phenomena, we can take only a small part of the cultural expressions into consideration here, looking at some of the perceptions, attitudes and values of political and business élites on the integration of women into the public sphere and into decision-making positions.

Chapter 17 presents a description of the outcomes. It demonstrates that assumptions related to gender equality issues generally vary between respondents of different organisational ranks, resulting in a greater consensus of male and female viewpoints at the highest levels.

Theoretically inspired by the sociology of knowledge, chapter 18 illustrates the perceptions of gender inequality and the explanations of women's under-representation in leading positions.

Chapter 19 discusses the perspectives of political and business leaders within the framework of different welfare regimes.

Its arguments are followed in chapter 20 which shows that macro-social structures play a crucial role in shaping attitudes and values on gender equality in élites, and focuses on the interplay between macro-social factors and individual characteristics.

17
Hierarchies, Attitudes and Gender
Litsa Nicolaou-Smokoviti and Burt Baldwin

Introduction

This chapter focuses on the issue of attitudinal differences/similarities between leaders at top levels of power in politics and the economy, particularly as to how these differences are related to gender.

Theoretical framework – a basic hypothesis

It is often assumed that there is a high level of homogeneity amongst the members of top-level management. Senior executives are thought to have similar job-relevant characteristics (education, training, experience, etc.) and also many job-irrelevant characteristics (gender, race, ethnicity, religion, etc.). However, some scholars are beginning to look at the extent of stratification at the top management level (Useem and Karabel, 1986; Tharenou, Latimer, and Conroy, 1994). Useem and Karabel, for example, note that the 'social and educational backgrounds of top senior managers are far higher than those not only of the average citizen, but also of other senior managers as well' (1986: 184). What many researchers are finding is that those who occupy the very top-level management positions often differ significantly from those one or two levels down and that these differences can operate to keep some members of the top management team from ever getting to the very top. Top-level management is itself hierarchically structured.

In most organisations, access to the very top-level positions is controlled by those who already fill these positions. Exceptions to this general case may be found with regard to some political or military organisations, but for private business corporations this generalisation tends to be axiomatic. There are gatekeepers at the entrance to the very top management, and only those whom they select gain entrance. This is not to say that external pressures, both direct and indirect, may influence gatekeepers' decisions, but only that in most organisations who will gain entry to the very top is determined by those already there.

Studies of the factors determining one's advancement up the organisation's managerial hierarchy have been produced in relatively large numbers over the past three decades (Zellman, 1976; Riger and Galligan, 1980; Stewart and Gudykunst, 1982; Morrison and Von Glinow, 1990; Fagenson, 1990; Morrison et al., 1992; Stroh, Brett and Reilly, 1992; Blum, Fields, and Goodman, 1994; Ohlott, Ruderman and McCauley, 1994). However, there is almost a complete lack of empirically based, quantitative studies dealing with promotion to the very top of the senior management hierarchy. Organisations are reluctant to reveal their promotion practices in such a sensitive area (Powell and Butterfield, 1994). As far as the present authors are aware, no studies exist based on first-hand observations of what influences gatekeepers to select one or two people from a pool of eligible candidates for entrance to the very top.

Kanter (1977) and other writers have pointed out that uncertainty is highest at the top level of the organisation. This calls for a high degree of trust amongst top managers, leading to the speculation that those brought into the top will in many ways be like those who are already there. Useem and Karabel (1986) have found this to be the case with regard to education and social class variables. It is also likely to be the case with regard to attitudes and beliefs held by top managers, which are related to the organisation's activities and its cultural context.

If the need for mutual trust increases as we go from lower to higher levels of senior management, we would expect to find a higher level of attitudinal consensus at the very top level of the organisation than at lower levels of the top management team. It is unlikely that the gatekeepers to the top of senior management will recruit new members with work-relevant attitudes widely divergent from their own.

Our central hypothesis is that attitudinal homogeneity varies directly with position in the hierarchy: as we go from lower levels to higher, we will find higher levels of attitudinal homogeneity. We will assess this hypothesis by contrasting male to female attitudinal responses at different hierarchical levels. If indeed attitudinal homogeneity is high at the very top, there should be little difference between men and women at this level. As we go down the hierarchy, attitudinal differences between men and women are expected to increase.

A corollary of our basic hypothesis reflects the fact that in virtually all major business and political organisations men hold all or close to all the top positions. In so far as these men establish the attitudinal baseline for top management as a whole, we would expect to see a growing attitudinal consensus as leaders proceed from lower levels in the organisational hierarchy to higher levels. In other words, we hypothesise that, where lower-level managers have attitudes divergent from those of the top male managers, these attitudes will change in the direction of the top males as the individual goes from lower to higher levels in the managerial hierarchy.

Political and business leaders

Attitudinal consensus should be highest where the top management team has absolute control over who will be accepted to share power with them. As entrance to the top becomes influenced by factors beyond the control of the top management team, a lower level of attitudinal consensus would be expected. Thus, we would expect to find lower levels of confirmation for our hypothesis amongst political leaders, who are elected to their positions, than business leaders, whose position and advancement are determined by internal organisational considerations.

Given the nature of a country's political party system, a lower level of attitudinal homogeneity can be expected than will be found in typical private business organisations. One of the things which competing political parties do not share is a high degree of attitudinal homogeneity. This is not to say that attitudinal homogeneity will not be found in some areas (national security, foreign policy, etc.), but that the very basis for different political parties is the divergent interests and attitudes functional to them held by different sectors of the population.

A final consideration regarding attitudinal homogeneity of business and political leaders is the country's socio-economic system. With respect to the specific focus of this chapter, different socio-economic systems may endorse divergent perspectives on the role of women in society in general, and as high-level business and political leaders in particular. Gender equality, for example, is more consistent with socialist political ideology, which is based on egalitarian principles than with capitalist ideology with its emphasis on individualism and competitiveness.

Methodological considerations

Hierarchical level

The measurement of one's position in the hierarchical level amongst senior managers in business organisations or senior political leaders was based on responses given to a question eliciting the title to one's present job. The hierarchies in both political and business organisations were divided into four levels. For the business leaders, the top level was composed of those who listed themselves as 'chief executive of a corporation' (N = 183). The second hierarchical level was made up of those who noted that they were 'Member of the central board of a corporation' (N = 242). Those indicating that they were branch managers composed level three (N = 241) and senior managers level four (N = 61). Turning to the political leaders, the top level was composed of those who listed themselves as member of the national cabinet, president or vice-president of parliament or head of the majority party (N = 90). The second level contained leaders who noted that they were an elected governor, head of opposition party or president/vice-president of a parliamentary committee (N = 87). Level three contained those listing themselves as mayor of a major city, member of the national parliament, member of the national central board of a party or member of the central judiciary (N = 434), and level four peripheral offices (N = 18). For most of the analysis, levels three and four for both business and political samples are combined due to the low number of cases in level four. We ended up with 735 business leaders and 762 political leaders.

Attitudinal variables

There are two clusters of attitudinal variables, which will be used to assess our hypotheses dealing with attitudinal homogeneity and hierarchical level. The first cluster has a common theme: 'explanations' for why men occupy almost the entire top level management positions in virtually all social organisations.

Six such explanations are given. We will refer to these collectively as the 'Men in Power' set. They are:

1. This is what women prefer.
2. Women lack special training.
3. Women are isolated in a male environment.
4. Society is organised in such a way that women do not reach top positions.
5. It's due to the way women are raised.
6. Women's lack of informal contacts.

The second cluster of attitudinal variables does not have a specific theme, but addresses the general area of 'Women and Work.' As such, this attitudinal cluster will be referred to as the 'Women and Work' set. Two of the seven variables deal with the respondent's specific organisational affiliation:

1. Are women generally accepted in leadership positions in your area?
2. Are men and women treated equally in your organisation?

The next four questions deal with general level women and work-related questions:

3. Women have to achieve more than men for the same recognition.
4. Men should have more right to scarce jobs than women.
5. The family suffers when women work full-time.
6. A paid job is best for woman's independence.

The final question does not deal with women and work issues, but solely with the acquisition of power, be it by men or women:

7. Power is based on networks of informal relations.

We will test our hypotheses by comparing mean attitudinal differences between men and women at the different levels of the top management hierarchy. We will use the three category typology of countries described in the methodological chapter for testing our socio/economic system hypothesis.

In proceeding with our analysis, our primary concern will be with attitudinal consensus at different levels of the top management team. At this level of the analysis, we will not be concerned with the actual meanings of the attitudes, but with patterns of agreement and disagreement amongst top-level managers of both genders. We will look at important differences related to the meanings of the attitudes following this higher order analysis.

Major findings

Looking at all of the business leaders, regardless of their location in the senior management hierarchy, we notice widespread discrepancies between men and women managers (1 = strongly agree, 5 = strongly disagree).

For 11 of the 13 attitudes, statistically significant gender differences were found. For the 'Women and Work' items, disagreement was total: there was not one attitudinal variable where men and women substantially agreed with each other. For the 'Men in Power' set, gender disagreement was found for four of the six items. However, when gender attitudinal comparisons are carried out at different levels of the senior management hierarchy, the relationship between gender and attitudinal position becomes more complicated.

Looking at the top-level senior managers in business organisations, we find statistically significant attitudinal differences for only four of the 13 variables, two variables for each of the two clusters being examined. This indicates a much higher level of attitudinal consensus amongst top-level senior managers than is found when we look at all of the managers as a group. Turning to level 2 managers, the degree of attitudinal consensus drops. Statistically significant differences are found for only one of the 'Men in Power' variables, but for six of the seven 'Women and Work' items. Gender differences increase even more as we turn to level 3 managers. Here we find substantial differences on ten of the 13 items (four for the 'Women in Power' attitudinal cluster and six for the 'Women and Work' cluster). It is obvious that attitudinal consensus is highest amongst top-level senior managers and decreases as we proceed to level 2 and again as we go to level 3.

Turning to the political leaders, we find that when we consider the respondents as a whole, statistically significant gender differences emerge for 11 of the 13 attitudinal items.

As with the business leaders, disagreement between men and women political leaders was noted for all of the 'Women and Work' items and for four of the 'Men in Power' items. When we look at the pattern of attitudinal agreement across hierarchical levels, we also find a pattern similar to the one found for business leaders. For the political leaders, however, attitudinal consensus is high for both levels 1 and 2, but then drops substantially as we move on to level 3. At this level, statistically significant disagreements are noted for nine of the 13 items; this drops to just three out of 13 disagreements for level 2 leaders and four out of 13 for leaders at level 1. These findings, combined with those noted for the business leaders, argue that, for both business and political organisations, attitudinal homogeneity is relatively high at the top levels of senior management, but decreases substantially as we go down the levels.

The above findings support our basic hypothesis that attitudinal homogeneity varies with level in the top management hierarchy: the higher the level in the managerial hierarchy, the greater the degree of attitudinal homogeneity.

For the purposes of assessing our secondary hypothesis, we will consider the attitudes of the men at the top of the senior managerial hierarchy (level 1) to be the baseline for assessing differences in attitudes amongst top managers at different levels of the hierarchy. We can thus compare men and women separately at different levels of the hierarchy with men at level 1 to test our hypothesis as it applies to gender. Do managers lower in the hierarchy change their attitudes to become consistent with the top male managers as the former advance in the hierarchy?

The numbers indicate a partial confirmation of our second hypothesis, which is consistent for both business and political leaders: attitudinal differences between men at level 1 and men at level 3 are virtually non-existent. Given our two attitudes sets, men at level 3 have almost identical attitudes as our baseline group of level 1 males. However, for women, substantial attitude differences are noted between men at level 1 and women at level 3. For women business and political leaders, statistically significant attitudinal differences are found for seven out of the 13 items, although there are some differences with regard to the particular items on which there is disagreement. Clearly, then, as women become members of the top senior management team, their attitudes become more consistent with those held by male top-level senior managers. No similar changes occur for men as they proceed from lower to higher levels in the hierarchy, as there is a very high degree of attitudinal homogeneity amongst the men at all levels. In other words, regardless of a man's position in the managerial hierarchy, his attitudes are very likely to be close to those held by the men at the very top of the hierarchy. Not so for women, except for those who are already at the top.

Tables 17.1 and 17.2 show that, disregarding hierarchical level, strong attitudinal differences exist between men and women top-level managers. By controlling for hierarchy, however, we find that the overall gender differences noted are primarily a reflection of gender differences at the lowest

Table 17.1 Comparisons of Attitude Clusters by Hierarchical Level and Gender: Business leaders (t-test)

Attitude Cluster	Hierarchical Level							
	All Cases		One		Two		Three	
	M	**F**	**M**	**F**	**M**	**F**	**M**	**F**
Men in power								
What women prefer	3.79	3.56*	3.31	3.75	3.41	3.59	3.43	3.65
Lack of training	3.66	3.62	3.71	3.64	3.50	3.60	3.74	3.63
Women isolated at work	2.85	2.75	2.78	2.92	2.78	2.71	2.96	2.67**
Way society organised	2.90	2.70*	3.00	2.89	2.75	2.76	2.96	2.58**
Way women raised	2.98	2.73**	2.89	2.53*	2.95	2.89	3.08	2.71**
Lack informal contacts	3.40	2.82**	3.45	3.06*	3.41	2.77**	3.37	2.75**
Women and work								
Women accepted as leaders	2.53	2.76**	2.68	2.62	2.49	2.79*	2.46	2.80**
Women treated equally	2.44	2.71**	2.44	2.26	2.47	2.70	2.54	2.96**
Women must achieve more	3.15	2.30**	3.12	2.38**	3.08	2.26**	3.26	2.29**
Scarce jobs go to men	4.07	4.40**	4.12	4.23	3.85	4.26**	4.21	4.58**
Family suffers if women work	2.75	3.47**	2.78	3.35**	2.73	3.64**	2.73	3.51**
Job best for independence	2.48	2.08**	2.23	1.96	2.62	2.19**	2.55	2 0.07**
Power informal networks	2.95	2.76*	2.95	2.91	3.09	2.75*	2.83	2.70
Total N	349	378	99	84	112	129	138	165

*p < 0.05, **p < 0.01.

level of the hierarchy. The largest attitudinal differences found are between women at level 3 and men *at any level*. As the women move from level 3 to level 1, their attitudinal differences with men decline substantially so that, as we approach the top of the hierarchy, gender differences have substantially decreased. For all 13 attitude items, the change in women's attitudes from level 3 to level 1 consistently move in the direction of men at level one.

Table 17.2   Comparisons of Attitude Clusters by Hierarchical Level and Gender: Political Leaders (t-test)

Attitude Cluster	Hierarchical Level							
	All Cases		One		Two		Three	
	M	**F**	**M**	**F**	**M**	**F**	**M**	**F**
Men in Power								
What women prefer	3.62	3.74	3.72	3.79	3.03	4.10*	3.73	3.92
Lack of training	3.68	3.51	3.89	3.79	3.83	3.79	3.73	3.83
Women isolated	2.95	2.63**	3.03	2.70	2.92	2.43	3.05	2.62**
Way society organised	2.63	2.42*	2.66	2.40	2.60	2.38	2.61	2.30**
Way women raised	3.02	2.74**	2.94	2.67	3.01	3.05	3.11	2.55**
Lack informal contacts	3.22	2.62**	3.13	2.32**	3.37	2.60**	3.21	2.55**
Women and Work								
Women accepted as leaders	2.41	2.80*	2.36	2.54	2.73	3.13	2.38	2.79**
Women treated equally	2.39	2.95*	2.38	2.93*	2.83	3.07	2.40	3.05**
Women must achieve more	2.96	2.00**	3.07	2.16**	2.47	2.90*	2.90	1.99**
Scarce jobs go to men	4.30	4.478*	4.49	4.40	4.38	4.32	4.32	4.47
Family suffers if women work	3.25	3.60**	3.37	3.16	3.23	3.71	3.26	3.55*
Job best for independence	2.51	2.08**	2.51	1.96*	2.35	1.82	2.59	2 0.27**
Power informal networks	2.77	2.61*	2.78	2.58	2.91	2.73	2.67	2.57
Total N	343	361	44	43	47	45	211	213

*p < 0.05, **p < 0.01.

Country groupings

A final consideration in our analysis of attitudinal differences by gender and position in the top-level management hierarchy is the grouping of countries by divergent socio-economic systems. We will follow the general typology used in this book.

Looking first at the business leaders, we find that for all three groups of countries there is a very high amount level of attitudinal homogeneity at

Table 17.3 Comparisons of Attitude Clusters by Level 1 Men vs Level 3 Men and Level 3 Women: Business and Political Leaders (t-test)

	Business leaders			Political leaders		
	Level 1 Men	Level 3 Men	Level 3 Women	Level 1 Men	Level 3 Men	Level 3 Women
Attitude Cluster						
Men in power						
What women prefer	3.31	3.43	3.65*	3.72	3.72	3.92
Lack of training	3.71	3.74	3.63	3.59	3.73	3.54
Women isolated	2.78	2.96	2.67	3.03	3.05	2.62*
Way women raised	3.00	2.96	2.58**	2.66	2.61	2.30*
Lack informal contacts	3.45	3.37	2.75**	3.13	3.21	2.55**
Women and Work						
Women accepted as leaders	2.68	2.46	2.80	2.36	2.38	2.72**
Women treated equally	2.24	2.55	2.96**	2.38	2.40	3.05**
Women must achieve more	3.12	3.26	2.29**	3.07	2.90	1.99**
Scarce jobs go to men	4.13	4.21	4.58**	4.49	4.32	4.47
Family suffers if women work	2.78	2.73	3.51**	3.37	3.26	3.55
Job best for independence	2.23	2.55*	2.07	2.51	2.59	2.73
Power informal networks	2.95	2.83	2.70	2.78	2.67	2.57
Total N	99	138	165	44	211	213

*$p < 0.05$, **$p < 0.01$.

the very top level of the senior manager hierarchy. In all three groupings there is only one attitude variable (a different variable for each of the three groups) where there is a statistically significant gender difference. For the less developed and social democratic countries a high level of attitudinal differences at level 3 is found. This is in sharp distinction to the free market countries, where we find six statistically significant differences at level 2, and ten differences at level 3. For these countries there is a clear progression in attitudinal homogeneity as we proceed from level 3 to level 1.

Turning to the political leaders, a pattern similar to that of the business leaders is found.[1]

There is a high degree of attitudinal homogeneity for the combined 1 and 2 levels for all three country groupings. For the free market and social democratic countries only one attitude variable is statistically significant between men and women leaders at the top level of the managerial hierarchy. For the less developed countries, the respective number is two. We thus find a high degree of attitudinal homogeneity at the top level for all three sets of countries. Looking at those managers at the low end of the hierarchy, we find a slight decrease in attitudinal homogeneity for the less developed and social democratic countries: two of the items differing significantly for the former set of countries and four items for the latter. For the free market countries, however, statistically significant differences are found between men and women lower level managers for twelve of the thirteen items.

Attitudinal content

Thus far we have been looking at the pattern of responses to the attitudinal items rather than to the actual meaning associated with each item. In this section, we will look at meanings to see if they are related to the patterns already discussed. Looking first at the business leaders, we earlier found that level one men and women managers differed on four of the thirteen attitude items they were asked to respond to (see Table 17.1). For three of these four items, statistically significant differences were found at all three levels indicating a fairly widespread disagreement between men and women throughout the top managerial hierarchy. Women were much more likely to agree with the item that men are in power because women lack informal contacts, that women have to achieve more than men for the same recognition, and that the family does not suffer if they work. Men and women differ on these items across all three levels. For the political leaders (see Table 17.2), disagreements were also found across all three levels for four items, two of which are the same as already noted for the business leaders: men are in power because women lack informal contacts and women have to achieve more than men for the same recognition. These two items separate men from women throughout the top-level management hierarchy for both business and political leaders.

Looking again at Tables 17.1 and 17.2 we find that, for both business and political leaders, men and women throughout the hierarchy are roughly in agreement that power in organisations is based upon informal networks. Women consistently endorse this attitude more than men, but the differences are statistically significant only for level 2 business leaders. Businessmen at level 2 in the hierarchy disagree more than any other group with the notion that power in organisations is based upon informal networks.

Conclusion

In this chapter we have examined the attitudes of leaders at top levels of power in politics and the economy, looking for differences and similarities, particularly as to how these relate to gender. We did find attitudinal differences at different levels of the hierarchy, but at the very top there is similarity of attitudes between the genders.

More specifically, our analysis led to the following conclusions: (1) attitudinal homogeneity increases as we go higher up in the power structure; (2) the dynamic underlying such a finding is that women who go from lower to higher levels are the ones who are changing their attitudes, thus accounting for the high level of attitudinal homogeneity at the top. Men, regardless of their level, agree on virtually all of the attitudinal items; (3) men and women throughout the hierarchy disagree over two central items: women feel that they have to achieve more than men for the same recognition, and women feel that the informal network is more important for obtaining power than do the men.

Our above findings conform in many ways to the findings of previous studies. In most organisations, access to the very top leadership positions is controlled by men who already fill these positions. This generalised trend tends to be axiomatic in private business, with a few exceptions in political organisations. We read about 'gatekeepers' at the entrance to the very top management level who determine entry to that very top level and select out of a pool of eligible candidates. What is required from prospective leaders is *high trust* that in many ways they will be like those who are already there, and *attitudinal consensus*, i.e. similar attitudes and beliefs with the top leadership team. By the fact that in virtually all major business and political organisations men hold all or close to all of the top-level positions, they establish the attitudinal baseline for top leadership as a whole. The specific mechanisms that lead few women to the top have still to be defined.

Despite the general trends for globalisation and convergence in such social issues as women's participation at top levels of leadership and power, there are divergent trends and national discrepancies, as shown in this research. Different socio-economic systems and cultural differences account for attitudinal differences in the groups of countries studied by gender and position in the top-level leadership positions. This means that gender perceptions, attitudes and behaviour are to a great extent culturally and socially defined.

Therefore, the gender differences on various hierarchical levels can be partly explained by one or a combination of the following reasons: (a) top male leaders recruit only women who conform; (b) stereotyping of roles as promoted by the mass media and perpetuated by the cultural and social environment; (c) economic and organisational conditions such as part-time employment – a fast-developing trend in the labour market – being negative for women moving up to top positions and expecting a competitive career with men; (d) contradictions and often a distorted picture of the 'successful woman' shaping men's behaviour patterns and limiting women's motivation for top careers (unless entry is already established in family businesses or political careers, where there is no gender competition); (e) social and economic gender inequality which remains strong in many countries.

Yet variables examined in this research (as, for example, informal contacts of women, organisation of society, upbringing of women, etc.) are subject to change and should not be considered in their static condition, but rather in the light of their inner dynamics and historical dimension.

At the end of the twentieth century, a crisis seems to afflict women, as attitudes, perceptions and actual social behaviour towards women are influenced negatively by economic conditions. On the other hand, some new developments seem to favour women, and appropriate legislation promotes and supports gender equality in a broader sense, at the national, European and international level. Improved education and increasingly delayed marriage and childbearing have created a pool of qualified women available for managerial positions.

In order to evaluate better the present situation and to estimate trends and prospects, the following should be further taken into consideration:

- trends in the labour market at the national, European and international level;
- trends in the area of education and professional training;
- anticipated legal and institutional arrangements regarding women's rights;
- the role of new technology and, more especially, information technology and its impact upon labour;
- the changing broader social perceptions and attitudes as to the role of women in the family, work and the broader social environment;
- demographic pressures as well as mobility and flexibility issues in the labour market relative to the abolition of national borders;
- the role of mass media, their influence on politics and shaping of the 'model' woman.

An examination of the above factors and trends within their historical context will throw further light on the reasons and the dynamics of the vast discrepancies in gender equality. Better understanding can create more appropriate conditions for bringing antagonistic partners closer together. There is a great need for further comparative longitudinal studies of gender equality issues and problematic areas which will permit comparisons and a follow-up of trends in which women themselves should be actively involved. As it was discussed in an international forum of ILO (1997), women themselves should take the burden of breaking through the 'glass ceiling', promoting gender equality at the top levels, complying with rising ethical considerations and social realities.

Note

1. Due to the overall low number of cases falling into levels 1 and 2, they have been combined for the country grouping analysis of political leaders so as to provide a sufficient basis for comparison.

18
Perspectives on Gender Cultures in Élites

Brigitte Liebig

Introduction

The transformation of gender relations in modern society is characterised by a considerable cultural lag. Strategies of gender equalisation based on structural changes often encounter a fairly unchanged symbolic order of gender difference and inequality. Conventional perceptions and feelings about gender, family, work and career apparently delegitimate endeavours to promote women's integration into public life, particularly at the level of leadership and authority. At the top of political and economic institutions, occupied by the heirs of the ruling classes of previous centuries (Bottomore, 1993), gender parity is still far from being achieved.

This chapter starts from the assumption that gender-related ways of thinking constitute a crucial determinant of women's upward mobility and success. Since patterns of meaning are strongly influenced by those having the power to define social reality (Berger and Luckmann, 1966), today's decision-makers are subjects of the analysis. Studying their modes of thinking about gender and power provides us with knowledge about societies' most powerful cultural potential for taking action. We will ask if they do perceive differences between men and women, and if their answers differ with regard to their sex, age or field of responsibility. By setting their views in relation to various social variables, we will try to identify those leaders who mostly encourage or resist the realisation of equal chances for women and men at the top and in society in general.

Towards a relational definition of gender culture

Numerous theoretical and empirical studies have illustrated that taken for granted beliefs about the characteristics and potentials of men and women influence gender specific allocations of functions and positions, decisions about recruitment and promotion, and the construction and evaluation of jobs (e.g., Acker, 1991; Cockburn, 1991; Wetterer, 1992, 1995; Collinson,

D.L. and Hearn, 1996). Yet, a review of international studies reveals the existence of a variety of gender definitions in relation to historical, national, socio-cultural, economic and political contexts (Adler and Izraeli, 1988, 1994; Hearn and Parkin, 1988; Weiss, 1988; Adler, 1993). Comparative studies give cause to assert that, besides some universal characteristics, cultural and symbolic constructions of gender hierarchies vary according to the specific frames of reference and power relations by which they are constituted. This seems to be true for the political as well as the economic field: developments concerning political institutions in many countries of the industrialised world suggest that contextual factors, such as the persistent pressure of women's groups, gender equality legislation, growing legitimacy concerns of parties or simply the devaluation of the factual power of politics have had a crucial influence on the growing numbers of women in politics over the last two decades (cf. Epstein, 1988; Lovenduski and Norris, 1989; Dahlerup, 1991). Similarly, statistical data on occupational gender segregation confirm the argument that various determinants, such as a rapid growth in the demand for occupational experts together with a shortage of male human potential, an increasing female clientele, new theories of management, governmental action programmes or the depreciation of special occupational fields on the market can facilitate the entry of women into formerly male occupations, corporations and industries (cf. Kanter, 1977; Vianello and Siemienska, 1990; Berthoin and Izraeli, 1993; Adler and Izraeli, 1994; Reskin and Ross, 1995).

Recognising these results, a relational perspective on gender construction will be applied.[1] In other words: it will be argued that perceptions of gender difference and inequality, definitions of political or managerial activity, and attitudes towards the appropriateness of leadership for women always have to be analysed in relation to the social contexts within which they are developed. Gendered connotations of leadership and career, of economic and political profiles reflect an active approach to the social reality within which this knowledge is produced. These gendered meanings, gendered experiences and identities, as they translate, interpret and mediate historical and social conditions, shall be defined here[2] as 'gender cultures'.

Acceptance of occupational gender equality

The last decades of the twentieth century were marked by fundamental social changes. These were paralleled by an increasing critique of traditionally established social hierarchies, referring to socially constructed differences between ethnicities, beliefs, social strata, and between men and women. Increasing female participation in the educational and occupational system, a growing self-determination of the female body, and the invention of new household technologies were some of the factors calling in question the confinement of women to the private sphere (Beck-Gernsheim, 1983).

As the awareness of gendered social inequalities came out of the politicised circles in universities and women's interests groups, it affected the whole of society. In many industrialised countries gender inequalities became a valid item on the political agenda. However, faced with the inertia of equalisation processes, it seems reasonable to ask if and to what extent these changes actually touch the lives and minds of those people who are the opinion leaders and main actors in processes of social and cultural change – in our case, top executives and political leaders.

How do today's élites interpret gender relations, which places do they assign to men and women in the public and private sphere? How do they perceive the situation of women within their own working domain at the top of society? Do different national, institutional, generational, educational or family backgrounds have an impact on the interpretation of social gender reality? These questions will be approached here by looking at responses to a number of statements presented in the questionnaire. In each case responses were given on a Likert scale reaching from high (strongly agree) consent to complete rejection (strongly disagree).

First, we will look at attitudes concerning the sexual division of labour in general. All items proposed refer to the legitimacy and consequences of women's employment:

- Having a paid job is the best way for a woman to be an independent person.
- Family life suffers when the woman has a full-time job.
- When jobs are scarce, men should have more right to a job than women.

Based on these items, an additive index has been created which allows us to discern different orientation patterns in relation to individual, organisational and institutional variables.[3] Polarising values of the index have been classified as either 'high' or 'low' acceptance of working women, while values in between these extremes were defined as expressions of 'indifference'.[4]

The data demonstrate a significantly greater acceptance of occupational gender equality by female leaders in both economic and political élites relative to their male colleagues, although they are of approximately the same age, work at the same level and within the same organisation. Nevertheless, professional women can count on more respect within political than business circles, a result which is primarily caused by comparatively high rates of acceptance by male political leaders. Besides that, a generational effect is clearly visible: men belonging to the younger generation[5] give answers that are significantly more egalitarian than older men. If we select the division of labour within private life as a background variable which might especially influence male perspectives on gender and work, the results show that respondents living in traditional households, i.e. with unpaid working female partners, develop little understanding for working

Table 18.1   Index: 'Acceptance of Occupational Gender Equality' (%)

	Low	**Indifferent**	**High**	**N**
Total	35.3	31.7	33.0	(1,433)
men	47.7	29.6	22.7	(692)
women	23.8	33.6	42.6	(741)***
business	37.3	34.4	28.3	(721)
politics	33.3	28.9	37.8	(712)***
Men				
business	51.6	32.4	16.0	(343)
politics	43.8	26.9	29.2	(349)***
women				
business	24.4	36.1	39.5	(377)
politics	23.1	31.0	45.9	(364)
age-class				
Men				
1910–45	52.9	28.6	18.5	(384)
1946–70	41.0	30.9	28.0	(307)**
Women				
1910–45	23.5	31.7	44.8	(328)
1946–70	24.0	35.1	40.9	(413)
Partners				
men				
paid work	40.9	31.6	27.5	(396)
no paid work	60.3	29.1	10.7	(234)***
Women				
paid work	23.0	33.8	43.2	(521)
no paid work	20.0	44.4	35.6	(45)
primary sector	37.9	36.2	25.9	(58)
industry	38.3	32.2	29.5	(227)
trade	56.8	22.7	20.5	(44)
services	39.6	28.6	31.9	(91)
banks/insurance	25.6	41.4	33.1	(133)
others	34.4	45.3	20.3	(64)*
Party ideology				
Men				
left	28.0	28.8	43.2	(118)
centre	40.0	32.0	28.0	(100)
right	60.0	21.0	19.0	(100)***
Women				
left	15.2	27.2	57.6	(125)
centre	25.7	30.3	44.0	(109)
right	24.7	37.0	38.4	(73)

***p = 0.001; **p = 0.01; *p = 0.05.

women in general, while men living in dual-earner or dual-career (Papanek, 1973) partnerships more often express favourable attitudes. Evidently, this cannot be observed within the group of female leaders, in which partners in unpaid work are rare. At the organisational level the data reveal the trade sector as an area of low acceptance for working women, whereby rather backward orientations dominate the top of economic organisations in general.[6] On the other hand, political leaders tend to respond in accordance with the ideology they represent: here both genders answer mostly in consensus with their party orientation. That means that women do not favour occupational gender equality to the same degree across different party ide-ologies, although they still rate distinctly higher for equality than their male colleagues within the parties regardless of their left, centre or right philosophy.

As mentioned previously, several studies offer evidence that gender-stereotypical attitudes change parallel to economic, political and cultural transformations; and records of sex segregation document a strong relation between the numeric presence of women in occupational fields and domi-nant cultural orientations regarding occupational gender equality (Reskin and Padavic, 1994; Reskin and Ross, 1995). The findings suggest that cross-national differences in the acceptance of working women could be related to numerical indicators of gender equality, such as the female representa-tion in educational, occupational and political institutions in a nation. Table 18.2 shows the strength of correlation between these variables.

Highly significant, though not very marked, relationships between most of the variables listed here and the acceptance of occupational gender equal-ity in national élites support the thesis of an interaction between cultural and structural evolution. The data illustrate a close connection between women's representation within the higher educational system, the labour force, trade unions and political institutions, and the respect that members representing national élites have for them actually being there. Notably high coefficients result from setting the orientation pattern in relation to women's representation in parliament and political parties in 1991 and ten years before. Besides that, an increasing number of women in top positions of political leadership also seems to affect attitudes about equality at work in a positive way; only in relation to top civil service do we observe resis-tant or slowly changing modes of thinking concerning this question.

Attribution patterns of women's under-representation at the top

The gendered character of occupational and organisational activities, the fact that authority, competence and leadership are perceived as a certain kind of masculinity and in contrast to female characteristics has been the subject of many studies already (cf. Witz and Savage, 1992; Collinson D.L.

Table 18.2 Numerical Presence of Women in Educational, Occupational and Political Fields and Scores of Acceptance (Correlation Coefficients)

Female Percentage	**Acceptance of Occupational Gender Equality**			
	1981		**1991**	
	r	**r**	**r**	**N**
With university degree	0.07*	1,156	0.08**	1,156
In employment	0.14***	1,315	0.17***	1,375
Employed in dependent job	0.07*	957	0.09**	1,243
Employed in independent job	0.11***	871	0.10***	1,260
In unions	0.06	930	0.16***	1,101
In parties	0.23***	622	0.20***	694
In parliament	0.07**	1,319	0.25***	1,321
In senate	0.06	780	0.11***	910
In top positions of unions	0.10**	688	0.12***	1,090
In top positions of parties	0.15***	634	0.11***	861
In top civil service	−0.12***	894	0.04	995
In top political executive positions	0.04	922	0.10***	1,066

*** $p = 0.001$; ** $p = 0.01$; * $p = 0.05$.

and Hearn, 1996). But, apart from that, we do not know very much about the ways gender differences are culturally produced and maintained within the élites themselves. One way to approach this question is to analyse how members of today's political and economic élites interpret the sustained under-representation of women at the top. From the many possible explanations provided by everyday knowledge as well as from social science research only some of the most popular have been selected here. There are:

1. this is what women prefer;
2. women lack specific training;
3. society is organised so that women are prevented from reaching top positions;
4. it is due to how women are reared;
5. women lack powerful informal contacts;
6. women are isolated in a mainly male environment.

The statements imply two opposite orientation patterns: the first, based primarily on a social argumentation; the second, on individualistic patterns of thinking. While according to the 'individualistic' perspective, success or failure of female upward mobility is interpreted as the effect of a personal decision or deficit (as supposed by the first two items), 'social' ways of thinking prefer interpretations that situate the exclusion of women from top jobs within the context of social processes on the level either of society or of face-to-face interaction (as supposed by the rest of the statements). These two categories have been used as components of the index given in Table 18.3.[7]

Though on the whole indifference prevails, gender differences which cross-cut all other social categories characterise the responses: irrespective of leaders' institution their level of formal education, their partnership models, the generation they belong to, the industry they work in or the party ideology they defend, women answer in significantly more social terms than their male colleagues. But, besides this remarkable distinction, the differences within the gender categories should not be ignored: female politicians rate definitely more often in social ways than their business colleagues of the same sex, while men in both fields of society show greater cognitive unity. At the same time, we discover generational effects in the group of male respondents, whereby younger age seems to cause primarily a higher degree of indifference: a non-social orientation. Educational backgrounds have been listed here in order to show the bigger number of highly educated women who tend to interpret success as individual achievement first, while the proportion of individualistic vs. social orientation of men does not vary significantly in respect to the educational variable. However, it should be noted that non-traditional forms of division of labour within the household obviously might raise men's preference for social explanations. While few variations show up when orientation patterns are contrasted between industries, political ideology once more causes a strong polarisation. And again it affects primarily the group of men: as anticipated, respondents of the left tend towards social explanations, whereas members of right-wing parties argue more individualistically.

Perception of gender (in)equality

The refusal to accept women as superiors and doubts about their ability to meet the requirements of leadership are crucial elements of the subtle mechanisms that uphold women's exclusion from élites (cf. Collinson D.L., Knights and Collinson M., 1990; Collinson D.L. and Hearn, 1995). But how do female leaders feel about these cultural barriers in the political institutions and business corporations they head? And how do male executives and politicians perceive the quality of gender relations within the same organisations? Related (self-)perceptions not only reflect the situation of women in various organisations and national élites from a subjective, female or male point of view, but may constitute women's actual workplace equality and the career opportunities of junior female generations. Also here the respondents were asked, as we saw in the previous chapter in a different perspective, to assess the situation with the help of a rating scale:

Table 18.3 Index: 'Explanation Patterns for Women's Under-representation at the Top' (%)

	Individualistic	Indifferent	Social	N
Total	29.2	38.1	32.6	(1,385)
Men	35.3	41.7	23.5	(671)
Women	23.5	34.7	41.7	(714)***
Business	31.2	39.6	29.2	(695)
Politics	27.3	36.6	36.1	(692)*
Men				
business	37.2	41.1	21.6	(333)
politics	33.4	42.3	24.3	(338)
Women				
business	25.6	38.1	36.4	(360)
politics	21.5	31.2	47.3	(353)*
Age-class				
Men				
1910–45	38.9	37.3	23.8	(370)
1946–70	30.9	47.2	21.9	(301)*
Women				
1910–45	25.7	35.2	39.1	(307)
1946–70	21.9	34.2	43.8	(406)
Education				
Men				
low/middle	36.7	37.9	25.4	(319)
high	34.6	45.2	20.2	(341)
Women				
low/middle	21.5	32.0	46.5	(353)
high	25.6	37.4	37.1	(356)*
Partner[a]				
paid work	33.6	43.0	23.4	(381)
no paid work	41.4	38.8	19.8	(227)
Industry				
Total	30.9	39.6	29.5	(539)
Party ideology				
Men				
left	22.0	43.2	34.7	(118)
centre	32.6	46.3	21.1	(95)
right	45.3	34.7	20.0	(95)**
Women				
left	22.3	25.6	52.1	(121)
centre	22.3	31.1	46.5	(103)
right	17.6	31.1	51.4	(74)

*** p = 0.001; ** p = 0.01; * p = 0.05.
[a] Male respondents only.

- men and women are treated equally in your organisation;
- women are generally accepted in positions of leadership in your field;
- women have to achieve more than men to receive the same degree of recognition in your field.

In order to identify some of the individual, institutional and organisational conditions, which eventually provoke differences of perceptive patterns, an index has been created based on the total of responses given. Starting from the extreme values, the resulting range has been classified into either 'positive', 'indifferent' or 'negative' perceptions.

More than a third of all respondents believe that their political and economic organisations possess a rather high level of equality, and are convinced that in their own work environment female leadership is usually accepted. Yet, a considerable number also perceive deficiencies. Once more the results reveal a striking gap between the perspectives of male and female respondents, whereby men of the same age, position and organisation tend twice as much to assess gender equality as achieved. The gender gap in perception is even more pronounced within political institutions, where half the male respondents consider gender equality as already realised, while many female politicians take a much more critical view – this also compared to their female colleagues working in top management. This time, generational experience and educational background have no effect on the perspectives, neither within male nor female élite groups; and the way men evaluate female career chances and workplace conditions in general is obviously not influenced by the employment situation of their wives or partners. Besides more negative views expressed by male and female managers of industry and trade, corporate gender equality is perceived preponderantly positively across all types of economic organisations listed here. On the contrary, political ideology once more causes attitudinal differences between men: male members of right-wing parties significantly rate more optimistically than respondents from centre and left ideological backgrounds, irrespective of the fact that at the same time even left-wing men assess the situation rather positively compared to their female party colleagues.

Results like this raise questions about the appropriateness of assessments of members of élites in general: To what degree does their very personal perspective correspond to reality in the respective organisations and their management bodies? To answer this question, the subjective statements will be contrasted with the actual numbers of women in those organisations and élite groups, which have been evaluated by the respondents. Table 18.5 presents the results of an analysis which correlates the individual perceptions with the actual number of women in their respective corporations and parties.

In the majority not very strong and partly negative correlations suggest that the relation between the numerical parity of men and women in the

Table 18.4   Index: 'Perception of Gender Equality at the Workplace' (%)[a]

	Negative	Indifferent	Positive	N
Total	25.9	38.5	35.6	(1,372)
Men	17.4	34.2	48.4	(661)
Women	33.9	42.5	23.6	(711)***
Business	23.7	40.2	36.1	(662)
Politics	28.2	36.9	34.9	(710)
Men				
business	18.2	36.0	45.9	(314)
politics	16.8	32.7	50.6	(346)
Women				
business	28.8	44.1	27.1	(347)
politics	38.9	41.1	20.0	(365)**
Age-class				
1910–46	24.4	37.4	38.2	(684)
1947–70	27.5	39.6	32.9	(687)
Education				
low/middle	26.8	38.2	35.0	(665)
high	25.3	38.8	35.8	(695)
Partner[b]				
paid work	15.7	34.1	50.1	(381)
no paid work	19.5	33.2	47.3	(226)
Industry				
primary sector	19.6	47.8	32.6	(46)
industry	29.5	38.2	32.4	(207)
trade	27.9	39.5	32.6	(43)
services	23.5	41.2	35.3	(85)
banks/insurance	21.1	40.7	38.2	(123)
others	21.2	44.2	34.6	(52)
Party ideology				
Men				
left	27.1	33.1	39.8	(118)
centre	15.3	36.7	48.0	(98)
right	9.1	27.3	63.6	(99)***
Women				
left	46.1	35.2	18.8	(128)
centre	41.0	43.8	15.2	(105)
right	36.5	41.9	21.6	(74)

*** p = 0.001, ** p = 0.01.
[a] In all cases high correlations (r > 0.72) between the single items and the total value existed, indicating that the index measured only the interesting dimension 'perception of gender (in)equality'. The reliability coefficient of the scale was α = 0.63.
[b] Male respondents only.

Table 18.5   Numerical Presence of Women and Perception of Gender Equality in Organisations and Élites (correlation coefficients)

Percentage of Women In 1991	Perception of Gender Equality in Respective Élites					
	Men		Women		Total	
	r	n	r	n	r	n
In respective corporations						
employed	0.03	196	−0.02	212	−0.02	408
highly professional	0.05	143	0.00	150	0.00	293
in top management	23***	199	0.00	196	0.04	395
In respective parties						
members	0.04	196	−0.08	202	−0.02	398
in top positions	−0.02	238	−0.10	234	−0.08	472

*** p = 0.001.

respective fields and the perception of gender equality is not very strong or even the reverse (see also chapter 12 for a commentary on Kanter's thesis). This means that the increase of the quantitative presence of women either is not enough to have an effect or it goes together with a growing sensitivity towards inequalities within organisations and their élites. This tendency in particular characterises the political field, where perceptions of inequality can be noted more often in parties with higher numbers of female members and women in top positions. The same mechanism operates in business on the level of female employees: i.e., both male and female élites give lower equality scores, the higher the number of women in the respective corporations; a result indicating also the lack of legitimacy of business organisations with high numbers of female employees, but low numbers of female managers. However, at least in the case of male élite groups, a significant correspondence between positive evaluations and the actual number of women in the top management of their corporations exist. According to these findings, the perceptions of male respondents appear more directly related to numerical gender parity than do the perceptions of female politicians: a difference that might give a hint of the different frames of reference which men and women leaders adopt evaluating the situation.

Gender cultures providing opportunities

An overview of the three-orientation patterns under study reveals overlapping characteristics, which allow us to distinguish fundamental differences between gender cultures of different social groups. First, it is women who generally answer in more progressive terms supporting statements which in their consequences will facilitate women's access to the labour market and their upward mobility. Basically, it is the group of female left-wing top political leaders who provide the most favourable gender cultures for women's integration and progress in public and professional life as well as for female leadership. While the thinking of the female élite is characterised by a relatively high degree of unanimity with regard to women's issues, the convictions of male leaders appear divided: so, it is primarily the younger generation of men which evaluates gender relations on the basis of more egalitarian ideals. Well-balanced power relations within the private sphere, as it has been operationalised by the intra-familiar division of labour, sometimes also contribute to more unprejudiced male attitudes. And left, centre and right party ideologies provoke significant differences between dominant orientation patterns of men concerning gender equality. But, beyond all disagreements, it should be noted that political élites – in contrast to business leaders – on the whole advocate the importance of paid employment for women's lives and favour social and critical attitudes when asked about the actual state of gender equality in society and organisations. Across industries, the thinking of corporate élites demonstrates a lower standard of gender equality, notwithstanding the different degrees of horizontal and vertical gender segregation within economic fields (Rubery and Fagan, 1995).

Finally, the data reveal a close relation between orientation patterns and structural indicators of equality, such as the numerical presence of women in politics and business. It becomes obvious that the progressivity of basic assumptions on gender mostly corresponds to a comparatively higher level of equalisation, while the lack of the latter seems to blur the sense for its non-existence and its desirability. In other words, gender cultures of élites are not only providers of structural gender equality, but products of the structural relations and mechanisms which they determine.

Implications for action

Gender policies aimed at the equal representation of women within the political and economic sphere always should be accompanied by political steps, which increase the legitimacy of changing social realities. In order to realise equal gender rights, we need a deeply rooted culture of equality, which helps structural measures to achieve broad societal acceptance (Liebig, 1997). Only by a continuous articulation of gender definitions and inequalities can this be achieved. As a battlefield for the maintenance and change of dominant categories to perceive the world (Bourdieu, 1984), the political arena probably is one of the most important providers of cultural change towards gender equality. To improve the integration of female protagonists into the political field, therefore, is a necessary step on this road; it is the precondition for the regendering of occupational and organisational activities, and the reinterpretation of authority, competence and leadership. A further imperative step is that economic organisations and élites choose an active and positive approach to integrate women, not only in order to redeem their social responsibility, but to make use of the competitive advantages of a management which does value diversity (Cox and Blake, 1991). Their readiness to invent egalitarian ways of thinking reflects their general intelligence to adapt to social and economic transformations, and their capacity to master the challenges of the twenty-first century. But, finally, redefinitions of gender relations will in the end only be successful when supported and followed by the convictions of a vast majority of people.

Notes

1. The basis for this approach is provided by the sociology of knowledge (Mannheim, 1964).
2. For more reflections on gender cultures cf. Hofstede (1991) or Collinson D.L. and Hearn (1996).
3. Previously it was tested to see if the three items contribute to the measurement of the index in the same way: All items discriminated significantly, with correlation coefficients of $r > 0.62$. The new range of values was created on the basis of the 1st and 4th quartile, i.e. by putting 25 per cent of respondents with the highest values and 25 per cent of respondents with the lowest values respectively into one category.
4. For Hungary and Russia all tables list statements of political leaders only; for the USA only statements of business leaders are included; Norway's data rely exclusively on women's responses.
5. Categories have been constructed along the median ($N = 46.00/N = 1,686$) of the total age–class distribution.
6. Not illustrated in the table are gender differences of acceptance in all industries except for members of the primary sector and of 'other', i.e. not further identified sectors.
7. Items were previously tested for homogeneity and reliability ($\alpha = 0.50$).

19

The Social Construction of Gender

Lis Højgaard and Johanna Esseveld

Introduction: The social construction of gender

In this chapter we want to explore how the cultural discourse on gender affects gender construction and the ways in which it differentiates the male and female top leaders included in our study. More concretely, we will look at the extent to which a series of statements on women and men position the two groups of leaders differently within two types of contexts: one being a symbolic context, that is the content of the statements, and the other being a structural context, that is the overall social conditions, what we have called welfare state regimes, in which the female and male leaders are situated. The purpose of this endeavour is to discuss the meaning of cultural embeddedness for the social construction of gender.

The theoretical point of departure is, as indicated above, constructivist. In line with this approach we see gender as constituted by actions in social space, orchestrated by structural processes and a symbolic order of gender that can be distinguished analytically, but in practice are interwoven in a particular pattern: the cultural discourse on gender. Gender is thus conceived as a cultural dynamic that is created, renewed and maintained in interactive processes, which are integral parts of the reproduction of the social order. The interactive processes that shape, enact and change the cultural discourse on gender comprise the interaction of the genders, each gender's interaction with itself and the interaction between social praxes/social structures and the symbolic universe of gender. Gender is something we do and something we think (West and Zimmerman, 1987; Gherardi, 1994; Højgaard, 1996).

The cultural discourse on gender encompasses deep-rooted transpersonal universes of meaning and is structured as a binary opposition between femininity and masculinity. This differentiation creates the basis for the cultural discourse on gender which permeates the culture in its totality and which, in addition, is often a differentiation linked to power. In other words, one is either a man or a woman and every culture praxis has significance for and is interpreted as either masculine or feminine, is assigned feminine or masculine connotations and is inscribed in a relation of power. The assignation of masculine or feminine is not always fixed and unambiguous, but is fluid and ambiguous (Gherardi, 1994). Nevertheless, the basic logic of the cultural discourse on gender is differentiation. The ascription of difference to the two sexes takes place at numerous levels of social life and one of the ways to deconstruct the cultural discourse on gender is to focus on the contesting areas of difference and similarity, and to identify the context in which this contest occurs. One such contesting area is topleadership, where the attempt to identify the type, range and meaning of difference and similarity is widely debated (Eagly and Johnson, 1990; Ely, 1995; Alvesson, 1997; Korac Kakabadse A., Korac Kakabadse N. and Meyers, 1998).

The cultural discourse on gender – attitude statements

The cultural discourse on gender has, of course, numerous expressions, but for the purpose of the argument of this chapter we will focus on the attitudinal questions included in our questionnaire, which consist of a number of statements on the social position of women and men. We see these statements as expressions of the cultural discourse on gender and we analyse them with respect to their ability to differentiate between men and women and thereby contribute to the ongoing construction of gender.[1]

These statements are, thus, parts of the available cultural constructs that feed the social world with intelligibility with respect to the positions of men and women and represent a range of explanations to choose from. Since we want to discuss the meaning of contexts or cultural embeddednes for the social construction of gender, we have chosen to analyse the following two sets of statements, which differ in their embeddedness.

The first set covers six widely used and general explanations, which were referred to in the two previous chapters, as to why there are more men than women in society's top posts. More specifically these are:

1. that's what women want;
2. women don't have the proper education;
3. women are isolated in a mainly male environment;
4. the way society is organised prevents women from achieving top jobs;
5. it's due to women's upbringing;
6. women lack the crucial informal contacts.

These six statements represent different contextualisations in the explanations they offer on the low representation of women in top positions: an individual context, a cultural/environmental context in an abstract form (which can be compared to the more immediate or concrete reference to the respondents' own field or organisation in the second set of statements), a mixture of individual and societal context and finally a societal context.

A clear-cut individual context is only represented in statement 1, which explains the low level of representation of women in top positions with individual women and their preferences. It is worth noting that the explanation is restricted to women and that there is no explicit statement on the choice of individual men, as for instance: 'that's what men want' or 'that's because men do not want women in top positions'. The latter type of statement is missing, not because it was left out by accident, but because it does not exist in the collective discourse on gender construction in this area.[2] Only in statement 3 is there an explanation why there are more men than women in top positions. This statement can be interpreted to mean that men as a group exclude women as well as that male cultures, independent of individual men, exclude them. It is, thus, ambiguous and this goes for statement 6: 'women lack the crucial informal contacts' as well. This lack of contacts can be interpreted to be either women's self-inflicted problem or due to their exclusion by others, men or women. Statements 3 and 6 represent the cultural/environmental context component. Statement 2 expresses a mixture of individual and societal context. It can be understood both as a statement on the choice of women not to educate themselves as well as a statement that society does not provide women with a proper education. Statements 4 and 5 place the explanation with social conditions in general.

The second set of statements represent a concrete cultural contextualisation, in that it includes three statements that deal with women's and men's relation to their own organisation and/or field of reference:

7. women are normally accepted in leadership positions in my field;
8. men and women are treated equal in my organisation;
9. in my field, women have to achieve better than men to get the same re cognition.

These three statements refer to similar contexts, but differ in content. They can be placed on a continuum from what one might call a gender-neutral position in the second statement to a moderate expression of possible unequal treatment of female and male leaders in the first statement, to an overt expression of discrimination in the third statement.

Symbolic and structural contextuality

As mentioned above we are planning to look at how these statements – as representations of cultural discourses on gender – differentiate female and male leaders within two types of contextualities: *a symbolic contextuality* expressed in the content of the statements as discussed above and *a structural contextuality* expressing the overall social conditions in which female and male leaders are placed and express their opinions on the statements. We make use of these contexts to suggest that responses to statements not only will differ by gender, but will also differ due to the particular cultural and social contexts the leaders are embedded in.

By symbolic contextuality we understand the meaning incorporated in the sentences both in the sense that they express differences in agreement/disagreement between people and in the sense that they express a variety of gender neutral/discriminatory content.

The structural contextuality is provided through a model that places the countries included in the study in different welfare state regimes, which are expected to contextualise the international discourse on gender (meaning that responses from the male and female leaders will differ in different regimes).

Four welfare regimes

In order to test the hypothesis that the contexts of different welfare regimes play a role in the construction of gender, we divided the 27 countries included in our study into four groupings, through a combination of Gøsta Esping-Andersen's (1990) model for studying variations in welfare states, in which class relations are central, with feminist critiques and redefinitions of theories of the welfare state. In his attempt to explain changing modes of societal organisation, Esping-Andersen suggests that modern welfare states can be differentiated through their logic of organisation, their social stratification effects and their employment regimes. These criteria in turn are used by him to present three ideal typical welfare state regimes: social democratic welfare states, liberal and conservative regimes. While at a theoretical level his typology presupposes that the family is to be given a central place together with state and market, at an operational level the key analytical relationship is the one between state and market. Class inequalities and class politics are central to his theorising, and gendered social relations are largely neglected and/or underdeveloped (Daly, 1994; Borchorst, 1994).

Feminist researchers have proposed different ways through which this imbalance can be re-addressed. From them, we choose two approaches that focus on differences within and among welfare states.[3] These are the approaches by Jane Lewis (1992) and Ann Schola Orloff (1992). Lewis categorises welfare states into three models on the basis of whether women are viewed as workers and/or mothers: strong, moderate and weak breadwinner models. In the first type of welfare state, women are mainly recognised as wives and mothers and in a weak breadwinner model women are mainly treated as workers. In moderate breadwinner welfare states, women are recognised as both mothers and workers. Orloff (1992) distinguishes different types of families or households according to whether they are based on a traditional gender division of labour – with a male breadwinner and an economically dependent wife – or on a division of labour where care and economic responsibilities are more equally distributed.[4]

We combined the above-mentioned approach by Orloff with Esping-Andersen and came up with three groupings:

A. individually-based welfare regimes;
C. traditional welfare regimes based on a nuclear family and a traditional division of labour;
B. Welfare regimes between A and C, where both individual and family provide the basis for its social policies.

To these we added a fourth grouping – D – in which we placed the countries that until the late 1980s/early 1990s had state-based welfare regimes and which were excluded from the above theorising and models of welfare states.

The countries were placed into each of the four groupings in the following way:

A. Individual	B. Individual/Family	C. Traditional	D. Former state
Australia	Austria	Belgium	Hungary
Canada	England	Greece	Poland
Denmark	France	Israel	Russia
Finland	Germany	Ireland	Slovenia
Iceland	Japan	Italy	Czech Republic
New Zealand	the Netherlands	Portugal	
Sweden	USA	Spain	
		Switzerland	

In the analysis of the nine statements, we will compare the differences in the responses of the male and female top leaders in these four welfare state regimes. The existing literature on gender and welfare regimes suggests that individual welfare regimes, such as the ones found in the Scandinavian countries, are friendlier than others to women. An underlying assumption in this literature is that there is a correspondence between social practices and social discourses in different types of welfare states (Siim, 1988; Borchorst, 1994). Following this literature, the expectation is that countries with traditional divisions of labour and low representation of women in politics and business accept more traditional discourses on gender and portray more disagreement between the genders, whereas countries with more equal divisions of labour are expected to accept less traditional discourses on gender as well as present more agreement between the genders. In relation to the welfare regimes presented above, the greatest gender differences, then, are to be expected in the traditional welfare regimes, slightly lower differences in the individual/family regimes and fewest differences in the individual regimes.[5]

The analysis

The top leaders were asked to state their degree of agreement with these statements on a five-point Likert scale from totally agree to totally disagree. As we mentioned before, the first set of statements includes a number of standard explanations as to why there are more men than women in top positions in society in general, which we earlier named cultural discourses on gender and leadership. The second set of statements includes opinions about gender that relate to a more specific context, namely the field or organisation a particular top leader represents.

In the analysis we combine the symbolic and structural contextualization and present the answers to the nine statements in Tables 19.1 and 19.2.

In the following analysis we will, on the one hand, explore the power of the nine statements to differentiate male and female responses within each country grouping and thus the extent to which gender dichotomies are constructed in each welfare regime. On the other hand, we will compare the groupings with each other and thus explore the differences between the welfare regimes with respect to similarities and differences between the genders.

The power of differentiation within each welfare regime

The individual welfare regime

Table 19.1 shows that women and men voice similar attitudes only with regard to two of the statements. Both reject the individual statement 'that's what women want' and the mixed individual and societal statement 'women don't have the proper education' as explanations for why there is a lower representation of women than men in society's top positions. The table also shows that men disagree, although in different degrees, with all of the six statements. They disagree least with statements 3 and 4: 'women are isolated in a mainly male environment' and 'the way society is organised prevents women from achieving top positions'. This means that the men, even though as a group they don't agree with any of the statements, are leaning towards societal explanations and are somewhat ambiguous with respect to the environmental explanations. The women, on the other hand, agree with four of the six statements. Again, there are differences in the level of agreement amongst them. They agree most strongly with statement 6: 'women lack the crucial informal contacts' and statements 3 and 4. The women then voice fairly strong agreement with the environmental explanations and with the societal explanations.

Table 19.2 shows that of the three field-related statements it is the third 'in my field, women have to achieve more than men to get the same recognition', that draws the strongest disagreement between men and women.

Table 19.1 Leaders' Responses to Six General Statements, by Sex and Country Groupings[a]

	A. Individual			B. Individual/Family			C. Traditional			D. State-modified			E. Total		
	Men	Women	diff	Men	Women	diff	Men	Women	diff	Men	Women	diff	Men	Women	diff
Women want	-71	-95	24	-60	-81	21	-57	-56	1	+9	-14	23	-48	-61	13
Lack education	-79	-72	7	-68	-47	21	-66	-57	9	-106	-114	8	-76	-60	16
Women isolated	-4	+47	51	+11	+35	14	+27	+41	14	-24	-7	17	+5	+33	28
Society	-1	+47	48	+35	+61	26	+36	45	9	-6	+11	17	+21	+30	9
Upbringing	-11	+24	35	-22	+33	55	+25	+33	8	+14	+14	0	-2	+28	30
Informal channels	-24	+61	85	-24	+49	73	-35	+16	51	-58	-15	43	-32	+29	61

[a]The statistics for male and female respondents are calculated as follows. A point system is used, where those who strongly agree with a statement are given 2 points, those who agree 1 point, neither agree nor disagree 0 points, disagree −1 point and strongly disagree −2 points. These points are subsequently multiplied by the percentage of respondents within a particular response-category and these in turn are added/subtracted from each other.

Table 19.2 Leaders' Responses to Three Field-related Statements, by Sex and by Country Groupings

	A. Individual			B. Individual/Family			C. Traditional			D. State-modified			E. Total		
	Men	Women	diff	Men	Women	diff	Men	Women	diff	Men	Women	diff	Men	Women	diff
Women accepted as leaders	93	49	44	49	33	16	43	1	42	62	40	22	60	28	32
Equal treatment	86	35	51	30	-2	32	63	13	50	92	49	43	64	22	42
Women to achieve better	-20	80	100	11	76	65	-13	94	107	-30	66	96	-11	93	104

Men disagree and women strongly agree with this statement that refers to overt discrimination.

It is characteristic for the countries included in this welfare regime that men and women disagree on a majority of the statements: as a matter of fact, disagreement between them is greater than in any other type (total disagreement rate: 443).[6] This may be taken to indicate a rupture in gender construction in this regime. The disagreement is most strongly expressed as far as the discriminatory statement amongst the field-related statements and the combined individual/societal explanations of the general statements are concerned.

The individual/family welfare regime

Table 19.1 shows that the women and men in this welfare regime voice similar attitudes towards four of the six statements, and disagree on only two statements, namely 5 and 6. These represent the environmental and societal explanations for why there is a disproportionately high representation of men in top positions and suggest that this is due to women's upbringing and lacking of crucial informal contacts. The highest gender differences concern statement 6. Men disagree with four of the six explanations and agree only with statements 3 and 4. The latter, which include an environmental and societal explanation, suggest that the reason why there are few women in top positions is due to their isolation in a mainly male environment and to the way society is organised. The women in this welfare regime support the same four statements as do the women in the individual welfare regime, but there are differences in the strength of their agreement. For the women in this grouping, it is the societal explanation of statement 4 that shows the highest degree of agreement. The women also support the environmental statements 3 and 6 to a lesser degree than the women in grouping A.

Table 19.2 shows that women disagree with the statement that men and women are treated equally in the respondents' organisations, whereas men agree with it. Women and men agree on the other two field-related statements, although in different degrees. Women voice much stronger agreement than men on the third statement 'in my field, women have to achieve more than men to get the same recognition'. As in the individual welfare regime, the gender difference is highest for this statement.

The disagreement rate for this grouping is smaller than in grouping A: 200 for the general statements and 113 for the field-related statements. The pattern of difference is similar to the one in the group A. The high difference on the discriminatory statement can once more be said to constitute a rupture for gender construction.

The traditional welfare regime

In the countries included in this welfare regime, women and men voice the same attitudes on five of the general statements. They only differ in their responses to statement 6. Men disagree, whereas women agree with the explanation that 'women lack the crucial informal contacts'. As in the previous regimes, then, the strongest disagreement between men and women is in their response to statement 6. The men agree on three and disagree on three of the statements. They give support to the societal statements 4 and 5 as well as to the environmental explanation 3 that women are isolated in a mainly male environment. The women agree with four of the six statements. Like the men, they agree most strongly with the societal statement 4 'the way society is organised prevents women from achieving top jobs'.

Table 19.2 shows that women neither agree nor disagree with statement 1 that women are normally accepted in leadership positions in the respondents' field. The table also shows that there is strong agreement amongst the women with statement 3 'in my field women have to achieve better than men to get the same recognition'. We interpret statement 1 as a moderate discriminatory explanation, whereas statement 3 is an explicit discriminatory statement.

There is an interesting gender discrepancy in this regime to the two sets of statements. The responses of the men and women to the general statements show the smallest rate of disagreement (92) on the general statements and the highest (199) on the field-related statements among the four welfare regimes. This might indicate that the rupture for gender construction is weak in the general statements and relatively strong in the field-related statements.

The state welfare regime

Even in this regime, the women and men voice similar opinions on four of the six statements. Apart from statements 2, where both men's and women's responses are in line with the other regimes, even though the level of disagreement is higher, the patterns of disagreement differ from the others. Both men and women disagree with statements 2 'women don't have the proper education', 3 'women are isolated in a mainly male environment' and 6 'women lack the crucial informal contacts'. The degree of disagreement, with the exception of statement 2, is higher amongst the men than the women. The difference between men and women is negligible for statement 2: both men and women largely disagree with this combined individual/societal explanation. In fact, the level of disagreement for both genders is the highest in this case among the four welfare regimes. Male and female responses differ in relation to two statements: the former agree and the latter disagree with statement 1 'That's what women want', while the opposite is true with the statement 'the way society is organised prevents women from achieving top positions'. On the whole, the men agree with an individual statement (1) and a societal statement (5), while women agree with the societal explanations of statements 4 and 5.

With respect to the field-related statements, this welfare regime shows similar patterns of attitudes and differences as the regimes A and C. Even here, the strongest differences in the responses of men and women concern the discriminatory statements.

Characteristic of this regime is that the rate of disagreement is not very high (108 for the general statements and 161 for the field-related statements), and that men and women both reject the environmental explanations in favour of societal explanations. It is also noteworthy that the men in this regime are the only men who support the individual explanation and that the women are the only women who disagree with statement 6: 'women lack the crucial informal contacts'. The level of disagreement is lower than that of the men, however: so much less, in fact, that the difference marks this statement among all. The rupture of gender construction is more difficult to detect in this cluster. Women and men only disagree with the discriminatory statement.

Discussion

The symbolic context, understood as the specific content of the statements, clearly differentiates the male and female leaders within each regime in two ways: according to generality/locality and according to discriminatory content. The more locally anchored[7] and the more discrimination against women is expressed in a particular statement, the stronger is its power of differentiation. With respect to locality, the field-related statements carry on the average a higher value of differentiation than the general statements, and of the general statements it is the environmental more than the societal explanations that demonstrate the most differentiating power. With respect to discriminatory content, it is the statement with the most explicit discriminatory content among the field-related statements, namely statement 2, that carries the strongest discriminatory power. Amongst the general statements, statements 3 and 6 have an ambiguously discriminatory content. Statement 6 carries the most differentiating power of these two across the four country groupings. It is, in other words, statements that either openly or ambiguously express discrimination against women that hold the strongest power to differentiate women and men. Many more women than men agree with these discriminatory statements. It is interesting, however, that, of the two ambiguous general statements 3 and 6, statement 6 gets most support from the women and is most strongly refuted by the men. Fewer men refute statement 3. In our description of the statements above, we suggested that statement 3 was the only statement that could be interpreted to attribute to men the explanation of why there are so few women in top positions, because it explicates that women are excluded in a male environment, whereas statement 6 offers no clues as to why women lack crucial informal contacts. It is an ambiguous statement that does not indicate who is at fault: it could be men, society or even other women.

Power of differentiation between the clusters

The structural context of the different welfare regimes appears to have the power of differentiating between the country groupings in two ways: there are large differences between the welfare regimes in relation to the differences between male and female responses to the general statements. To take but one example: men and women in individual, individual/family and traditional regimes all disagree with statement 1, whereas men and women in state regimes differ in their responses. There are also differences in the levels of disagreement amongst the responses in those three regimes. Men and women in the traditional welfare regime disagree to the same degree, whereas there is a higher level of disagreement amongst the women than amongst the men in the individual and individual/family regimes.

   The analysis also shows marked differences in the pattern of gender agreement/disagreement between the clusters. The gender differences in attitudes are strongest in the individual welfare regimes, both with respect to the total disagreement rate and with respect to the number of statements men and women disagree on. The individual welfare regime is followed by the individual/family welfare regime. Here the disagreement rate is lower and there are fewer statements disagreed upon. The results from the traditional welfare regimes and the state regimes are more contradictory. On the one hand, there are weak differences between the genders in relation to the general statements, but, on the other, the differences between the responses of the male and female leaders are high for the field-related statements. This relatively high gender unanimity on the general statements and relatively high degree of discrepancy in relation to the field-related statements seems to suggest that gender construction in the traditional welfare regimes and the state regimes is rather complex. This also suggests the importance of field-related statements for the construction of gender.

Conclusion

The purpose of the analysis of this chapter was to discuss the meaning of contextualisation – or cultural embeddedness – for the construction of gender.

   With respect *to the symbolic contextualisation*, the differences between the two sets of statements – the general and field-related statements – show that there is a correlation between degree of contextualisation and gender differences. This conclusion is strengthened by the fact that it was the environmental statements amongst the general statements that showed the most powerful differentiation. These statements are characterised by their embeddedness and in that respect are in line with the field-related statements.

With respect to *the structural contextualisation* represented by the four welfare regimes, the analysis also showed marked differences in gender construction.

The patterns of gender construction, then, differ according to contextualisation both with respect to locality, i.e. welfare regimes, and with respect to types of discourse: general versus field-related.

Another interesting finding of this study is that the gender differences in responses in the individual welfare states are larger than the differences in responses from the top leaders of more traditional welfare regimes. This result goes counter to the expectation we presented at the beginning of this chapter, based on existing literature about welfare states, namely that countries with traditional divisions of labour and low representation of women in politics and business are expected to accept more traditional discourses on gender and portray more gender disagreement, whereas countries with more equal divisions of labour are expected to accept less traditional discourses on gender as well as present more gender agreement. In relation to the four welfare regimes presented above, the highest gender differences were expected in the traditional welfare regimes, slightly lower differences were expected in the individual/family regimes and least differences in the individual regimes. The findings do not support this ranking and point, in fact, in another direction. They indicate that the gender equality in social practices found in the countries included in the individual welfare regime may not foster equality in attitudes amongst its citizens. The study also suggests that equality in social practices is counter-balanced by differences in the discourse on gender. We suggest that this can, perhaps, be seen as an expression of the basic logic of the cultural discourse on gender: differentiation.

Notes

1. This means that we do not see them as fostered by individual gendered psychologies as if they were expressions of a deeper lying coherent personality structures or world outlooks, but as culturally available choices.
2. We are not arguing that people do not make statements to that effect, but would argue that those who do are usually accused of partisan views.
3. This means that we leave aside feminists who emphasise the gendered nature of welfare states, e.g. by claiming that the ideologies underlying welfare state policies reinforce women's secondary status or that welfare states are dependent on women's unwaged care work (see e.g. Siim, 1988; Fraser, 1989).
4. Her categorisation overlaps to a large extent with classification of welfare states in Europe on the basis of the role played by religion (see e.g. Siaroff, 1994). European countries, then, can be divided according to whether they belong to Catholic or Protestant spheres of influence. In the former, women are encouraged to focus on

their familial roles and are discouraged from working for pay, while the latter present more diverse discourses on women's role and family.

5. The state regimes cannot be interpreted according to these writings on gender and the welfare state.

6. The disagreement rate is calculated by adding the differences between male and female responses to the six general and three field-related statements to each other.

7. An exception here is that the individual explanation amongst the general statements, in a sense the most local of all, does not carry much differentiating power.

20
Élites' Value Orientations

Renata Siemienska

An analysis of the composition of the political and economic élites and the ways in which they were recruited has shown that the degree of their continuity differed in the various states and over different periods of time, that sometimes the changes were evolutionary and at other times the continuation was severed (e.g. Czudnowski, 1982).

A peculiar situation appeared in Central and Eastern European countries in the late 1980s and early 1990s. At that time, those countries embarked on the road to economic and political transformation, a shift from an authoritarian system to a democratic one and from a centrally planned economy to a free market one. A question arose whether the changes in the system would be accompanied by a turnover of political and economic élites or whether the old élites would be able to retain their influence in both or one sphere. Systematic analyses carried out in the early 1990s have shown that, despite some differences, in Russia, Hungary and Poland (Wasilewski, 1992; Wasilewski and Wesowski, 1992, Siemienska, 1994; Szelenyi, Treiman and Wnuk-Lipiñski, 1995; Jasinska-Kania, 1998) the political élites circulated to a much greater extent than the economic élites, whose reproduction took place on a relatively larger scale due to a gradual transformation of the socialist economy into one based on private ownership.

Some questions arise: to what extent do value orientations of élites in post-communist countries differ from (i) value orientations of élites in states with stable and relatively new democracies; and (ii) value orientations of the societies of the general publics democratic and post-communist countries? What factors differentiate them?

The recognition of the range of the existing gender inequalities and the acceptance of the given model of relations between women and men in society is particularly significant, as the members of élites make decisions regarding others or have influence over the policy of decision-making groups, to which they belong. We assume – in accordance with several psychological theories – that these people have a tendency to undertake actions which are consistent with their systems of values, even though this does not at all mean that their behaviours will always be directly inspired by them (Van Deth and Scarbrough, 1995). The élites' members may also describe the way their values affect their own possibilities in public life, affect the formation of their individual aspirations, determine their cultural and social capital (as these terms are defined by Bourdieu, 1984; Hale and Kelly, 1989; Guy, 1992).

We assume that the different ways of entering public life by women in communist and non-communist countries have influenced value orientations and attitudes of (élite) members towards gender equality.

We may basically distinguish two types of models for the professional activisation of women after World War II: 'externally controlled', more typical for the countries of Central and Eastern Europe throughout the last 50 years, and 'internally controlled', which better describes the situation which existed at that time in Western Europe and many non-European countries (Vianello and Siemienska, 1990). The first model was characterised by the fact that the change in the behaviour of women took place as a result of external pressure on them (and the family), the pressure of political power, which also controlled the distribution of economic goods. Changes in the sphere of awareness, a departure from the traditionally defined social roles for the sake of a non-traditional model based on partnership between men and women, took place at a very slow rate. In fact, women had to combine professional work with the roles traditionally ascribed to them. The propaganda of that period treated the problem of gender equality as 'taken care of'. The situation was perceived by members of the communist societies not as requiring a re-evaluation of the roles of men and women, so that the burden of numerous duties would be distributed more evenly, but as the existence of 'excessive equality between the genders'. The only way out of the situation – in the opinion of a significant part of society – was a return to the traditional division of roles (Siemienska, 1986; Vianello and Simienska, 1990). Other factors which have strengthened traditional conceptions of women's role in the societies were (to point out the most important): the relations between men and women in private life, to a large extent brought over from the traditional peasant societies, were 'frozen' by the communist system; there was no possibility of realising one's value orientations, which gave rise to a desire for 'withdrawal' from public life; an 'automatic' attainment of certain rights and so-called privileges of welfare state, which in the context of imposed duties and forced behaviours were perceived as a way of reinforcing the inequalities between women and men and their exploitation; lack of possibility of organisation (e.g., women's interest groups, including feminist groups), so typical of democratic societies, but contrary to the conception of society under communism (Einhorn, 1993; Wolchik, 1994).

All these factors hindered or even counteracted the transformations in the sphere of values and attitudes throughout the last few decades. Nevertheless, certain processes in the sphere of awareness, as far as changes of attitudes with respect to the role of women in society are concerned, did take place, being associated mainly with an increase in the education level of women. The relationship between the level of education and the perceived need to grant women equal rights and greater independence is a tendency, which is generally observed in the world.

What was characteristic of the 'Western' model were mainly the changes in the awareness of women regarding their place in social life, which became an important factor drawing them to look for work outside the family. The existing feminist movements in non-communist countries significantly contributed to the diffusion of the idea of women's rights and their role in society.

Neither of the models appeared in a 'pure' form. Nevertheless, their dominance in given countries was the reason why in the late 1980s and early 1990s, when the communist system was collapsing, the expectations of the members of the post-communist societies and of Western European and North American countries clearly differed as far as the conceptions of the desired roles of women and men were concerned. At that time, the societies of Central and Eastern Europe expected that the transformations would bring changes enabling the realisation of the hitherto unfulfilled dreams of prosperity, part of which is a life-style based on the traditional family model, according to which it is mainly the woman who takes care of the home and children and the man provides the financial means (Siemienska, 1996a; 1996b).

The following hypotheses will be tested in this chapter:

1. Similarities in the systems of values of élites and society should be greater in countries currently undergoing the process of transformation, where the replacement of élites is taking place on a larger scale.
2. The presence of the feminist movement in a country (or the lack of one) should influence the degree of difference in the value orientation between women and men of their political and economic élites. Where it has a long tradition, these differences should be tendentially large, while where society is divided into two opposite blocks: 'us' – society, and 'them' – the imposed (e.g. communist) authorities, they should be small.
3. In countries with a strong orientation towards post-materialist values (Inglehart, 1990; 1997), political and economic élites more frequently recognise the existing gender inequalities in public life.
4. The political and economic élites have their respective specific traits, even though it is also known that often they are mutually reinforced. People with a strong position in the economic élite combine it periodically, for example, with a political career, and vice versa.

Owing to the specific traits of the compared countries, their different history and the different degrees of participation of women in public life, the following groupings have been adopted:

1. Scandinavian countries (Denmark, Finland, Norway, Sweden), which stand out because of their particularly high rate of women's participation in public life and an active feminist movement;
2. the relatively new democracies in Western Europe (Portugal, Spain and Greece), with relatively lower living standards;
3. post-communist countries at the stage of political and economic transformations (Czech Republic, Poland, Slovenia, Hungary, Russia);
4. stable democracies in Western Europe (Austria, Belgium, France, Germany, Holland, Italy, Switzerland, Great Britain, and Ireland);
5. non-European democratic countries (United States, Canada, New Zealand, and Australia, Israel), whose development was affected by mass immigration.

The impact of culture, politics and economic growth on élites' value orientation

The attitudes towards gender equality are usually associated with more basic values and attitudes concerning a social order. Inglehart (1990; 1997) found that people attaching great significance to post-materialist values are more frequently in favour of gender equality and a less traditional family model, and that the type of value orientation is determined by a series of factors both on the level of society as a whole and at the individual level. He defines 'materialist' values as those which emphasise economic and physical security, while 'post-materialist' values are those which emphasise self-expression and the quality of life. Post-materialists are not non-materialists, still less are they anti-materialists. The term 'post-materialist' denotes a set of goals that are emphasised after people have attained material security, and because they have attained material security (Inglehart, 1997: 35).

The analyses presented below allow us to find out what kind of value orientation prevails in élites in different types of societies and also to state which factors – apart from individual traits and experiences of the respondents – are conductive to the appearance of people in the élites with a post-materialist orientation.

The value orientation was examined by using Inglehart's four-item battery, from which the respondents selected two most important goals, which should be realised over the next ten years. It included two materialist goals, 'maintaining order in the nation' and 'fighting rising prices', and two post-materialist ones: 'giving people more say in important government decisions' and 'protecting freedom of speech' (Inglehart, 1977; 1990; 1997).

The results of our analyses show – comparing the findings with the earlier obtained results on representative national samples (Inglehart, 1990; 1997) – that groups of countries clearly differ between each other as far as

Table 20.1   Differences in Élites' Value Orientation among Groups of Countries (%)

Region/Value Orientation	Political Élite:			Business Élite:		
	Total	**Men**	**Women**	**Total**	**Men**	**Women**
Scandinavia:						
Materialist	05	11	–	15	15	15
Post-materialist	27	17	34	12	12	12
Mixed	68	72	66	73	73	73
Southern Europe:						
Materialist	12	5	18	15	17	13
Post-materialist	35	31	40	21	30	13
Mixed	53	64	42	64	53	74
Western Europe:						
Materialist	15	14	15	15	21	9
Post-materialist	36	34	39	23	19	27
Mixed	49	52	46	62	60	64
Non-European democracies:						
Materialist	6	8	4	16	17	15
Post-materialist	37	35	40	20	19	22
Mixed	57	57	56	64	64	63
Post-communist countries:						
Materialist	15	19	12	23	23	24
Post-materialist	15	13	16	10	12	8
Mixed	70	68	72	67	65	68

orientations towards values are concerned, both in the case of entire societies as well as people in the top positions in the political and economic structures (Tables 20.1 and 20.2).

The degree of similarity in orientations of materialist v. post-materialist values between societies as a whole and the members of the élites is very different in the particular countries. As a rule, élites are more post-materialistically oriented compared to the inhabitants of their countries (Table 20.2).[1]

Inglehart (1990; 1997) shows that the existence of a stable democratic system over a longer period of time, the accompanying satisfaction of society with living conditions, an increase in the education level are associated with post-materialist values. He also found that young people are characterised by a greater orientation of post-materialist values, as are persons who had better economic conditions when they were growing up.[2]

Table 20.2 Economic and Social Structure, Political, and Cultural Variables and Value Orientation

	GNP/ Capita 1990*	Per cent in Higher Education*	Years of Continuous Democracy*	Level of Democracy, 1990*	Subjective Well-being of Society**	Post-materialist Values of Society 1990 %***		Post-materialist Values of Politicians %		Post-materialist Values of Economic Elite %	
						M	F	M	F	M	F
Austria	19,000	33	49	14	59	26	24	54	36	18	35
Belgium	17,580	37	75	14	77	27	20	50	58	40	23
Britain	16,080	25	75	14	75	22	18	33	38	15	46
Canada	20,380	70	75	14	69	30	21	na	na	na	–
Czech Republic	3,190	18	04	4	32	11	10	29	38	12	13
Denmark	22,440	32	75	14	85	17	15	30	59	21	27
Finland	24,540	47	75	14	76	33	25	7	15	7	–
France	19,590	40	37	13	67	28	23	27	64	36	43
Hungary	2,780	15	4	9	28	5	3	25	7	na	na
Ireland	10,370	26	75	14	80	18	20	na	na	na	na
Italy	16,882	20	49	14	66	26	19	18	19	–	6
Japan	25,840	31	49	14	54	10	10	54	58	31	14
Netherlands	17,570	34	75	14	85	33	37	36	30	33	18
Norway	22,830	43	75	14	81	11	8	na	33	na	17
Poland	1,690	22	4	9	58	11	9	4	7	19	4

Portugal	4,950	18	18	13	51	13	12	43	46	36	21
Russia	3,430	20	0	5	-1	8	4	-	14	na	na
Slovenia	3,000	18	3	2	23	9	4	6	16	-	6
Spain	11,010	34	17	14	65	24	17	23	22	23	8
Sweden	23,780	33	75	14	86	23	22	na	33	-	-
Switzerland	32,250	26	75	14	86	26	22	22	23	-	25
United States	21,810	75	75	14	77	24	21	30	22	25	31
(W.)Germany	22,360	32	46	14	70	29	28	na	na	na	na

*GNP per capita 1990 from World Bank *World Development Report 1993*; the percentage of the college-age population enrolled in higher education in 1988 is from the World Bank, *World Development Report 1993*, 294–95; years of continuous democracy and the level of democracy in 1990 based on the Freedom House score, which range from 2 (low) to 14 (high) are from Freedom House, *Freedom in the World 1990* from Inglehart (1997) *Modernization and Postmodernization. Cultural, Economic and Political Change in 43 Societies*.

**The subjective well-being index for a particular society is the mean of two differences – the percentage of respondents answering happy minus the percentage unhappy, and the percentage satisfied minus the percentage dissatisfied. The index was constructed by Inglehart on a basis World Values Survey 1990–1993 (Inglehart 1997).

***Score of post-materialism is based on four items battery developed by Inglehart (described in the text). Data from: Inglehart, Basañez and Moreno (1998) *Human Values and Beliefs: A Cross-Cultural Sourcebook*.

Our goal was to find out to what extent his theory, supported on the national level, is confirmed in a case of élites and whether value orientation of society influences their value orientation. Therefore, the multiple regression analysis model included variables of two types: (a) macro-economic and characterising the level of development of democracies in the various countries (GNP/capita, 1990, percentage in higher education, percentage of people with post-materialist orientation in total population of each country, level of democracy in 1990, subjective well-being and group of countries with a specific history); (b) regarding the members of the studied élites (gender, age group, family's economic position when the respondent was 14, total years of the respondent's education). The multiple regression analysis was carried out separately for persons from the world of politics and business. In the case of the former, the most important predictors explaining the orientations were (1) the subjective well-being of society (beta –0.30, p 0.0009), (2) level of democracy in 1990 (beta 0.24, p 0.003), (3) GNP/capita in 1990 (beta 0.10, n.s.), (4) index of post-materialist orientation (1 mat, 2 mixed, 3 p = mat) (beta 0.07, n.s.), (5) gender (beta 0.06, n.s.), (6) the percentage of people in higher education (beta 0.05, n.s.). The model as a whole was statistically significant (adjusted R^2 = 0.021).

In the case of business leaders the interactions between the various predictors were different. The most important predictors were: (1) level of democracy in 1990 (beta 0.32, p 0.000), (2) belonging to generations born before 1935 (beta –0.25, p 0.000), (3) subjective well-being of society (beta –0.18, p 0.02), (4) percentage of persons with a post-materialist orientation in society as a whole (beta –0.15, p 0.06), (5) living in Scandinavian countries (beta 0.11, p 0.05), (6) the percentage in higher education in the particular country (beta 0.08, n.s.). The model as a whole was statistically significant (adjusted R^2 = 0.083).

The predictors included in the model to a larger extent explained the value orientation of people who attained top positions in business compared to those active in politics.

Summing up, the broader context of political and economic nature as well as the value orientation of society affect – as expected – the value orientation of people found at the top of the political and economic ladders, who to a certain degree are representative of the populations of their countries. What is characteristic of the élites in our study is that in all groups of countries the members of political élites are much more post-materialistically oriented than the members of the economic élites (see also Aberbach, Putnam and Rockman, 1981). The smallest differences are observed between both élites in the post-communist countries, a result which may be due to the fact that these élites are just forming and are frequently made up of people who had been previously active in the political élite or in the opposition or outsiders to these categories. The gender of the respondents is a predictor to a greater extent differentiating the attitudes of people from the world of

politics from those of business. Women are more post-materialistically oriented; this pattern is clearly visible among the members of political élites
and appears often also in the economic élites. The lower, compared to
all other groups of countries, post-materialist orientation of the members
of élites in the post-communist countries confirms earlier findings
(Siemienska, 1996b) as well Inglehart's theory.

The perception of gender inequality as a barrier to advancement

The analyses in this section aim at tracing the connection between value
orientation and recognition of the existing barriers in women's advancement; they are also an attempt to answer the question: to what extent are
the élites representative of their societies as far as orientations towards values
and attitudes towards gender inequality are concerned.[2]

Our study demonstrates that various aspects of the inequalities between
women and men appear with varying intensity in the different groups of
countries. They are relatively most frequently stressed by the élite members
of 'non-European democratic countries' and the 'new democracies of Southern Europe'; and least frequently by the élites in post-communist countries.
In addition, in some of country groups, in certain cases the attitudes and
opinions of women and men are very similar, whereas in others they clearly
differ. But, generally speaking, women more frequently than men are aware
of the inequalities as well as the barriers of a cultural and social nature,
which make it more difficult for women to enter the political and economic
élites. For example, the number of women and men who do *not* agree with
the statement that women prefer men in decision-making positions and that
women lack specific experience to perform such roles is quite similar.
Women, on the other hand, far more frequently than men believe that they
are isolated in the mainly male professional environment, that they are not
elected (or appointed) to the highest positions, and also that they must
achieve more than men in order to get noticed (see Tables 20.3 and 20.4).
Also more than men, women believe that earning money is the best way to
ensure women's independence. Far more frequently than men, women disagree with the opinion that men should take priority when there are not
enough jobs (Table 20.5).

Members of the political élite are more aware than the members of economic élites of the inequalities and the social and cultural barriers imped-
ing women's progress into top positions.

The low values of the indices (Figures 20.1a–b, 20.2 a–b and 20.3 a–b) stem
partly from the fact that a large number of the respondents – both women
and men – are not strongly convinced that the problem of discrimination
exists, and also what place women should hold in society. The answers (both
'agree' and 'disagree') given by members of élites can be considered more as

Table 20.3 Sources of Women's Social Discrimination: Perceptions of Macro-social and Cultural Barriers Faced by Women in Reaching Top Positions (Answers 'strongly agree'* or 'strongly disagree'**) (%)

	Women Prefer Men in Top Positions**		Women Lack Specific Training**		Women are Isolated in a Mainly Male Environment*		Women are Prevented from Reaching Top*		Due to How Women are Brought up*		Women Lack Informal Contacts*	
	M	F	M	F	M	F	M	F	M	F	M	F
Political élite												
Scandinavia	38	33	36	25	3	3	14	12	–	6	2	11
Southern Europe	45	41	25	28	19	27	14	16	9	7	7	7
Western Europe	28	34	28	26	7	19	19	34	4	15	6	18
Non-European democracies	35	47	27	30	18	21	12	24	5	5	4	19
Post-communist countries	6	12	28	32	5	4	16	18	3	7	4	11

Business élite

	M	F	M	F	M	F	M	F	M	F	M	F
Scandinavia	11	25	36	30	5	6	2	14	4	7	–	6
Southern Europe	31	19	25	34	17	21	5	17	2	17	2	15
Western Europe	23	27	29	26	7	11	12	16	7	15	2	9
Non-European democracies	20	37	14	15	14	22	7	13	–	6	3	11
Post-communist countries	8	14	29	54	3	7	9	6	16	11	2	3

Table 20.4 Gender Inequality at Work. Perception of Gender Inequality in Reaching Top Positions (Answers 'strongly agree'* or 'strongly disagree'***) (%)

| | Political Élite | | | | | | Business Élite | | | | | |
| | Women are Accepted in Leadership Positions in the Field** | | Men & Women Treated Equally in my Organisation** | | In My Field Women Have to Achieve More than Men to Receive Recognition* | | Women are Accepted in Leadership Positions in the Field** | | Men and Women Treated Equally in my Organisation** | | In my Field Women Have to Achieve More than Men to Receive Recognition* | |
	M	F	M	F	M	F	M	F	M	F	M	F
Scandinavia	2	10	–	1	1	27	4	11	2	2	14	13
Southern Europe	9	9	2	15	19	52	7	9	–	5	5	34
Western Europe	2	7	3	14	13	43	5	9	6	9	9	32
Non-European democracies	2	10	–	16	12	48	1	7	–	9	5	40
Post-Communist countries	2	13	3	3	9	40	2	3	–	3	5	34

Table 20.5 Concept of Women's Role in Public and Private Life (Answers 'strongly agree'* or 'strongly disagree'**) (%)

	Political Élite						Economic Élite					
	When Jobs are Scarce Men Should Have More Rights**		Family Suffers When Women Work Full-time**		Paid Job Best for Women's Independence*		When Jobs are Scarce Men Should Have More Rights**		Family Suffers When Women Work Full-time**		Paid Job Best for Women's Independence*	
	M	F	M	F	M	F	M	F	M	F	M	F
Scandinavia	80	93	45	32	41	49	69	84	11	30	27	50
Southern Europe	66	74	27	22	52	63	52	57	7	11	46	65
Western Europe	61	83	19	34	20	38	49	70	5	28	14	32
Non-European democracies	69	87	28	43	17	35	55	86	8	23	19	49
Post-Communist countries	27	15	17	8	17	31	28	27	12	17	28	42

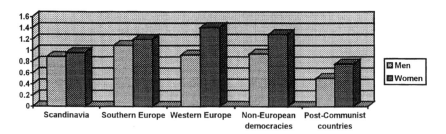

Figure 20.1a   Index 'Sources of Women's Social Discrimination'*: The political élite

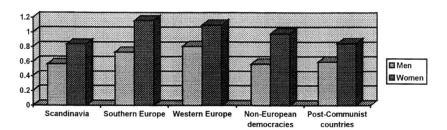

Figure 20.1b   Index 'Sources of Women's Social Discrimination'*: The business élite

*The index is based on the answers 'strongly agree' and 'strongly disagree' as shown in tables. The higher the score, the higher perception of sources of women's discrimination. '0' means that the respondent did not give any answer; '3' that the respondent answered 'strongly agree' or 'strongly disagree' to any questions included to the index

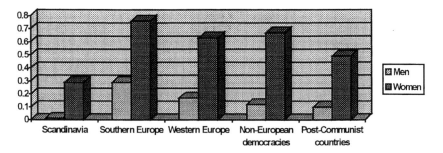

Figure 20.2a   Index: 'Gender Inequality at Work': The political élite

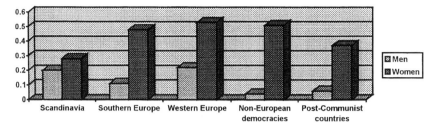

Figure 20.2b Index: 'Gender Inequality at Work': The business élite

*The index is based on the answers 'strongly agree' and 'strongly disagree' as shown in Table 20.2. The higher the score, the higher perception of women's discrimination. '0' means that the respondent did not give any answer; '3' the respondent answered 'strongly agree' or 'strongly disagree' to all the questions included to the index

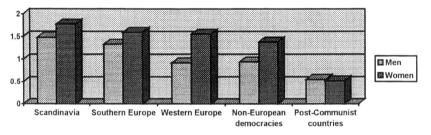

Figure 20.3a Index 'Concept of Women's Role in Public and Private Life': The political élite

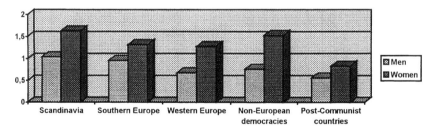

Figure 20.3b Index 'Concept of Women's Role in Public and Private Life': The business élite

*The index is based on the answers 'strongly agree' and 'strongly disagree' as marked in the Table 20.3. The higher the score, the less traditional is the concept of women's role. '0' means that the respondent did not give any answer; '3' that the respondent answered 'strongly agree' or 'strongly disagree' to all the questions included to the index

an expression of a 'political correctness' in modern societies than as the expression of their crystallised views. But we are not able to prove this assumption from the available data. In total, 790 respondents did not give even one 'strongly agree' or 'strongly disagree' response in the case of the index of 'Sources of Women's Social Discrimination', 1,325 in the case of the index 'Perceived Gender Inequality in Work' and 581 élite members in the case of the index 'Concept of Women's Role in Public and Private Life'.

Factors shaping élites' perception of gender inequality in public and private life

As stated earlier, women – members of both élites – perceive gender inequalities, as far as advancement opportunities are concerned, much more frequently than men, and younger women more often than older women. Members of the political élite with a post-materialist orientation notice them much more frequently than members of the economic élite. The higher is the mothers' education, the more frequently the members of political élites perceive this inequality, especially that women are isolated in a male environment and lack informal contacts. Also – though to a lesser extent – fathers' education influences the perception of the unequal possibilities for women and men.

The relationship found between the value orientation held and the perception of the unequal possibilities of women's advancement is consistent with the connection demonstrated by Inglehart between the more general value orientation and the preference for several other values in countries with different political experiences and different levels of economic development (Inglehart, 1990; 1997).

The degree of similarity between the attitudes of general populations and the attitudes of the members of their political and economic élites depends to a large extent on the content of the attitude. For example, granting priority to men in getting jobs is rejected in all countries by the élite members, with the exception of post-communist ones, where a significant number of women and men, often more women than men, are willing to accept it. Differences in the attitudes between 'society' and the élites are very large. The situation is different in the case of the concept of work as the best road to ensure independence for women. Élites and societies in most cases have identical opinions in this matter, and men are usually more willing to accept that women's work is a road to their independence (Table 20.6).

Two types of multiple regression analysis were carried out for each of the previously discussed indices to find out which predictors play a part in perceiving discrimination and forming the concept of women's role in society by the élite members: individual 'resources' of the respondents or the broader political, economic and cultural context.

The first type included the following variables as predictors: (a) macro-

Table 20.6 Attitudes of Societies and Political and Business Élites towards Gender Equality in Labour Market and Jobs as a Way to Gain Independence by Women (percentages of respondents who 'strongly agree' and 'agree')

Country	Men Have More Rights to a Job							Women's Path to Independence						
	Society in the early 1990s*			Political Élite		Economic Élite		Society in the early 1990s*			Political Élite		Economic Élite	
	T	M	F	M	F	M	F	T	M	F	M	F	M	F
Austria	50	54	48	–	6	22	–	74	71	76	80	88	61	90
Belgium	38	38	38	9	–	25	9	70	68	72	29	63	58	43
Britain	34	31	36	5	10	5	5	68	65	70	26	70	28	58
Canada	19	18	20	9	6	12	–	55	56	54	55	35	53	82
Czech Republic	55	57	52	31	–	–	–	55	50	59	23	54	73	67
Denmark	11	7	14	–	–	–	–	81	79	82	41	80	33	54
Finland	15	16	15	–	–	–	–	77	75	79	73	100	87	80
France	33	35	31	–	–	13	7	79	77	81	23	20	28	33
Hungary	42	41	44	14	47	na	–	48	49	46	40	53	na	na
Ireland	36	36	35	8	–	6	7	61	62	60	69	73	44	67
Italy	43	45	41	18	5	7	5	74	70	78	53	74	67	79
Japan	34	38	30	8	–	53	64	78	76	81	46	60	27	7
Netherlands	22	26	21	6	–	–	–	56	52	57	80	60	60	53
Norway	16	17	15	na	–	na	–	75	77	74	na	78	na	7
Poland	55	58	52	67	80	57	57	na	na	na	87	83	67	87
Portugal	34	35	32	–	–	8	–	80	75	85	47	73	86	71
Russia	40	46	36	25	55	na	na	58	51	63	37	78	na	na
Slovenia	29	34	25	32	74	20	15	73	69	77	84	80	67	95
Spain	31	30	31	7	7	–	–	79	75	83	86	86	93	93
Sweden	8	7	9	–	7	–	–	74	76	72	67	80	60	87
Switzerland	na	na	na	7	–	13	–	na	na	na	47	73	73	57
United States	24	26	23	na	Na	–	–	60	60	60	40	45	50	73
(W.)Germany	31	37	27	–	–	10	20	75	73	77	60	80	87	73

*Data from: Inglehart, Basañez and Moreno (1998).

Table 20.7 Predictors of 'Sources of Women's Social Discrimination', 'Gender Inequality' and 'Women's Role in Public and Private Life' (MCA – type I) (beta coefficients)[a]

Predictors:	Political Élite			Economic Élite		
	Sources of Women's Social Discrimination	Gender Inequality in Work	Women's Role in Public and Private Life	Sources of Women's Social Discrimination	Gender Inequality in Work	Women's Role in Public and Private Life
R's characteristics:						
1. Gender	0.143**	0.339***	0.163***	0.161***	0.262***	0.289***
2. Family's economic position when R was 14 years old	0.028	0.035	0.003	0.036	0.008	0.007
3. R born before 1935	−0.052	−3.33E-04	0.098*	−0.057	0.029	−0.119*
4. R born between 1936–1945	−0.060	−0.015	0.038	0.003	0.002	−0.040
5. R born after 1945	−0.002	−0.051	0.016	0.041	0.069	−0.070
6. R's post-mat. Orientation	0.152***	0.004	0.150***	−0.011	0.042	0.031
7. R's total years of education	−0.007	0.066	0.032	0.010	0.044	0.092

Characteristics of R's country:

8. years of continuous democracy	−0.181	−0.155	0.126	−0.186*	−0.048
9. Level of democracy in 1990	0.194	0.157*	0.201**	0.006	−0.011
10. Post-mat. orientation of society	0.238**	0.181*	0.259***	0.274***	0.132
11. Subjective well-being	−0.104	−0.053	0.812E-04	0.010	0.088
12. GNP/capita in 1990	−0.012	−0.268***	0.170*	−0.148	−0.068
13. percent in higher education in 1990	−0.030	0.072	0.173**	0.082	0.047
Adjusted R^2 (Type I)	0.06***	0.14***	0.16***	0.04**	0.05***
Adjusted R^2 (Type II)	0.14***	0.16***	0.19***	0.06**	0.09***

[a]Level of significance: *** $p < 0.001$; ** $p < 0.01$; * $p < 0.05$. Adjusted R^2 (type II) is shown in the table for the comparison with the model not including the groups of countries. All beta coefficients are for the Type 1 analysis.

economics and characterising the level of the development of democracy in the various countries (GNP/capita 1990, percentage in higher education, percentage of people with post-materialist orientation in total population in each country, the level of democracy in 1990, years of continuous democracy, subjective well-being); (b) regarding the members of the studied élites (gender, age group, family's economic position when respondent was 14, total years of the respondent's education).

The second type, in addition to the group of predictors given above under (a) and (b), included groups of countries with a different history and culture. As previously, the analyses were conducted separately for the members of the political and economic élites.

The multiple regressions (Types I and II) explained more perception and attitudes towards gender inequality by members of political than economic élites. The most important predictors are gender and characteristics of the respondents' countries. In general, women post-materialist oriented respondents, members of élites of more post-materialist oriented societies, with a higher level of democracy, living in countries with more experience of continuous democracy and a higher economic level are more sensitive to women's conditions and more often perceive their discrimination.

The inclusion of the country grouping in the analyses shows that it is an important predictor of the differences in attitudes and perception of gender inequality, showing the impact specific histories of different groups of countries have on this matter.

Conclusion

The systems of values of the various societies as a whole affect the perception by the élite members of both genders of inequalities and barriers encountered by women to promotion is concerned. But the perception of gender inequality, the concept of the social roles of women and men in the area of public and private life, like the general value orientation, are preconditioned by having a nation reach a certain level of economic development. Also important is the existence of a democratic system with its mechanisms for articulating interests, needs and methods for satisfying them. They include the way in which women are mobilised to go beyond their traditional roles and participate in public life, the existence of feminist movements, adequate legislation, etc.

The different experiences of recent decades have affected the attitudes and perception of both the populaces of societies and their élites, creating differences between the élites as well as between the country groups.

The findings clearly show that one of the tasks faced by all those who consider gender equality an important issue is to promote it as a basic human right, which will only be effective when it is also embodied in the cultural patterns embodied in everyday life.

Notes

1. Table 20.2 gives also the basic characteristics for the countries, which will be used in further analyses.
2. 14 years of age is adopted as the age when the hierarchy of values becomes crystallised.

General Conclusions

Gwen Moore and Mino Vianello

with contributions from Joanna Liddle, Maria José Alonso Sánchez, Eileen Drew, Michal Palgi, Alison Woodward, Jeannette Bakker, Jenny Neale, Judith Ziegler, Jaana Kuusipalo, Litsa Nicolaou-Smokoviti, Brigitte Liebig and Renata Siemienska

This study of women and men in leading business and political posts in 27 industrialised nations has revealed both gender differences and similarities in pathways to power, uses of power in office, combining private life and career, and the cultural dimensions of gender inequality in élites. Women in élite positions differ most notably from their male counterparts in their social and educational backgrounds and in their private lives. Fewer gender differences emerge in attitudes and activities related to leaders' power positions. In this concluding chapter we briefly review the major findings of the empirical sections and consider the theoretical and policy implications of our research.

Part I, 'Pathways to Power', investigates how and why women were able to enter positions of power and whether pathways to the top differ by gender. Two chapters (chapter 3 by Liddle and Michielsens, and chapter 4, by García de León, Alonso Sánchez and Rodriguez Navarro) ask whether the small number of élite women are simply exceptional individuals whose extraordinary talents propel them to leading positions, or if, by contrast, significant social and cultural characteristics distinguish women leaders from comparable men. They find that women decision-makers in politics and business, across the 27 countries studied, are able to draw on greater social resources than are equivalent men: a more privileged class background, higher educational level among relatives and a family culture in which mothers have higher social and economic visibility. On the basis of these findings, the authors conclude that certain identifiable patterns differentiate men and women in public power, and that women's access to power cannot be understood as simply exceptional, nor as the result of individual efforts alone, but that women who attain top positions have available additional structural and cultural resources on which they can draw as a replacement for the structural and cultural deficits implicit in their gender. These resources are forms of material, social and cultural capital, which help to explain how and why these women gained access to top leadership positions.

Also in Part I, Drew (chapter 5) finds gendered career paths even among top-level leaders in business and politics. When compared to their male colleagues, women leaders more often report conflicts between family and career and were more likely to have followed atypical career patterns.

Focusing on careers, power and attitudes of political élites, Carrilho (chapter 6) concludes that while men and women hold and manage power in similar ways, male politicians enjoy more party support than do their female colleagues.

From these analyses of pathways to power we conclude that gender divisions cannot be understood in isolation from other important social divisions in society such as class structures, and that gendered power must be conceptualised as both constituted by, and constitutive of, the social relations of gender and class.

Part II investigates facets of strategies, contexts and uses of power. Examining leaders' reports of having mentors and of mentoring junior colleagues, Palgi (chapter 7) finds that politicians and business leaders, especially women, commonly report that they had mentors. Leaders of both sexes cite mostly men mentors, especially from among their superiors. Mentoring patterns varied somewhat by country groupings, however. In social democratic countries, with clear policies of advancing and empowering women, women more often act as mentors for both men and women, while women rarely mentor men in the other societies.

Woodward and Lyon (chapter 8) find that political and business leaders of both sexes devote far more time to their jobs than do other workers in the same countries. Their findings support the hypothesis that in many ways women in top leadership positions follow the same patterns as men, such as the allocation of time to work and private life. Yet, even if women leaders are following the same time scheme as men, they make sacrifices in their private lives to a greater degree than do equally situated men.

The chapters by Bakker (chapter 9) and by Moore and White (chapter 10) assess élite women's and men's access to informal contacts and information. Both analyses report more gender similarities than differences in leaders' access to information and informal contacts.

Bakker finds that women and men leaders generally report adequate access to, and satisfaction with, informal channels of information on the job. Women's satisfaction with informal access is relatively greater in countries with high levels of women's participation in decision-making (as in the UN *Gender Empowerment Measure*) and in European Union countries with lower proportions of women in full-time employment.

Assessing reported frequency of contact with other élites and service on boards of directors, Moore and White conclude that in both business and (especially) politics, men are advantaged not only by more frequent access to top officials, but also by holding more corporate board seats than their women counterparts. This male advantage declines substantially among business (but not political) women and men with similar personal and organisational traits. In general, results are similar across country groupings, although in the less economically developed country grouping, politicians, especially women, report less frequent élite contacts than in the full market economy grouping.

Examining the effects of organisation structure on business women's and men's authority, Kavčič and Merkač (chapter 11) find larger variations across countries than between women and men in business posts. Nevertheless, businessmen rate their decision-making authority higher than similarly situated women rank their own authority, on average, both overall and in several types of organisations.

With reference not to office held, but to the amount of perceived power connected with an élite position, Vianello (chapter 12) shows that the hypothesis that women need more privileged conditions in order to exercise as much power as men is not supported, although high social status seems to increase somewhat women's ability to exercise power. Once in power, women exert it to the same extent men do. Factors conducive to perceived power exercise for male leaders are centred on interpersonal contacts, while for women they are more tied to family resources.

One conclusion from this Part II is that women's gender disadvantage appears to be greater in gaining access to a élite position than in performing well in that office. We find that the rare women 'above the glass ceiling' are less disadvantaged in exercising power than they might have been in achieving a leading position in the first place.

The chapters in Part III focus on careers and everyday lives. What emerges is that the life-style of male leaders to a great extent follows a traditional pattern, with marriage and children, and often a wife responsible for family tasks. Women leaders are forced to consider alternatives. Chapters examine aspects of leaders' private lives across sectors, age cohorts and country groupings (North/South Europe, welfare regime types).

Neale's review (chapter 13) indicates that male business leaders and female political leaders exhibit the most traditional patterns in balancing career and family. In contrast to women in business, many women in politics are trying 'to do it all', with a demanding career on top of a traditional female family role. Women business leaders less often have partners or children and rarely personally care for the household or children.

Diem-Wille and Ziegler's analysis (chapter 14) of two age cohorts (born before and after 1945) reveals gender differences in family and domestic work in both cohorts and offers little evidence that women's responsibility for household labour and childcare is disappearing in the younger generation of leaders.

The chapters in Part III examine cultural and structural effects on élite careers and family life. Kuusipalo, Kauppinen and Nuutinen (chapter 15) find that the dominant family models of Northern Europe (the dual-earner model) and Southern Europe (the male breadwinner model) affect leaders' ways of combining everyday life and a top-level career. In Northern Europe, women leaders can more easily combine family and career, and male leaders are less often free of family responsibilities. In Southern Europe, male leaders typically have a partner's support for family duties, and women leaders can count less on the support of partners and publicly funded childcare, relying instead on paid services and relatives for childcare.

Esseveld and Andersson (chapter 16) concur that leaders' career life-forms vary by gender and region, with men often living in traditional career life-forms and women in the single life-form. In Scandinavia and Eastern Europe, regions with official gender equality policies and long traditions of women's paid employment, gender differences in career life-forms are generally smaller. Yet, in all regions, women leaders do more family work than do their male colleagues.

This part confirms that even women in senior positions typically carry a double burden of career and family/household responsibilities. By contrast, their male counterparts have far less responsibility for housework and childcare. Nevertheless, women leaders often arrange different ways of combining their careers and everyday lives. It appears, however, that unless new models of combining public and private lives are institutionalised (for instance, with the adoption of widely available quality childcare), the conflict between the two will remain and the choices women have will be limited.

Part IV examines the ways gender is constructed within the traditionally male-dominated fields of top management and politics in the 27 nations studied. Beyond structural barriers to gender equality in élite posts, the authors investigate the role of cultural mechanisms in interaction with social contexts. They emphasise the interplay of cultural and structural factors at various organisational levels.

Results indicate that gender is a dynamic phenomenon, created and reproduced in interactive processes between cultural and social factors. Gender is part of the symbolic order of each culture and always related to power relations. We can, thus, speak of a 'cultural construction of gender'. This cultural construction can be analytically divided into the structural level, the action level and the attitudinal level – each interacting with the others. This part deals mainly with the attitudinal level, especially on explanations for gender inequality in élite posts.

These analyses show that societal values affect the perception of gender inequalities and of the barriers faced by women in attaining leadership positions (see especially chapters 18–20, by Siemienska, Liebig, and Højgaard and Esseveld). But this perception is influenced by structural factors such as levels of economic development and democracy (see Siemienska) and welfare regime types (Højgaard and Esseveld). Variations in attitudes are also found between genders and sectors, with business élites and male élites typically acknowledging less élite gender inequality. Within organisations, there is an interaction between cultural factors and the organisational hierarchy. Women in top-level positions tend to exhibit greater agreement with men at that level on explanations for gender inequality (see Nicolaou-Smokoviti and Baldwin, 1990). With cross-sectional data, we cannot determine whether women change their attitudes as they move up the hierarchy or whether this greater attitudinal homogeneity at the top results from selective promotion of women who fit in well with their senior male colleagues.

Within the organisational and national settings, substantial relations are also found between structures and cultural dimensions. These analyses suggest the value in distinguishing between micro- and macro-social structures. With that distinction, investigation of how these shape gender values among élites and of the interplay of macro-social factors and individual characteristics can clarify cultural dimension of gender inequality in élites.

Unlike most research on élites and leadership, we took women leaders as the starting point for our project. Continued male predominance in top positions required a non-probability sample, so we focused on women in the highest economic and political positions in each nation and on similarly placed men. This essential sampling strategy reflects the strong male advantage remaining in political and economic posts in each of these countries. Among the goals of this project was a clearer understanding of the rare 'women at the top' in comparison to their numerous male counterparts in industrial and post-industrial societies. After agreeing that economic and political élites are central in decision-making in the countries studied, we decided to study these two sectors and to include not just women but also men in similar élite positions. As a result, we compare men and women, different countries, and the business and political sectors. Our variable-oriented comparative design is well suited to discovering general patterns, but qualitative, case-focused studies are also necessary for a nuanced understanding of gender and power within societies.

With frameworks from élite, leadership and feminist theory, we tested varied hypotheses on gender and power. Consistent with previous élite studies (e.g., Putnam, 1976; Higley et al., 1992), we found that élites, especially women, across the 27 nations of the study tend to share privileged family and educational origins. While much of the recent literature on leadership stresses gender differences in areas such as informal access and management style, we found at least as many similarities as differences among the men and women in top positions in these societies. Feminist theory's attention to women's subordination in both the public and private spheres shaped many of the analyses, particularly those examining the overlap of élite careers and private lives. By comparing women and men in similar demanding careers, we were able to determine that élite men typically have the advantage of a supporting partner, while their women colleagues rarely enjoy such a luxury.

Since we have studied only those who have 'made it', rather than those who were not selected for élite positions, we cannot reach firm conclusions about differential access to élite positions. Still, our results strongly suggest that structural, political and cultural barriers hinder women's access to top positions in public life. Women in political and economic leadership posts in the 27 industrialised nations of our study come from more privileged social origins, on average, than do their similarly located male colleagues and report making more personal sacrifices for their careers. Nevertheless, once in power, women do not need a more privileged background than men to participate fully in decision-making and leadership. In brief, the small number of women who make it into powerful positions are not greatly disadvantaged relative to their far more numerous men colleagues in the formal and informal aspects of leading positions.

This study also shows that adoption of affirmative measures for gender equality – as in the social democracies and, to a lesser extent, the post-communist countries – facilitates women's access to and performance in élite positions. In the Nordic countries public policies, such as family leave and widespread public childcare, and extensive public discussion of gender equality as a societal goal appear to lead to more equal sharing of family tasks between men and women partners.

In studying occupants of top political and economic leadership posts in industrial and post-industrial societies, we have found gender differences, but also substantial similarities between men and women élites. These findings offer reason for cautious optimism that men's near-monopoly of powerful positions will continue to decline.

We do not know what consequences the access of large numbers of women to top positions in public life would have on the exercise of power, but we do know that women's exclusion from such posts is very slowly declining throughout the world. Élites in industrial and especially post-industrial societies are undergoing a change related, on the one hand, to economic affluence and widespread advanced education and, on the other hand, to enhanced concern with self-realisation, which often clashes with traditional cultural patterns. Our study illuminates a specific feature of this phenomenon: how the male monopoly of public power is opening up to women, and what this means for men and women, especially for those women who challenge tradition by aiming for top offices.

Although we do not know whether a massive presence of women at the top of public life will change the traditional mechanisms of power, until now a male monopoly, it seems reasonable to surmise that in the emerging culture of post-industrial society more collegial leadership styles, oriented towards post-materialist goals, are more effective than the hierarchical style of organisation that characterised early industrial society. As we have seen, women élites are more likely to have less hierarchical, more post-materialist orientations than male élites. They may actually make more effective leaders in the emerging society – until men also learn this style.

Appendix: Data about Countries

Silvia Sansonetti

Countries	Indicators			
	Population mid-year estimates in 1,000	**Fertility rate**	**Marriage rate**	**Divorce rate**
Australia	18,054	1.9	6.2*	2.70*
Austria	8,053	1.5	5.3	2.11*
Belgium	10,113	1.6	5.1	n.a.
Canada	29,606	1.7	5.4*	2.70°
Czech Republic	10,331	1.3	5.3	3.01
Denmark	5,228	1.8	6.7	2.63*
Finland	5,108	1.8	4.5	2.70*
France	58,143	1.7	4.4	1.96
Germany	81,642	1.2	5.2	2.04*
Greece	10,458	1.4	5.9	0.74*
Hungary	10,225	1.6	5.3*	2.28*
Ireland	3,582	1.9	4.6*	n.a. (1)
Israel	5,545	2.4	6.5°	1.39°
Italy	57,187	1.2	5.0*	0.48*
Japan	125,197	1.5	6.3*	1.56*
Netherlands	15,451	1.6	5.2	2.35*
New Zealand	3,542	2.1	6.3*	n.a.
Norway	4,360	1.9	4.6*	2.54*
Poland	38,588	1.6	5.4*	0.98
Portugal	10,797	1.4	6.9°	1.22°
Russian Federation	147,855	1.4	7.3*	4.60*
Slovenia	1,984	1.3	4.2*	0.80
Spain	39,210	1.2	5.0	n.a.
Sweden	8,831	1.7	4.4	2.54
Switzerland	7,040	1.5	4.8	2.23*
United Kingdom	58,258	1.7	5.9°	3.08°
United States	263,034	2.1	9.1*	4.57*

Indicators			
Electoral system in Parliament	**% Women in national lower chamber* (2)**	**Government form is**	**Government's members are**
Non-proportional	8.0	Parliamentary	Elected
Proportional	21.0	Parliamentary	Elected
Proportional	9.0	Parliamentary	Mixed
Non-proportional	18.0	Parliamentary	Elected
Proportional	10.0	Parliamentary	Appointed
Proportional	33.0	Parliamentary	Elected
Hybrid	39.0	Parliamentary	Mixed
Non-proportional	6.0	Semi-presidential	Mixed
Hybrid	21.0	Parliamentary	Elected
Non-proportional	6.0	Parliamentary	Mixed
Hybrid	11.0	Parliamentary	Appointed
Hybrid	12.0	Parliamentary	Elected
Non-proportional	9.0	Parliamentary	Elected
Proportional (5)	15.0	Parliamentary	Mixed
Non-proportional	3.0	Parliamentary	Mixed
Proportional	31.0	Parliamentary	Appointed
Non-proportional	21.0	Parliamentary	Elected
Proportional	39.0	Parliamentary	Elected
Proportional	13.0	Parliamentary	Mixed
Proportional	9.0	Parliamentary	Appointed
Hybrid	10.0	Presidential	Appointed
Proportional	14.0	Parliamentary	Appointed
Proportional	16.0	Parliamentary	Mixed
Proportional	34.0	Parliamentary	Mixed
Proportional	18.0	Parliamentary	Elected
Non-proportional	9.0	Parliamentary	Mixed
Non-proportional	11.0	Presidential	Appointed

Countries	Indicators			
	% Women in government as minister*	% Women in high positions* (3)	% 3rd level studies who are women (not vocat)	% 3rd level studies who are women (incl. vocat)
Australia	12.9	23.3	54.0 (6)	50.1
Austria	15.8	4.7	44.2 (7)	45.8
Belgium	11.1	15.4 (4)	44.0*	49.4*
Canada	13.6	19.7	55.7*	52.7*
Czech Republic	0.0	0.0	45.0	47.9
Denmark	29.2	10.7	52.8	51.8
Finland	15.0	17.4	49.8	52.9
France	6.9	11.5	55.1*	54.6*
Germany	16.0	5.2	40.7 (8)	43.2
Greece	4.0	7.7	50.3° (9)	49.5°
Hungary	0.0	6.0	50.0	52.7
Ireland	15.8	15.0 (4)	n.a.	49.1
Israel	4.3	4.9	53.5°	50.8°
Italy	12.0	15.6	51.8	52.5
Japan	6.3	8.0	31.6*	43.7*
Netherlands	31.3	10.3	n.a.	46.1*
New Zealand	8.3	16.5	55.6 (6)	55.4
Norway	35.0	48.8	54.9	54.6
Poland	6.7	11.8	53.6*	56.7*
Portugal	9.5	5.1	57.0	57.0
Russian Federation	0.0	2.6	52.7 (9)	55.3
Slovenia	5.0	12.5	59.6^ (8)	56.8^
Spain	14.3	0.0	52.5	52.5
Sweden	30.0	4.3 (4)	n.a.	54.9
Switzerland	16.7	0.0	40.2*	36.7*
United Kingdom	8.7	7.1	48.4	50.0*
United States	13.6	26.1	n.a. (10)	n.a.

Indicators		
N° of weeks for maternity leave	**% of wage during the covered period**	**Cash benefits source**
Federal 52 that may be shared between parents	unpaid (13)	
		Social Security
8(b) and 8(a)	Medium wage-private sector. 100% pub. servants.	
		Social Security
7(b) and 8(a)	82 for 30 days 75 thereafter	
		Unemployment Insurance
17	57 for 15 weeks	n.a.
n.a.	n.a.	Municipality
4(b) and 14(a)	100 up to a ceiling	Social Security
105 days	80 (14)	Social Security
6(b) and 10(a) (11)	84	Social Security and employer
6(b) and 8(a)	It Depends on the employee's seniority	
		Social Security
16	75	Social Security
24	100 or 65 up to a ceiling	Social Security
14	70 up to a ceiling	Social Security
12	75 up to a ceiling	Social Security
2 months(b) and 3 months(a)	80	
		Health Insurance/Social
14 6(b) and 8(a)	60	Social Security
6(b) and 10(a)	100	
14	unpaid	Employer/Social Security
12(b) and 6(a)	100 (15)	Social Security
16–18 (12)	100	Social Security
90 days	50 min. private sector 100 pubblic sector	
		Social Security (Private Sector)
70 days(b) and 70 days(a)	100	Department (Public Sector)
		n.a.
n.a.	n.a.	Social Security
16	75	Social Security
6(b) and 6(a)	Guaranteed level of cash benefits fixed by law	
		Employer
8(a) (16)	100 (16)	Social Security
14	90 for 6 weeks and then weekly flat rate	
Like a temporary disability for medical reason (16)	unpaid	

Countries	Indicators
	Childcare leave for mothers
Australia	(16)
Austria	Full-time until child is 2 or part-time until the child is 4 to be shared by the parents.
Belgium	Max. of 60 months workers can leave for any reason childcare included.
Canada	24 weeks, during the first year to be shared by parents (16)
Czech Republic	n.a.
Denmark	18 weeks for the mother and 10 weeks after birth available for both. 13 weeks up to 26 per year for each parent until the child is 8.
Finland	A max. of 170 working days to be shared between parents only with the mother's consent.
France	Until the child is 3 years old one year extendable twice. It is possible to work part-time.
Germany	Until the child is four the parents may share the leave. They may also work part-time for the same or another employer.
Greece	Until the child is 30 months, 3 months unpaid for each parent.
Hungary	Employees may request an absence for a maximum of 2 years available until the child reaches the age of two.
Ireland	4 weeks after maternity leave, additional unpaid leave.
Israel	Unpaid leave for a maximum of 12 months.
Italy	6 months any time until the child is 1 year old.
Japan	Parents can take unpaid child care leave until the child reaches the age of 1.
Netherlands	Workers are entitled to work reduced hours but at least 20 hours, for a maximum interrupted period of six months, until the child is 4.
New Zealand	Unpaid leave until the child is 5 for both parents for a total of 52 weeks.
Norway	1 year to be shared between parents.
Poland	Maximum of 3 years for each child under 4 years age. The leave may be split into a maximum of three periods.
Portugal	Between 6 months and 2 years until the child is 3 starting at the end of maternity leave. Parents cannot take the leave together.
Russian Federation	18 months paid leave and unpaid leave until child is 3. It is possible to work part-time.
Slovenia	n.a.
Spain	No more then 3 years from the child birth. Only one parent can exercise the right.
Sweden	Unpaid leave up to 18 months, partly as a full-time leave and partly part-time until the child is 3.
Switzerland	(16)
United Kingdom	No.
United States	12 weeks unpaid for either parent during 12 months after the birth of a child. (16)

Indicators		
Childcare leave (Cl): for fathers and Paternity leave (Pl)	**GNP per capita in P.P.P.$**	**% of labour force who are women**
Pl: one week at the birth	18,940	43
Cl: To be eligible the male employee must live in the same house as the child.	21,250	41
Cl: as mothers. Pl: 3 days chosen by the legally recognised father within 12 days	21,660	40
Cl: as mothers.	21,130	45
n.a.	9,770	47
Cl: as mothers. Pl: 2 weeks after the birth.	21,230	46
Cl: as mothers. Pl: 6 working days paid and 12 working days unpaid for the birth.	17,760	48
Cl: as mothers. Pl: 3 days for the birth.	21,030	44
Cl: as mothers.	20,070	42
Cl: as mothers.	11,710	36
Cl: as mothers.	6,410	44
Cl: in the case of the death or illness of the mother, the father is entitled to her right.	15,680	33
Cl: for invalidity or illness of spouse	16,490	40
Cl: as mothers (in substitution of the mother or when the father has sole custody of the child)	19,870	38
Cl: as mothers.	22,110	41
Cl: as mothers. Pl: a worker is entitled to an unspecified short period for a child birth.	19,950	40
Cl: as mothers. Pl: two unpaid weeks	16,360	44
Cl: as mothers. Pl: 2 weeks for the birth if the father lives with the mother.	21,940	46
Cl: the father is entitled to this right in the case of mother's incapacity	5,400	46
Cl: the father, in the case of mother's death is entitled to take leave to care for his child.	12,670	43
Cl: as mothers.	4,480	49
n.a.	12,110^ (17)	46
Cl: as mothers. Pl: 2 days for the birth.	14,520	36
Cl: as mothers. Pl: 10 days for the birth.	18,540	48
No	25,860	40
No	19,260	43
Cl: as mothers.	26,980	46

Countries	Indicators			
	Women activity rate	% of women part-time workers	% of women employers and own account workers	% Women in management
Australia	69.7 (18)	n.a.	n.a.	13.7° (23)
Austria	77.0^	26.0	8.7	3.8
Belgium	72.0 (19)	29.8	n.a.	n.a.
Canada	76.8	n.a.	n.a.	12.5° (23)
Czech Republic	74.9^	n.a.	6.8	3.6
Denmark	83.6^	35.5	6.2	2.8
Finland	80.7	15.7	9.1^ (21)	2.4 (23)
France	78.5 (19)	28.9	n.a.	n.a.
Germany	74.8	33.8	5.8	3.6
Greece	63.3	8.4	18.7	6.2
Hungary	69.4	n.a.	6.6	4.4
Ireland	64.5	23.1	7.8	2.8
Israel	65.1^ (18)	n.a.	4.8	2.2
Italy	59.8	12.7	n.a.	14.4 (23)
Japan	60.4	n.a.	8.9	0.8 (23)
Netherlands	72.0	67.3	7.9 (21)	5.8
New Zealand	67.6	n.a.	13.1	9.5
Norway	79.8	46.3	n.a.	4.7 (23)
Poland	78.6	n.a.	19.6 (22)	4.7
Portugal	79.7	11.6	23.0	6.3
Russian Federation	83.7 (20)	n.a.	n.a.	n.a.
Slovenia	92.8	n.a.	7.6	2.7
Spain	65.1	16.6	16.3	7.8
Sweden	83.2	41.0	5.4 (21)	n.a.
Switzerland	75.0 (19)	52.9	n.a.	10.0 (23)
United Kingdom	74.6 (19)	44.3	n.a.	11.8
United States	75.4	n.a.	6.7	12.8 (23)

Indicators				
% women employed in agriculture	% women employed in industries	% women employed in services	% of women unemployed	% of unemployed who are Women
3.0* (24)	11.0* (24)	80.0* (24)	8.0	40.6
8.5	16.5	74.8	4.3	50.2
1.0* (24)	11.0* (24)	72.0* (24)	12.2	54.1
2.5	11.9	85.6	9.2	43.7
5.3	31.4	63.2	4.0	53.4
2.5	15.0	82.3	8.6	56.2
5.5	14.4	83.9	16.7	46.0
4.0* (24)	17.0* (24)	78.0* (24)	13.9 (25)	53.4 (25)
3.1	20.1	76.6	11.1	50.7
23.9	13.9	62.1	15.4	58.5
4.6	24.8	70.5	8.7	37.2
3.2	17.3	79.1	12.2	37.7
1.2	14.9	83.4	8.6	54.1
7.6	21.8	70.5	16.7	51.4
6.5	25.0	68.1	3.2	41.42
2.1	9.4	83.0	8.8	51.2
6.6	14.2	79.0	6.3	44.5
2.9	10.2	86.7	4.6	43.0
22.5	21.0	56.5	14.7	50.8
12.6	22.7	64.7	8.1	51.0
10.0* (24)	35.0* (24)	56.0* (24)	8.7	45.8
11.7	59.4	44.5	7.0	44.3
7.3	14.0	78.6	30.6	51.0
1.6	11.7	86.5	6.9	42.6
4.0* (24)	19.0* (24)	74.0* (24)	3.9	50.4
1.2	13.9	84.4	6.8	34.5
1.6	13.2	85.2	5.6	46.2

Legend

The data refer to 1995. If they are not available for that year, the symbols used are the following: * = 1994, ^ = 1996, ° = 1993.

n.a. = if they are available for none of these years.

Indicators were created based on the *Handbook for producing National Statistical Reports on Women and Men* (United Nations, 1997). It was decided to have no provisional data and homogeneous data – the same source and the same year – when possible.

Where it is not specified, the percentage of women with a given characteristic is the ratio of women in the specific group to the total of women multiplied by 100. The percentage of people with a characteristic who are women is the ratio of women with a characteristic to the total women and men who have that characteristic multiplied by 100.

Population families and households

Country population mid-year estimates (*Demographic Yearbook* 47th issue 1995, 1997 United Nations).

Total fertility rate – the average number of children that would be born alive to a hypothetical cohort of women if, throughout their reproductive years, the age-specific fertility rates for the specified year remained constant per woman (*World Development Indicators* 1997, World Bank 1997).

Marriage rate – the number of recognised marriages performed and registered per 1,000 mid-year population. Recognised marriage is an act a ceremony or a process by which the legal relationship of husband and wife is constituted; the legality of the union is established by civil, religious or other means as recognised by the laws of each country (*Demographic Yearbook* 47th issue).

The divorce rate – the annual number of final divorce decrees granted under civil law per 1,000 mid-year population. Divorce decree confers on the parties the right to remarry under civil or religious and/or other provisions according to the laws of each country (*Demographic Yearbook* 47th issue).

(1) In Ireland divorce was introduced in 1997.

Public life and leadership

Notes: (2) If the parliamentary system is monocameral this is the percentage of women in parliament. (3) These percentages include deputy-ministers and high-ranking bureaucrats. (4) Not all levels lower then minister were considered. (5) In Italy, during the survey, there was an electoral system change (in 1994) from a proportional to a hybrid non-proportional system. The data refer to 1994, to be homogeneous with the others.

The sources are our survey and *World's Women 1995* (United Nations, 1995).

Education

According to the International Standard Classification of Education (ISCED, adopted in 1976) *Third level* refers to the sixth and the seventh ISCED levels, which include courses leading to a first university degree or equivalent such as BA/BSC, as well as those which lead to first professional degrees such as doctorates awarded after completion of study in medicine, engineering or law. They include also studies leading to a postgraduate university degree. They are intended to reflect specialisation within a given subject area. The second indicator is calculated considering the fifth ISCED level, including courses leading to a professional specialisation without a degree. The data refer to the academic year 1994/5, or when not available, the academic year before (*) or after (^); (°) indicates two academic years before.

Note: (6) the data refer to the whole year 1995, (7) the data include multiple counting of students enrolled in more then one field of study, (8) not including postgraduate students if registration is not required, (9) not including postgraduate students. (10) For the United States the last rate available is from 1990s Census.

The source is the *UNESCO Yearbook 1997*, United Nations, 1997.

Maternity and childcare

Notes: Maternity leave is measured in number of weeks. (b) means before the birth and (a) means after the birth.

(11) Starting from the third child 8(b) and 18(a), (12) 18 weeks starting from the second child, (13) Only federal servants with various percentages of the total wages in different regions, (14) A total of 275 working days, (15) Women can choose: either 100 per cent for 42 weeks or 80 per cent for 52 weeks, (16) for federal countries where law differs among states, data refer to federal law only.

All data refer to *Conditions of Work Digest, Maternity and Work* Vol. 13, ILO, 1994.

Work and economy

GNP is the sum of value added by all resident producers plus any taxes (less subsidies) that are not included in the valuation of output plus net receipts of primary income (employee compensation and property income) from non resident sources. It is converted to international dollars (one PPP $ has the same purchasing power over GNP as the US dollar in the US) using the purchasing power parity rates.

(17) For Slovenia the PPP$ GNP was available for 1996 only. *World Development Indicators 1997* and *World Development Indicators 1998* (World Bank, 1998).

Statistics on labour are based on *Labour Force Sample Surveys* in *International Labour Organisation Yearbook*, 1996 (*International Labour Organisation Yearbook 1996*, 1997) and 1997 (*International Labour Organisation Yearbook 1997*, 1998). These sample surveys include groups of persons who are often not covered in labour statistics, in fact the economically active population and economically non-active population are both considered. For employment all status groups are covered: employees, including paid family workers, employers, self-employed, members of producers' co-operatives, contributing family workers and workers not classifiable by status; usually no distinction is made between persons employed full-time and less then full-time. Regarding unemployment, Labour Force Sample Surveys include people seeking work for the first time who are generally excluded from other statistics. Generally the definitions of economically active population, unemployment and employment used for this type of statistics, follow the recommendations of the International Labour Organisation and are more comparable than those obtained by other sources. The reference period is one day or one week.

The employed: comprise all persons above a specific age who, during a specified period, either one week or day, were in paid employment – at work or with a job but not at work – or in self-employment – at work or with an enterprise but not at work.

The unemployed: comprise all persons above a specified age who, during the reference period, were: without work, currently available for work, seeking work.

The economically active population: comprises people who supply labour for the production of goods and services during a specified period (generally one year), it includes both employed and unemployed. The treatment of groups such as the armed forces and seasonal and part-time workers varies by country. Whereas the armed forces, the unemployed and first-time job-seekers are generally included, unpaid carers, housewives, students, members of collective households, inmates of institutions, the retired, people living entirely on investment income, people wholly dependent upon others and workers in the informal sector are not included.

To have homogeneous data for the percentage of labour force who are women, the source is *World Development Indicators 1997*.

For the percentage of women part-time workers only countries that adopt the same classification are considered. *Eurostat Yearbook* 1997 (Eurostat, 1997).

In calculating the percentage of women employers and self-employed, the indications in *International Classification by Status in Employment* (ICSE, 1993) were followed: employers and the self-employed operate alone or with one or more partners (who may or may not be members of the family household), operate a job where the remuneration depends directly upon profits derived from goods and services produced. The difference being that employers employ one or more persons on a continuous basis, the self-employed do not. The meaning of the continuous basis varies with the national definitions; generally members of producers' co-operatives and contributing family workers are not included.

Women in management is the ratio between: women classified as legislator, senior official and managers, following *International Standard Classification for Occupation* (ISCO-1988) or administrative and managerial workers – as ISCO 1968 indicates – and women employed in the whole year.

Percentages of women employed in different sectors are ratios between women employed in each sector, following the *International Standard Industrial Classification* (ISIC), Revision 2 or 3, divided by the total of women employed.

(18) Age 25–44. (19) Age 25–49 *Eurostat Labour Force Survey*. (20) Age 25–49. (21) Employers only. (22) Comprehensive of members of producer's co-operatives. (23) Indicates countries where ISCO 68 is still adopted (see ILO *Yearbook 1996*, 1997). (24) The source is *World Development Indicators 1998*. (25) These rates are compiled by national authorities using the official estimates.

Bibliography

Aberbach J. D., Putnam R. D., Rockman B. A. with the collaboration of Anton T. J., Eldersveld S. J., Inglehart R. (1981), *Bureaucrats and Politicians in Western Democracies*, Harvard University Press.

Acker J. (1991), 'Hierarchies, jobs, bodies: a theory of gendered organizations', in Lorber J. and Farrell S. (eds), *The Social Construction of Gender*, Sage: 162–79.

Adam B. (1990), *Time and Social Theory*, Polity Press.

Adam B. (1993), 'Within and beyond the time economy of employment relations: conceptual issues pertinent to research on time and work', *Social Science Information* 32(2):163–84.

Adler N. and Izraeli D. (1988), 'Women in management worldwide', in Adler N. and Izraeli D. (eds), *Women in Management Worldwide*, Sharpe: 3–16.

Adler, N. (1993), 'An international perspective on the barriers to the advancement of women managers', *Applied Psychology: An International Review*, 42(2):289–300.

Adler N. and Izraeli D. (eds) (1994), *Competitive Frontiers. Women Managers in a Global Economy*, Blackwell.

Adler N. (1996), 'Global women political leaders: an invisible history, an increasingly important future', *Leadership Quarterly* 7(1):133–61.

Ahrne G. et al. (1985), *Klasssamhällets förändring* (Changes in Class Society), Arkiv.

Airsman L. A. and Bam D. S. (1993), 'A comparative study of the occupational attainment processes of white men and women in the United States: the effects of having ever married, spousal education, children and having ever divorced', *Journal of Comparative Family Studies* 24(2), Summer: 171–87.

Allen S. (1997), 'Gender relation and research on work' in Holmer J. and Karlsson J. C. (eds), *Work – Quo Vadis? Re-thinking the Questions of Work*, Ashgate Publishing Company.

Almond G. and Verba S. (1963), *The Civic Culture: Political Attitudes and Democracy in Five Nations*, Princeton University Press.

Alvesson M. (1997), 'Kvinnor och ledarskap. En översigt och problematisering' (Women in leadership. An overview and problematisation) in Nyberg A. and Sundin E. (eds), *Ledare, makt och Kön*, SOU.

Alvesson M. and Billing Y. D. (eds) (1997), *Understanding Gender and Organisations*, Sage.

Andersson G. (1993), *Leva för jobbet och jobba för livet. Om chefs familjers vardag och samlevnadsformer* (To live for work and work to live. Bosses' families' daily life and life forms), Symposium.

Andersson G. (1996), 'Karriär, kön, familj' (Career, gender, family), in Nyberg A. and Sundin E. (eds), 135.

Andrew C., Coderre C. and Denis A. (1994), 'Women in management: the Canadian experience' in Adler N. and Izraeli D. (eds), 377–87.

Aschaffenburg K. and Maas I. (1997), 'Cultural and educational careers: the dynamics of social reproduction', *American Sociological Review*, 62:573–87.

Atkinson A. (1997), *Creating Culture Change: Strategies for Success*, Rushmere Wynne.

Baltzell E. D. (1958), *Philadelphia Gentleman: the Making of a National Upper Class*, Free Press.

Barrett M. (1980), *Women's Oppression Today*, Verso.

Becker G. (1985), 'Human capital, effort, and the sexual division of labor', *Journal of Labour Economics*, 3(1):33–58.

Beck-Gernsheim E. (1983), 'Vom 'Dasein für andere' zum Anspruch auf ein Stück 'eigenes Leben': Individualisierungsprozesse im weiblichen Lebenszusammenhang', *Soziale Welt*, 3:307–40.

Beck-Gernsheim E. (1993), *Das halbierte Leben. Männerwelt Beruf, Frauenwelt Familie*, Fischer-Taschenbuch-Verlag.

Beck-Gernsheim E. and Beck U. (1995), *The Normal Chaos of Love*, Polity.

Beechey V. and Perkins T. (1987), *A Matter of Hours: Women. Part-time Work and the Labour Market*, Polity.

Bell, D. (1970), *El Advenimiento de la Sociedad Postindustrial*, Alianza.

Berger P. and Luckmann T. (1966) *The Social Construction of Reality*, Doubleday.

Bernadoni C. and Werner V. (1987), *Ohne Seil und Haken. Frauen auf dem Weg nach oben*, Deutsche Unesco-Kommission.

Berthoin A. and Izraeli D. (1993), 'A global comparison of women in management. Women managers in their homelands and as expatriates', in Fagenson, Ellen (ed.), *Women in Management. Trends, Issues, and Challenges in Managerial Diversity*, Sage: 52–96.

Billing Y. D. and Alvesson M. (1994), *Gender, Managers and Organizations*, de Gruyter.

Bischoff S. (1990), *Frauen zwischen Macht und Mann. Männer in der Defensive. Führungskräfte in Zeiten des Umbruchs*, Rewohlt Verlag.

Blanchard K. and Johnson S. (1981), *The One Minute Manager*, Berkeley Books.

Blossfeld H. P. and Shavit Y. (eds) (1993), *Persistent Inequality: Changing Educational Attainment in Thirteen Countries*, Westview.

Blum T. C., Fields D. L. and Goodman J. S. (1994), 'Organization-level determinants of women in management', *Academy of Management Journal*, 37:241–68.

Borchorst A. (1994), 'Welfare regimes, women's interest and the EC', in Sainsbury D. (ed.), *Gendering Welfare States*, Sage.

Bottomore T. (1993), *Élites and Society*, Routledge, 1993.

Bourdieu P. (1977), *Outline of a Theory of Practice*, Cambridge University Press.

Bourdieu P. (1983), *La Distinción. Crítica Social del Juicio*, Taurus.

Bourdieu P. (1984), 'Espace social et genèse de "classe"', *Actes de la Recherche en Sciences Sociales*, 52/53.

Bourdieu P. (1984), *Distinction. A Social Critique of the Judgement of Taste*, Harvard University Press.

Bourdieu P. (1985), *Question de Sociologie*, Minuit.

Bourdieu P. (1986), 'The forms of capital', in Richardson J. (ed.), *Handbook of Theory and Research in the Sociology of Education*, Greenwood.

Bourdieu P. (1987), 'What makes a social class? On the theoretical and practical existence of groups', *Berkeley Journal of Sociology*: 1–17.

Bourdieu P. (1988), *Homo Academicus*, Stanford University Press.

Bourdieu P. (1989), 'Social space and symbolic power', *Sociological Theory*: 14–25.

Bourdieu P. and Passeron J. C. (1970), *La Réproduction*, Minuit.

Bourdieu P. and Passeron J. C. (1979), *The Inheritors*, University of Chicago Press.

Brodsky M. A. (1993), 'Successful female corporate managers and entrepreneurs: similarities and differences', *Group and Organization Management*, 18(3).

Burke R. J. and McKeen C. A. (1990), 'Mentoring in organizations: implications for women', *Journal of Business Ethics* 9:317–32.

Burton M. and Higley J. (1987) 'Invitation to élite theory. The basic contentions reconsidered', in Domhoff G. and Dye T. (eds), *Power Élites and Organizations*, Sage.

Burzio F. (1945), *Essenza e Attualità del Liberalismo*, Einaudi.

Calas M. and Smircich L. (1993), 'Dangerous liaisons: the 'Feminine-in-Management' meets globalisation', *Business Horizons*, March–April.

Chafetz J. S. (1988), *Gender Equity: an Integrated Theory of Stability and Change*, Sage.

Chapman J. (1993), *Politics, Feminism and the Reformation of Gender*, Routledge.

Charles, N. (1993), *Gender Divisions and Social Change*, Harvester-Wheatsheaf.

Cockburn C. (1985), *Machinery of Dominance: Women, Men and Technical Know-how*, Pluto.

Cockburn C. (1991), *In the Way of Women, Men's Resistance to Sex Equality in Organisations*, Macmillan.

Coleman J. S. and Fararo T. J. (eds) (1992), *Rational Choice Theory, Advocacy and Critique*, Sage.

Collinson D. L., Knights D. and Collinson M. (1990), *Managing to Discriminate: The Reproduction and Rationalization of Sex Discrimination*, Routledge.

Collinson D. L. and Hearn J. (1994), 'Naming men and women: Implications for work, organization and management', *Gender, Work and Organization.* I(1) January: 2–22.

Collinson D. L. and Hearn J. (1995) 'Men managing leadership', *International Review of Women and Leadership*, 1(2):1–24.

Collinson D. L. and Hearn J. (eds) (1996), *Men as Managers, Managers as Men. Critical Perspectives on Men, Masculinities and Management*, Sage.

Connell R. W. (1987), *Gender and Power: Society, the Person and Sexual Politics*, Polity.

Coole D. (1996) 'Is class a difference that makes a difference?', *Radical Philosophy* 77, May/June: 17–25.

Coser L. and Coser R. (1974) 'The housewife and her greedy family', in L. Coser and R. Coser (eds), *Greedy Institutions: Patterns of Undivided Commitment*, Free Press: 89–100.

Cox T. and Blake S. (1991), 'Managing cultural diversity: implications for organizational competitiveness', *Academy of Management Review*, 5(3):45–56.

Coyle A. (1989), 'Women in management: a suitable case for treatment', in *Feminist Review*, 31, Spring.

Crompton R. (1993), *Class and Stratification*, Polity Press.

Czudnowski M. (ed.) (1982), *Does Who Governs Matter?*, Northern Illinois University Press.

Dahl R. A. (1956), *A Preface to Democratic Theory*, Chicago University Press.

Dahl R. A. (1971), *Polyarchy*, Yale University Press.

Dahl R. A. (1989), *Democracy and its Critics*, Yale University Press.

Dahl R. A. (1991), *Modern Political Analysis*, Prentice-Hall.

Dahlerup D. (1991) 'Strategien auf dem Weg von einer kleinen zu einer grossen Minderheit – Frauen in der skandinavischen Politik', in Schaeffer-Hegel B. and Kopp-Degethoff H. (eds), *Vater Staat und seine Frauen*, Bd. 2, Pfaffenweiler, Centaurus: 71–88.

Daly M. (1994), 'Comparing welfare states: toward a gender friendly approach', in Sainsbury D., *Gendering Welfare States*, Sage.

Davidson M. J. and Cooper C. L. (1992), *Shattering the Glass Ceiling*, Paul Chapman.

Davies K. (1989), *Women and Time, Weaving the Strands of Everyday Life*, Avebury.

Department of Labor Women's Bureau (1992), *File No. 92*.

Diamond E. E. (1987), 'Theories of career development and the reality of women at work', in Gutek B. A. and Larwood L. (eds), *Women's Career Development*, Sage: 15–27.

Diamond E. E. (1998) *'Gender and Working Conditions in the European Union'* in report prepared by K. Kauppinen and I. Kandolin for the European Foundation for the Improvement of Living and Working Conditions, Dublin.

Diem-Wille G. (1996), *Karrierefrauen und Karrieremänner. Eine psychoanalytisch orientierte Untersuchung ihrer Lebensgeschichte und Familiendynamik*, Opladen.

Djilas M. (1957), *The New Class*, Praeger.

Dogan M. and Pelassy D. (1984), *How to Compare Nations: Strategies in Comparative Politics*, Chatham House.

Dogan M. and Higley J. (eds) (1998), *Élites, Crises and the Origins of Regims*, Rowman and Littlefield.

Dogan M. (ed.) (1989), *Pathways to Power: Selecting Rulers in Pluralist Democracies*, Westview.

Domhoff G. W. (1998), *Who Rules America? Power and Politics in the Year 2000*, Mayfield.

Dorso G. (1955), *Dittatura, Classe Politica e Classe Dirigente*, Einaudi.

Dreher G. and Ash, R. (1990), 'A comparative study of mentoring among men and women in managerial professional and technical positions', *Journal of Applied Psychology*, 75:539–46.

Drew E. (1987), 'New structures of work, an irish perspective', *International Journal of Manpower*, 8(2).

Drew E. (1990), *Who Needs Flexibility? Part-time Working . . . The Irish Experience*, Dublin: Employment Equality Agency.

Drew E. and Emerek R. (1998), 'Employment, flexibility and gender' in Drew E., Emerek R. and Mahon E. (eds), *Women, Work and the Family in Europe*, Routledge: 89–99.

Duane-Richard A. M. (1988) 'Gender relations and female labour: a consideration of sociological categories' in Jenson J. et al.

Eagly A. H. and Johnson B. T. (1990), 'Gender and leadership style', *Psychological Bulletin* 108(2):233–56.

Einhorn B. (1993), *Cinderella Goes to Market. Citizenship, Gender and Women's Movements in East Central Europe*, Verso.

Elchardus M. and Glorieux I. (1994), 'The search for the invisible 8 hours: the gendered use of time in a society with a high labour force participation of women', *Time and Society*, 3(1):5–27.

Elias P. and Main B. (1982), *Women's Working Lives: Evidence from the National Training Survey*, University of Warwick: Institute for Employment Research.

Ellis G. and Wheeler J. (1991), *Women Managers: Success on Our Own Terms*, Penguin Books.

Ely R. (1995), 'The power in demography: women's social construction of gender identity at work', *Academy of Management Journal*, 38(3):589–634.

Epstein C. F. (1970), *Woman's Place: Options and Limits in Professional Careers*, University of California Press.

Epstein C. F. and Coser R. L. (eds) (1981), *Access to Power: Cross-National Studies of Women and Élites*, George Allen and Unwin.

Epstein C. F. (1981), *Women in Law*, University of Illinois Press.

Epstein C. F. (1988), *Deceptive Distinctions. Sex, Gender, and the Social Order*, Sage.

Epstein C. F. (1994), 'A different angle of vision: notes on the selective eye of sociology', *Social Science Quarterly*, December: 645–56.

Epstein C. F., Seron C., Oglensky B. and Saute R. (1999), *The Part-Time Paradox: Time Norms, Professional Life, Family and Gender*, Routledge.

Esping-Andersen G. (1990), *The Three Worlds of Welfare Capitalism*, Polity.

Esseveld J. (1988), *Beyond Silence. Middle-aged Women in the 1970's*, Lund University.

Esseveld J. (1997), 'Om kvinnliga förtroendevalda, makt och könsrelationer i fack-föreningar' (About women representatives, power and gender relations in unions) in Nyberg A. and Sundin E. (eds), *Ledare, makt och Kön*, SOU, Stockholm, 135.

Etzioni-Halevy E. (ed.) (1997), *Classes and Élites in Democracy and Democratization a Collection of Readings*, Garland.

European Commision (1997), *Women and Employment in the European Union*.

European Commission (1995), *Frauen und Männer in der Europäischen Union*, Eurostat.

European Commission (1997), *Gender Equality and the Reconciliation of Working, Family and Personal Life: a Review of Documents Produced by Five International Organisations*.

European Commission (1996), *Women in Decision-Making*.

European Foundation for the Improvement of Living and Working Conditions (1998), *Gender and Working Condition in the European Union*.

EUROSTAT Yearbook '96. *A Statistical Eye on Europe 1985–1995*.

Evans M. (ed.) (1994), *The Woman Question*, Sage.

Fagenson E. (1990), 'At the heart of women in management research: theoretical and methodological approaches and their biases', *Journal of Business Ethics*, 9:267–74.

Fagenson E. A. and Jackson J. J. (1994), 'The status of women managers in the United States', in Adler N. J. and Izraeli D. N. (eds), 388–404.

Fiedler F. E. (1967), *A Theory of Leadership Effectiveness*, McGraw-Hill.

Fine B. (1992), *Women's Employment and the Capitalist Family*, Routledge.

Fisichella D. (1996), *La rappresentanza politica*, Laterza.

Flanders M. (1994), *Breakthrough: the Career Woman's Guide to Shattering the Glass Ceiling*, Chapman.

Folbre N. (1994), *Who Pays for the Kids?*, Routledge.

Fraser N. (1989), *Unruly Practices: Power, Discourse and Gender in Contemporary Social Theory*, University of Minnesota Press.

Frey (1993), 'The perception of power: regarding what is perceived', *Revue Inter-nationale de Sociologie*, 1–2:156–82.

Friberg T. (1990), *Kvinnors vardag. Om kvinnors arbete och liv. Anpassningsstrategier i tid och rum* (Women's everyday life. About Women's work and life. Strategies in time and space), Lund University Press.

Funk N. and Mueller M. (1993), *Gender Politics and Post-Communism: Reflections from Eastern Europe and the Former Soviet Union*, Routledge.

García de León Mª. A. (1982), *Las Élites Femeninas Españolas (Una Investigación Sociológica)*, Queimada.

García de León Mª. A. (1991), *Las Mujeres Políticas Españolas*. Dirección General de la Mujer, Madrid.

García de León Mª. A. et al. (eds) (1993), *Sociología de la Educación*, Barcanova.

García de León Mª. A. (1993), 'Masculino y femenino en el sistema de enseñanza español', in M. A. García de León et al.

García de León Mª. A. (1994), *Élites Discriminadas*, Anthropos.

Gelb J. (1986), 'Movement strategies: inside or outside the "system" – feminism in Britain: politics without power?' in Dahlerup D. (ed.), *The New Women's Movement Feminism and Political Power in Europe and the USA*, Sage: 103–21.

Gherardi S. (1994) 'The gender we think, the gender we do in our everyday organizational lives', *Human Relations*, 47(6): 591–610.

Gibson J., Ivancevich J. and Donnelley J. (1988), *Organizations*, Business Publications,.
Giddens Anthony (1991), *Modernity and Self-Identity – Self and Society in the Late Modern Age*, Stanford University Press.
Goldthorpe J. (1997), 'Current issues in comparative macrosociology: a debate on methodological issues,' in *Comparative Social Research*, 16.
Guy M. E. (ed.) (1992), *Women and Men of the States*, Sharpe.
Haavio-Mannila E., Dahlerup D., Eduards M., Gudmundsdottir E., Halsaa B., Hernes H. M., Haenninen-Salmelin E., Sigmundsdottir B., Sinkkonen S. and Skard T. (1985), *Unfinished Democracy: Women in Nordic Politics*, Pergamon.
Hale M. M. and Mae Kelly R. M. (eds) (1989), *Gender, Bureaucracy, and Democracy*, Greenwood Press.
Hall D. (1976), *Careers in Organisations*, Goodyear.
Hansson C. G. (1996), *Fackliga karriärer* (Union Careers), Boreá.
Hantrais L. (1993), 'The gender of time in professional occupations', *Time and Society* 2(2):139–57.
Harragan B. L. (1977), 'Games mother never taught you', reprinted in Frost P. J., Mitchell V. and Nord W. R. (eds), *Organizational Reality*, HarperCollins, (1992):188–202.
Harriman A. (1985), *Women/Men/Management*, Praeger.
Headlee S. and Elfin M. (1996) *The Cost of Being Female*, Praeger.
Hearn J. and Parkin W. (1988), 'Women, men and leadership. a critical review of assumptions, practices, and change in the industrialized nations' in Adler N. and Izraeli D. (eds), 17–40.
Heller F. (ed.) (1992), *Decision-making and Leadership*, Cambridge University Press.
Hennig M. and Jardim A. (1976), *The Managerial Woman. The Survival Manual for Women in Business*, Pocket Books.
Hernes H. M. (1987), *Welfare State and Womanpower: Essays in State Feminism*, Norwegian University Press.
Hernes H. M. (1984), 'Le rôle des femmes dans la vie politique en Europe', in Conseil de l'Europe, *La Situation des Femmes dans la Vie Politique*, Pt. III
Hersey P., Blanchard K. H. (1977), *Management of Organizational Behaviour: Utilizing Human Resources*, Prentice-Hall.
Higley J., Deacon D. and Smart D. (1979), *Élites in Australia*, Routledge and Kegan Paul.
Higley J., Hoffmann-Lange U., Kadushin Ch. and Moore G. (1992), 'Élite integration in stable democracies', *European Sociological Review* 77:35–48.
Hirdman Y. (1990), 'Genussystemet' (The Gender System), in *Demokrati och makt i Sverige* (Democracy and Power in Sweden), SOU.
Hochschild A. (1997), *The Time Bind*, H. Holt & Co.
Hodge B. J. and Anthony W. P. (1988), *Organization Theory*, Allyn and Bacon.
Hofstede G. (1991), *Cultures and Organizations. Software of the Mind. Intercultural Cooperation and its Importance for Survival*, McGraw-Hill.
Højgaard L. (1996) 'Working fathers – caught in the web of the symbolic order of gender', *Acta Sociologica*, 40:245–61.
Højrup Th. and Christensen L. R. (1988), 'Strukturel livsformsanalyse' (Structural life-forms analysis), *Nord Nytt, Nordisk tidskrift for folkelivsforskning*, 37.
Holter H. (1970), *Sex Roles and Social Structure*, Universitetsforlaget.
Hood J. C. (1983), *Becoming a Two-Job Family*, Praeger.
ILO (1997), *Yearbook of Labour Statistics*.
Inglehart R. (1977), *Silent Revolution*, Princeton University Press.

Inglehart R. (1990), *Culture Shift in Advanced Industrial Society*, Princeton University Press

Inglehart R. (1997), *Modernization and Postmodernization. Cultural, Economic and Political Change in 43 Societies*, Princeton University Press.

Inglehart R., Basanez M. and Moreno A. (1998), *Human Values and Beliefs: A Cross-Cultural Sourcebook.*, The University of Michigan.

Ishida H. (1993), *Social Mobility in Contemporary Japan: Educational Credentials, Class and the Labour Market in a Cross-National Perspective*, Macmillan.

Ishida H. et al. (1995), 'Class origin, class destination, and education: a cross-national study of ten industrial nations', *American Journal of Sociology*, 10(1):145–93.

Ivanko S. (1980), *Raziskovanje in projektiranje organizacije* (Organization research and designing); Delo – Gospodarski vestnik.

Jaarboek Emancipatie '98, *Tijd en ruimte voor arbeid en zorg* (Yearbook Emancipation '98, Time and space for labor and care), VUGA Uitgeverij B.V.

Jacobs, J. A. (1992), 'Women's entry into management. Trends in earnings, authority and values among salaried managers', *Administrative Science Quarterly* No. 37: 282–301.

Jaffee, D. (1989), 'Gender inequality in workplace autonomy and authority', *Social Science Quarterly* 70, 2: 375–90.

Jasinska-Kania A. (1998), 'Kim są przedstawiciele lokalnych elit władzy?' (Who are representatives of local authorities?), in Wiatr, Jerzy (ed.), W*adza lokalna w warunkach demokracji* (Local Authorities in Conditions of Democracy), Institute of Sociology, University of Warsaw: 35–45.

Jencks Ch. et al. (1972), *Inequality: a Reassessment of the Effect of Family and Schooling in America*, Basic Books.

Jenson J., Hagen E. and Reddy C. (1988), *Feminizatiuon of the Labour Force Paradoxes and Promises*, Polity.

Johnson G. and Scholes K. (1997), *Exploring Corporate Strategy*, Prentice-Hall.

Joseph B. (1994), *Envy in Everyday Life. Psychic Equilibrium and Psychic Change*, Routledge.

Kanter R. M. (1977), *Men and Women of the Corporation*, Basic Books.

Kast F. E. and Rosenzweig J. E. (1985), *Organization and Management*, McGraw-Hill.

Kauppinen-Toropainen K. (1994), 'Women under a glass ceiling: breaking the masculine gender stamp of the manager', in *Women at the Top: a Study on Women as Leaders in the Private Sectors*, Statistics Finland, Studies No. 211:50–62.

Kavčič B. and Antončič V. (1978), *Samoupravna urejenost in gospodarska uspecnost delovnih organizacij* (Self-management realisations and economic efficiency of work organizations); Delavska enotnost.

Kavčič B. (1991), *Sodobna teorija organizacije* (Contemporary Organization Theory), DZS.

Knights D. and Odin P. (1995) '"It's About Time!" The significance of gendered time for financial services consumption', *Time and Society*, 4(2):205–31.

Korac-Karabadse A., Korac-Karabadse N. and Meyers A. (1998), *Demographics and Leadership Philosophy: Exploring Gender Differences*, Paper given at The Manchester Conference of Gender, Work and Organization.

Kotthoff H. and Wodak R. (1997), *Communicating Gender in Context*, John Benjamins.

Kovac J. (1990), *Uresnicevanje strategije podjetja s pomocjo organizacijske strategije* (Realisation of the Companies' Strategy with Organizational Strategy), FSPN.

Kuusipalo J. (1994), 'Women as political actors in the Finnish welfare states', in Anttonen A. (ed.), *Women and the Welfare State: Politics, Professions and Practices*, Department of Social Policy. University of Jyväskylä, Working Papers No. 87:52–72.

Langevin, A. (1984), 'Le caractère sexué des temps sociaux', *Pour*, No. 95:75–82.

Lasswell H. D. et al. (1952), *The Comparative Study of Élites: an Introduction and Bibliography*, Stanford University Press.

Lasswell H. D. (1936), Politics: *Who Gets What, When, How*, Free Press.

Lasswell H. D. and Kaplan A. (1950), *Power and Society*, Yale University Press.

Leira A. (1994), 'The "woman-friendly" welfare state?: The case of Norway and Sweden', in Lewis J. (ed.), 49–71.

Lewis J. and Ostner I. (1991), *Gender and the Evolution of European Social Policies. CES workshop on Emergent Supranational Social Policy: The EC's Social Dimension in Comparative Perspective*, Center for European Studies, Harvard University.

Lewis J. (1992), 'Gender and the development of welfare regimes', *Journal of European Social Policy*, 2(3):159–73.

Lewis J. (1994). 'Introduction: women, work, family and social policies in Europe' in *Women and Social Policies in Europe. Work, Family and the State*, Edward Elgar. 1–24.

Lewis S. and Lewis J. (eds) (1996), *The Work–Family Challenge: Rethinking Employment*, Sage.

Liebig B. (1997), *Geschlossene Gesellschaft. Aspekte der Geschlechterungleichheit in wirtschaftlichen und politischen Führungsgremien der Schweiz*, Rüegger.

Lijphart A. (1977), *Democracy in Plural Societies: a Comparative Exploration*, Yale University Press.

Lijphart A. (1984), *Democracies: Patterns of Majoritarian and Consensus Government in Twenty-one Countries*, Yale University Press.

Likert R. (1961), *New Patterns of Management*, McGraw-Hill.

Likert R. (1967), *The Human Organization*, McGraw-Hill.

Lindenberg, S. (1991), 'Social approval, fertility, and female labour market behaviour', in Siegers J. J., de Jong-Gierveld J. and van Imhoff E. (eds), *Female Labour Market Behaviour and Fertility. A Rational Choice Approach*, Springer.

Lipovec F. (1987), *Razvita teorija organizacije* (Developed Organization Theory), Obzorja.

Lovenduski J. (1986), *Women and European Politics: Contemporary Feminism and Public Policy*, University of Massachusetts Press.

Lovenduski J. and Norris P. (1989), 'Pathways to Parliament', *Talking Politics*, 8(4).

Mannheim K. (1964), *Wissenssoziologie, Auswahl aus dem Werk*, Luchterhand.

Marshall G., Newby H., Rose D. and Vogler C. (1988), *Social Class in Modern Britain*, Hutchinson.

Martin J. and Roberts C. (1984), *Women and Employment: a Lifetime Perspective*, Department of Employment/OPCS.

McPherson J. M. and Smith-Lovin L. (1986), 'Sex segregation in voluntary associations', *American Sociological Review* 51:61–79.

Melucci A. (1996), *The Playing Self: Person and Meaning in the Planetary Society*, Cambridge University Press.

Mercure D. and Wallemacq A. (eds) (1988), *Les Temps Sociaux*, De Boeck-Wesmael.

Meyer K. (1986), 'The influence of gender on work activities and attitudes of senior civil servants in the United States, Canada, and Great Britain,' in Moore G. and Spitze G. (eds), *Women and Politics: Activism, Attitudes and Office-Holding. Research in Politics and Society, Vol. 2*, JAI: 283–300.

Miliband R. (1969), *The State in Capitalist Society*, Basic Books.

Miller J. (1986), *Pathways in the Workplace: the Effects of Gender and Race on Access to Organizational Resources*, Cambridge University Press.

Mills C. W. (1956), *The Power Élite*, Oxford University Press.

Mizruchi M. (1996), 'What do interlocks do? An analysis, critique, and assessment of research on interlocking directorates', *Annual Review of Sociology* 22:271–98.

Mobley M. G., Jaret C., Marsh K. and Lim Y. Y. (1994), 'Mentoring, job satisfaction, gender, and the legal profession', *Sex Roles*, 31(1–2):79–98.

Moore G. (1979), 'The structure of a national élite network', *American Sociological Review* 44:673–91.

Moore G. (1988), 'Women in élite positions: insiders or outsiders?', *Sociological Forum* 3:566–85.

Moore G. (1992), 'Gender and informal networks in state government', *Social Science Quarterly*, 73:46–61.

Morgan G. (1986), *Images of Organization*, Sage.

Morrison A. M. and Von Glinow M. A. (1990), 'Women and minorities in management', *American Psychologist*, 45:200–8.

Morrison A. M., White R. P., Van Velsor E. and the Center for Creative Leadership (eds) (1992), *Breaking The Glass Ceiling: Can Women Reach the Top of America's Largest Corporations?*, Addison-Wesley.

Moss P. (1996) 'Reconciling employment and family responsibilities: a European perspective', in Lewis S. and Lewis J. (eds), *The Work Family Challenge*.

Nagel Th. (1975), *The Descriptive Analysis of Power*, Yale University Press.

Nagel Th. (ed.) (1995), *Other Minds: Critical Essays, 1969–1994*, Oxford University Press.

Nicolaou-Smokoviti L. and Baldwin B. (1990), *Alienation and Burnout in the Case of Women Professionals in Greece*, Paper presented at the 12th World Congress of Sociology, International Sociological Association.

Nicolaou-Smokoviti L. (1998), 'Women managers in Greek banking organizations: a model for interpreting women's participation in management', in the volume published in honour of Vasilios Sarsentis, University of Piraeus.

Noe R. A. (1988), 'Women and mentoring: a review and research agenda', *Academy of Management Review*, 13:65–78.

Nordic Council of Ministers (1995), *Women and Men in the Nordic Countries. Facts and Figures 1994*.

Norris P. (1987), *Politics and Sexual Equality The Comparative Position of Women in Western Democracies*, Wheatsheaf.

Norris P. and Lovenduski J. (1995), *Political Recruitment: Gender, Race and Class in the British Parliament*, Cambridge University Press.

Norris P. (1996) 'Women politicians: transforming Westminster?', in Lovenduski J. and Norris P. (eds), *Women in Politics*, Oxford University Press: 91–104.

Odendahl T. and Youmans S. (1994), 'Women on nonprofit boards', in Odendahl T. and O'Neill M. (eds), *Women and Power in the Nonprofit Sector*, Jossey Bass: 183–221.

OECD (1985), *The Integration of Women into the Economy*.

Oeuvrard F. (1993), 'Tendencias actuales de la sociologìa de la educaciòn en Francia', in Garcìa de Leon M. A., *Sociologìa de la Educacaciòn en Francia*, Barcanova.

Ohlott P. J., Ruderman M. N. and McCauley C. (1994), 'Gender differences in managers developmental job experiences', *Academy of Management Journal*, 37:46–67.

Orloff A. S. (1992), 'Gender and the social rights of citizenship: state policies and gender relations in comparative research', *American Sociological Review*, 58(3):303–28.

Palgi M. (1994), 'Women in the changing kibbutz economy', *Economic and Industrial Democracy*, 15(1):55–74.

Papanek H. (1973), 'Men, women and work: reflections on the two-person career', *American Journal of Sociology*: 857–72.

Parasuraman S. and Greenhaus J. H. (1993), 'Personal portrait: the life-style of the woman manager' in Fagenson E. A. (ed.), *Women in Management*, Sage: 186–211.

Pateman C. (1989), *The Disorder of Women*, Stanford University Press.

Pollert A. (1996), 'Gender and class revisited; or, the poverty of patriarchy', *Sociology* 30(4).

Powell G. N. and Butterfield D. A. (1994), 'Glass ceiling phenomenon: an empirical study of actual promotions to top management', *Academy of Management Journal*, 37:68–86.

Przeworski A. and Teune H. (1971), *Values and the Active Community: a Cross-National Study of the Influence of Local Leadership*, Free Press.

Putnam R. D. (ed.) (1976), *The Comparative Study of Political Élites*, Prentice-Hall.

Quinn J. B., Minzberg H. and James R. M. (1988), *The Strategy Process*, Prentice-Hall.

Ragin C. C. (1987), *The Comparative Method: Moving Beyond Qualitative and Quantitative Strategies*, University of California Press,

Ramsey K. and Parker M. (1992), 'Gender, bureaucracy and organizational culture', in Witz A. and Savage M. (eds), *Gender and Bureaucracy*, Blackwell, 253–78.

Randall V. (1987), *Women and Politics an International Perspective*, Macmillan.

Rantallaiho L. (1993) 'Reshaping the gender contract', OECD Conference, *A Mirror to the Future*, Helsinki.

Reskin B. and Padavic I. (1994), *Women and Men at Work*, Pine Forge.

Reskin B. and Ross C. (1992), 'Jobs, authority and earnings among managers: the continuing significance of sex', *Work and Occupations*, 19, 4:342–65.

Riger S. and Galligan P. (1980), 'Women in management: an exploration of competing paradigms', *American Psychologist*, 35:902–10.

Rogers B. (1988), *Men Only an Investigation into Men's Organisations*, London: Unwin-Hyman.

Rosenbaum, J. (1984), *Career Mobility in a Corporate Hierarchy*, Academic Press.

Rosener J. B. (1990), 'Ways women lead', *Harvard Business Review*, November–December.

Rubery J. and Fagan C. (1995), 'Gender segregation in societal context', *Work, Employment and Society*, 9(2):213–40.

Rubery J., Fagan C. and Smith M. (1995), *Changing Patterns of Work and Working Time in the European Union and The Impact on Gender Divisions*, Report for the Equal Opportunities Unit, Commission of the European Communities.

Rueschemeyer D. E., Stephens H. and Stephens. J. D. (1992), *Capitalist Development and Democracy*, University of Chicago Press.

Sartori G. (1976), *Parties and Party Systems*, Cambridge University Press.

Sartori G. (1993), *La democracia después del comunismo*, Alianza Editorial.

Sartori G. (1997), 'The changing roles of women in the United States', special issue of *U.S. Society and Values* (Electronic Journals of the U.S. Information Agency), 2(2).

Schumpeter J. (1941), *Capitalism, Socialism and Democracy*, Harper.

Scott, J. (ed.) (1990), *The Sociology of Élites*, Edward Elgar.

Seron C. and Ferris K. (1995) 'Negotiating professionalism: the gendered social capital of flexible time', *Work and Occupations* 22(1):22–47.

Siaroff A. (1994), 'Work welfare and gender equality: a new typology', in Sainsbury D. (ed.), *Gendering Welfare States*, Sage.

Siemienska R. (1986), 'Women and social movements in Poland', in *Women and Politics* 6(4):5–35.

Siemienska R. (1994), 'Women managers in Poland: in transition from communism to democracy', in Adler N. J. and Izraeli D. N. (eds), 243–62.

Siemienska R. (1996a), 'Women's political participation in Central and Eastern Europe: a cross–cultural perspective', in Wejnert B., Spencer M. and Drakulic S. (eds), *Women in Post-Communism*, JAI: 63–92.

Siemienska R. (1996b), *Kobiety: nowe wyzwania. Starcie przeszłości z teražniejszošcą* (Women: New Challenges. Clash of the Past and the Present), Institute of Sociology, University of Warsaw.

Siim B. (1988), 'Towards a feminist rethinking of the welfare state', in Jonasdottir A. and Jones K. (eds), *The Political Interest of Gender*, Sage: 160–86.

Smith L. P. and Smith J. S. (1994), 'The feminization of leadership?', *Training and Development*, February.

SOU 1990 (1990), *Demokrati och makt i Sverige* (Democracy and Power in Sweden), Maktutredningens huvurapport.

Spelman E. (1988), *Inessential Woman: Problems of Exclusion in Feminist Thought*, The Women's Press.

Stewart L. P. and Gudykunst W. B. (1982), 'Differential factors influencing the hierarchical level and number of promotions of males and females within an organization', *Academy of Management Journal*, 25:586–97.

Stroh L. K., Brett J. M. and Reilly A. (1992), 'All the right stuff: a comparison of female and male managers' career progression', *Journal of Applied Psychology*, 77:251–60.

Szelenyi I., Treiman J. D. and Wnuk-Lipiñski E. (eds) (1995), *Elity w Polsce, w Rosji i na Wêgrzech. Wymiana czy reprodukcja?* (Élites in Poland, Russia and Hungary. Exchange or Reproduction?), Institute of Political Studies – Polish Academy of Science.

Tannenbaum A. S. (ed.) (1968), *Control in Organizations*; McGraw-Hill.

Taylor D. et al. (1985), *Women: a World Report*, Methuen.

Teune H. (1990), 'Comparing countries: lessons learned', in Else Øyen et al., *Comparative Methodology, Theory and Practice in International Social Research*, Sage.

Tharenou P., Latimer S. and Conroy D. (1994), 'How do you make it to the top? An examination of influences on women's and men's managerial advancement', *Academy of Management Journal*, 37:899–931.

Thompson J. D. (1967), *Organizations in Action*, McGraw-Hill.

Treiman D. J. (1974), *Occupational Prestige in Comparative Perspective*, Academic Press.

United Nations (1997), *Human Development Report*, Oxford University Press.

Useem M. (1984), *The Inner Circle*, Oxford University Press.

Useem M. and Karabel J. (1986), 'Pathways to top corporate management', *American Sociological Review*, 51:184–200.

Valdez R. L. and Gutek B. A. (1987), 'Family roles. A help or a hindrance for working women?', in Gutek B. A. and Larwood L. (eds), *Women's Career Development*, Sage: 157–69.

Van Deth, J. W. and Scarbrough E. (1995), 'The concept of values', in: Van Deth J. W. and Scarbrough E. (eds), *The Impact of Values*, Oxford University Press.

Veldman A. and Wittink R. (1990), 'De kans van slagen. Invloeden van culturen en regels op de loopbanen van vrouwen' (The chance of success. Influences of cultures and rules on women's careers), Stenfort Kroese Uitgevers.

Verba S., Nie N. H. and Kim J. O. (1971), *The Modes of Political Participation – A Cross-National Analysis*, Sage.

Verba S., Nie N. H. and Kim J. O. (1978), *Participation and Political Equality – A Seven-Nation Comparison*, The University of Chicago Press.

Verba S. and Orren G. R. (1985), *Equality in America: The View From the Top*, Harvard University Press.

Vianello M. and Siemienska R., with Damian N., Lupri E., Coppi R., D'Arcangelo E. and Bolasco S. (1990), *Gender Inequality. A Comparative Study of Discrimination and Participation*, Sage.

Vianello M.(1996), 'Genere, stile manageriale e clima organizzativo', in *Quaderno n.2*, Dipartimento di Contabilità Nazionale e Analisi dei Processi Sociali, Università di Roma 'La Sapienza'.

Wajcman J. (1996), 'Women and men managers' careers and equal opportunities', in Crompton R., Duncan G. and Purcell K. (eds), *Changing Forms of Employment Organisations, Skills and Gender*, Routledge.

Walby S. (1986), *Patriarchy at Work*, Polity.

Walby S. (ed.) (1988), *Gender Segregation at Work*, Open University Press.

Walby S. (1990), *Theorising Patriarchy*, Basil Blackwell.

Walby S. (1997), *Gender Transformations*, Routledge.

Wasilewski J. (1992), 'Dilemmas and controversies concerning leadership recruitment in Eastern Europe', in Lewis P. (ed.), *Democracy and Civil Society in Eastern Europe*.

Wasilewski J. and Wesolowski W. (eds) (1992), *Początki parlamentarnej elity: Posłwie kontraktowego Sejmu* (The Beginning of Parliamentary Élite: Deputies of the Contract Parliament), Warsaw, IFIS.

Weiss J. W. (ed.) (1988), *Regional Cultures, Managerial Behavior, and Entrepreneurship. An International Perspective*, Quorum Books.

West C. and Zimmerman D. H. (1987), 'Doing Gender', *Gender and Society*, 1(2):125–51.

Wetterer A. (ed.) (1992), *Profession und Geschlecht: Über die Marginalität von Frauen in hochqualifizierten Berufen*, Campus.

Wetterer A. (ed.) (1995), *Die soziale Konstruktion von Geschlecht in Professionalisierungsprozessen*, Campus.

Wildenmann R., Kaase M., Hoffmann-Lange U., Kutteroff A. and Wolf G. (1982), *Führungsschicht in der Bundesrepublik Deutschland 1981*, Mannheim: Lehrstuhl für Politische Wissenschaft und Lehrstuhl für Politische Wissenschaft und International Vergleichende Sozialforschung.

Wilson Schaef A. (1981), 'The female system and the white male system: new ways of looking at our culture', reprinted in Frost J. P., Mitchell V. and Nord W. R. (eds), *Organizational Reality*, HarperCollins: 132–42.

Witz A. and Savage M. (1992), 'The gender of organizations', in Savage M. and Witz A. (eds), *Gender and Bureaucracy*, Blackwell: 3–62.

Wolchik S. (1994), 'Women in transition in the Czech and Slovak Republics: the first three years', *Journal of Women's History* 3(5):100–7.

Wolf, W. C. (1979), 'Sexual stratification: differences in power in the work setting', *Social Forces* 58, 1:94–107.

Wolf, W. C. and Fligstein, N. D. (1979), 'Sex and authority in the workplace: the causes of sexual inequality', *American Sociological Review* 44:235–52.

Woodward J. (1965), *Industrial Organizations: Theory and Practice*, Oxford University Press.

World Bank 1995, *World Development Report*.

Wright E. O. (1985), *Classes*, Verso.

Zerubavel E. (1981), *Hidden Rhythms*, University of Chicago Press.

Zey M. (ed.) (1992), *Decision-making. Alternatives to Rational Choice Models*, Sage.

Index of Names